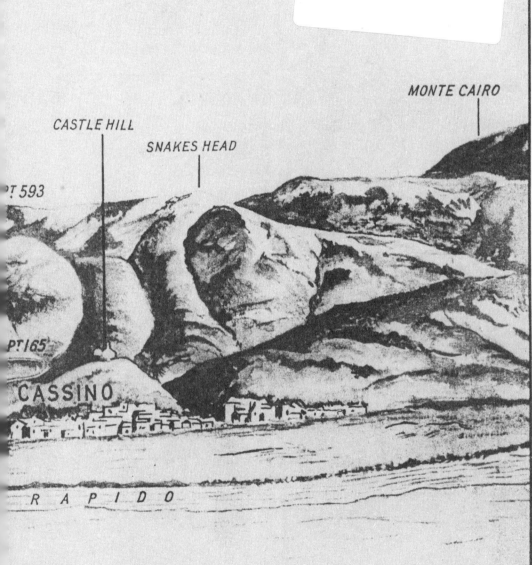

MONTE CAIRO

CASTLE HILL

SNAKES HEAD

PT 593

PT 165

CASSINO

R A P I D O

Wool, War and Westminster

WOOL, WAR AND WESTMINSTER

Front-line Memoirs of Sir Paul Bryan, DSO, MC

Tom Donovan
London

First published in 1993 by
Tom Donovan Publishing Ltd.
52 Willow Road
Hampstead
London NW3 1TP

© P.E.O.Bryan, 1993

ISBN: 1-871085-11-X

Desk-top typeset by Custom Business Systems, London W1

Printed by Antony Rowe Ltd., Chippenham, Wilts

For my daughters

Contents

Twenty-nine photographic illustrations appear between pages 153-152
Numbers 6, 7, 8, 10, 11, 12, 13 and 14 are reproduced by kind
permission of the Trustees of the Imperial War Museum, London.

Maps

Author's note and Acknowledgement

I wrote this book for my daughters, who have kindly helped me with the 'family' chapters.

I would like to thank Denis Forman for his help and advice; Shaun Stewart, Gordon Defrates, John Maling and Jack Nixon for supplementing my war memories with theirs; Bill Baker for his admirable battle maps of the Tunisian campaign; Michele Topham for her co-ordinating; Pauline Hukin for her typing and her ever patient re-typing and my wife Cynthia for brightening my prose and correcting my puncuation.

Part One: My Early Life

1
Japan

I was born in Japan in 1913, the seventh of the nine children of the Reverend Doctor John Thomas Ingram Bryan, MA, PhD.

My grandfather, John Bryan, was born in 1840 at Clonyquin, a farm at Port Arlington near Dublin, said to have been granted to the Bryans in 1649 after the family arrived from France. He emigrated in the 1860s to Prince Edward Island, Canada, to join his uncle, an army man who had bought land there but was having difficulty in clearing it on his own.

Then comes the mystery of why my father's birth certificate bears the words 'born in Albany, New York, on the 12 May 1868.' Apparently, when his mother was due to have her baby she decided she would like the child to be born in Ireland, but things did not go quite to plan and John Thomas Ingram Bryan was born en route at Albany. She then decided to go back to Prince Edward Island, where she bore another seven children.

With the small capital with which he had been endowed by his father on leaving Ireland, John Bryan in time bought a farm on the Foxley river, not far from his uncle's. Most of the farm was still forest land that wanted clearance and cultivation.

When I knew my father he seldom talked about his childhood days in Prince Edward Island. Little did I realise how harsh a life he had lived and how physically exhausting. Every journey; to the school, to the shop, to a neighbour, was a matter of several miles, sometimes on skates, often trudging through snow. To get the wood for next winter's warmth and for cooking all the year round involved hard work for father and son, with whole days spent wielding axes and loading wood onto a sleigh for transport three miles to their house. Nowadays a forester with a power saw can do more in half an hour without effort than those two could manage in an exhausting day.

Of the rest of the Bryan family four became farmers, one a prosperous manufacturer of pharmaceutical products in Boston. A sister married a Mr Henderson in Boston, another sister did not get married but inherited Foxley Farm.

In 1973 I got an unexpected opportunity to see the land where my father was brought up. That year was the centenary of the political junction of Prince Edward Island with mainland Canada and celebrations went on throughout it. As part of the celebration distinguished figures from the Queen downwards made official visits to the Island. Many worthy bodies, including a parliamentary delegation, did the same. As I was the only Member of Parliament who could claim family ties with the Island I was a ready made leader for the delegation.

On arrival at the airport at Charlottetown we were greeted by the Speaker of the local parliament, who devoted his time to us for a whole week. In his opening speech he expressed doubts about the possibility of being able to show us all the Island had to offer in the space of a week. We rather wondered whether it would fill a day.

To see the actual land where my father's family farmed was naturally of intense interest, but I think my most moving moment was seeing my father's handwriting, which I knew so well, in the records of the meetings of the Parish Council at St Pauls, Charlottetown, where he had been the vicar. I found a number of relatives, but only a few with the name of Bryan, and they seemed nice sound people but none in positions of any great distinction. Most of the islanders are of Irish or Scottish descent, many of the Scots having come as a result of the highland clearances.

I once asked his brother, John, then in his eighties and on his first visit to England, how it was that my father, from such a primitive home background, progressed to the Prince of Wales College in Charlottetown, the ambition of every bright boy in the island. He answered simply: 'Our mother was a very good reader.'

After his education at Prince of Wales College, and the University of Toronto, my father was ordained by the Bishop of Toronto and became the Vicar of St Paul's, Charlottetown. The exact timing of his progression to Japan is uncertain, but his curriculum vitae shows him to have attended both the University of California and the University of Pennsylvania, collecting a number of degrees. He also served as Rector at the Church of the Advent, Philadelphia.

Armed with all these academic distinctions my father and his first wife moved on to Japan, where as a lecturer in the Faculty of Letters at the Tokyo Imperial University he became an authority on the country, its history and its literature. Why he chose to move to Japan when he seemed to be doing well in America I do not'know, but it may have been connected with his first wife's poor health. She died not long after their arrival in Japan leaving him with a son, my half brother Arthur.

He then married my mother, Lucy Silver Hall, daughter of William Silver Hall, who was working in Japan as an engineer de Havillands. His family came from Ashby de la Zouche. When Mother was eight and Oliver, her brother, was six, her mother died and she went to live with her Aunt Lucy at Ilkley. Mother's father's first wife was descended from the Barbers, a family which was destined to feature much in my adolescent life.

I lived in Japan until the age of seven. As the seventh in a family of nine you might think that my memories would be of life in a crowd of brothers and sisters, but it was not quite like that: my half-brother, Arthur, was many years older and I had never seen him; my next two brothers, Awdry and Austin, had been sent to Canada to be educated at Ridley College; my younger sister, Kathleen, had died at birth so that left me with my three sisters, Margo, Sylvia and Helen, five, three and two years older than me respectively.

We lived in what I remember as a large house in Tokyo - no doubt destroyed with the rest of that city by US bombers in the Second World War - and went to school at a convent to which I trailed wearily behind my sisters every day. In winter my galoshes kept on coming off in the sticky mud.

My first day at the convent was the most memorable. A nun had died and was lying in state for us all to see and pay our respects. I was goggle-eyed.

In the summer we went like many expatriates to Karuizawa in the Japanese Alps, where I was born. We rented a large wooden house and went every Sunday to a church with huge open windows through which the youngest children were handed to the *amahs* before the sermon. Sometimes I took the collection with my cousin, Farquhar McCrae, my mother's nephew and the son of a missionary. He did one side of the church and I did the other. I was hugely impressed when a large man at the back of the church, having already put a coin in Farquhar's bag, called me over and put one in mine too. I was not surprised that Farquhar followed his father into the mission field for even at that age he was out to improve his fellow men. I still smart from the recollection of his breaking one of those rare silences at a family dinner table with the words 'Paul, keep your mouth shut when you eat.'

I have almost no memories of my father in Japan. He spent his days either at the University or in his study endlessly writing. I do remember that he had a dramatic turn of phrase. Describing an accident on the local erupting volcano, Asama Yama in Karuizawa, when a boulder landed on a climber, he said: 'And it squashed his leg flat as a kipper.' Describing Goliath with his heavy armour from the pulpit once he said 'There he stood looking like any junk shop.'

His liking for onomatopoeia comes out in his poem *Buddhist Bells* published in his book *Films of Blue* in 1908. It should be read slowly and aloud:

> Low the boom of Buddhist bells
> Slowly, slowly how it swells
> Full and far through Shiba dells;
> Every dull repeated tone,
> In its endless sob and moan
> Sends a shiver to the bone

My father's poetry was not always so gloom and doom laden:

> The Antiphon
>
> Faint and far the cuckoos call
> Breaks the silence of the morn:
> A tenor to the waterfall -
> Music of the mountains born
>
> Come, Love, to the window seat;
> Hark that echo from the hill'
> How the cuckoos mistress sweet
> Answers him with ready will.

Note: Antiphon - 'Song sung by two parties each responding to the other.'

My father left his indelible stamp upon the future of his sons by his choice of Christian names. My eldest brother was condemned to a girl's name for life because he had to be named after Bishop Awdry. My second brother, Austin, carries the name of an obscure poet, Lowell, and I an even more obscure poet, Elmore.

I am surprised how little I remember about my mother in Japan considering how much I loved her. The amahs, all nice, seemed to dominate our lives and we were quite at home with the Japanese language. When visiting Karuizawa on a train in 1985 I heard the Japanese lady in the seat behind singing a lullaby to her baby. I found I could remember both the Japanese words and the tune.

My mother used to read to us and teach us songs at the piano. The stories and songs I remember best would now be considered violent, racist or both by modern standards.

The book I enjoyed most and which survived to entertain my children too was Struwwel Peter, a collection of what you might call violent parables, for every story taught a lesson.

There was cruel Frederick:

> He caught the flies, poor little things
> And then tore off their tiny wings.
> He killed the birds, and broke the chairs,
> And threw the kitten down the stairs.'

But he paid the price, for, trying to whip the dog, 'Poor Tray,' he got badly bitten. The final highly satisfactory picture is of Frederick in bed, the doctor at his bedside whilst:

> Good dog, Tray, is happy now
> He has no time to say bow-wow,
> He seats himself in Frederick's chair
> And laughs to see the nice things there.
> The soup he swallows sup by sup
> And eats the pies and puddings up.

One racist song I remember, I think by Robert Louis Stevenson, goes:

> Little Indian, Sioux or Crow
> Little frosty Eskimo
> Little Turk or Japanee
> Oh, don't you wish that you were me.
> Oh, don't you wish that you were me.

You have curious things to eat
While I am fed on proper meat
You must dwell beyond the foam
While I am safe and live at home.
While I am safe and live at home.

In those days all little British boys, whether 'safe living at home' or the sons of expatriates abroad, considered themselves not as other boys. This is clearly illustrated in a picture which shows the little English boy looking self-satisfied in the centre of a ring of foreign contemporaries, each in his national costume.

When Cynthia and I visited Karuizawa in 1985 it had greatly changed since my childhood. The English church was there with its big windows as was our wooden house. But the village itself has become a Japanese Gleneagles with golf courses and the huge modern Prince Hotel with its 2000 inmates all with Prince rackets and apparently all dressed by Messrs Lilywhite. As I had not been to Karuizawa for 65 years and as Margo and Helen were both born there too it seemed appropriate to telephone them, Margo in London and Helen in Sydney. They were surprised.

I believe my sisters had quite a social time in Japan, with parties at the British Embassy and so on, but I have no memories of this apart from great celebrations on Empire Day when I had to carry the Union Jack. My three sisters were always pleasant to me - at least I cannot remember them ever being nasty - with Helen, the nearest to me in age, not unnaturally being the closest.

When I was seven we left Japan for England, travelling via Canada where we were to pick up my two brothers. We sailed in the NYK ship *Haruna Maru*. Though far from well off, for some reason we travelled first class. On the first night I was left in the cabin whilst the rest of the family had supper in the restaurant, and was woken up by an appalling clatter of cranes working to store away the deck cargo in the hold. I couldn't think what was happening and I ran into the passage and asked a passing old lady, 'Are we sinking?'

On the second night things had turned in my favour for by then my sisters were sea-sick and I ate up their ice-creams. During the voyage to Vancouver I met up with a friendly Japanese family and spent much of the time with them. At Vancouver we transferred to the Canadian

Pacific Railway for a five day train journey across Canada, definitely not first-class; all our meals were taken picnic-style in our compartment. There was an observation car at the back where we spent a lot of time, especially in the more exciting parts of the journey as we crossed the Rocky Mountains.

I have no memory whatever of my father on the boat to Canada and only one on the train. That was at Winnipeg, where to my horror the train moved off whilst he was in the station buying bread. It had, in fact, only shunted a few hundred yards to make way for another train. I can still see my father puffing down the track with a big loaf under each arm.

The train was like those seen in the Wild West films. The steam engine had a cow-catcher on the front and on one occasion we did in fact stop for a cow. Going over the Rockies a second engine joined our own to help it up the steep gradients.

Our destination in Canada was the village of Winona, in Ontario, where we were to pick up my brothers, Awdry and Austin. They were then 14 and 12 years old respectively. They had been sent there three years previously, presumably because my father considered that the education at Ridley College would be superior to anything available in Japan.

My brothers had been spending their school holidays with the vicar of Winona in whose care they had got completely out of hand.

We had been brought up very strictly in every sort of way. Endless pleases and thank-yous; no elbows on the table; hand up when you yawn; wash hands before meals. Prayers were never missed (Pray God, bless Father and Mother, all my brothers and sisters, and help me to be a good boy; Amen); immaculate pronunciation - 'Oh,' not 'ow'; 'white' not 'wite.'

Canada seemed to have purged my brothers of all this careful training. My mother was horrified. I was entranced - especially to hear my brother, Austin, shouting at the Reverend West from behind a gate, 'All right - chase me, you monkey' when the Vicar was trying to correct him for some fresh outrage. Life took on a more promising prospect if this was how one could hope to behave once one had reached the age of 12.

When we had relieved the Reverend West of the burden of my brothers, we boarded the Canadian Pacific Liner *Empress of Canada* at Montreal. We sailed at a snail's pace out of the St Lawrence River for fear of icebergs of which we counted 37, all seemingly far enough from the ship for safety, but the grown-ups tried to dramatize with tales that a huge icebergs in view was only the tiniest tip of what was under the water. My memories of the journey to Liverpool are confined to my brothers' continuing bad behaviour and broad Canadian accents. This went on until they were finally deposited a few weeks later at St John's School, Leatherhead, a school then almost entirely filled with sons of clergymen, where the cane was *de rigueur.*

* * *

Our first house in England was 31 Central Hill, Upper Norwood, a large cold Victorian house within the SE19 district of London, rented from a clergyman.

My father spent most of his time travelling around the country speaking on behalf of the Society for the Propagation of the Gospel, or as a University extension lecturer for Cambridge University. When at home he sat in his office endlessly writing. All his life his spare time was spent writing articles, or more often stories, usually for Blackwoods or for American magazines. With so many children and in an ill-paid profession he must have been constantly short of money, especially as his primary aim in life was to give his family a good education. This was not surprising for his own life was a triumph of education over humble beginnings. He succeeded in paying for three of his sons to go to Cambridge and no doubt my youngest brother, Michael, would have gone there too, had he survived the war.

My father was nearly always grumpy at meals - the only time we saw him. He grumbled at the food, accusing it of being full of preservatives, particularly Formaldehyde, of which I have not since heard. He got angry when the loo got clogged up, accusing us in general of using too many sheets of paper when 'one was plenty.' Though the tone of his voice was severe his words were moderate - 'Just imagine' was his strongest expletive.

My poor mother was constantly making excuses for him by explaining what a tiring life he led on our behalf. This was true enough, for travelling up and down the country in the 1920s by bus and train in all weathers was no fun. I can see him setting off, a big man, in his heavy coat and wondered why he needed such a big suitcase.

I must not give the impression that my father was all gloom. He had a sense of humour. He seldom generated humour but he was capable of collapsing into uncontrollable laughter. In the war, in his old age, he would weep with laughter at Tommy Handley's ITMA programme. Nor can the inventor of 'Chucky Choodle,' a game which has entertained three generations of Bryan children, be without some feeling for the mind of a child.

Making every allowance for the pressures on his own life, his constant bullying of my saintly mother was disgraceful. With six children and little help, setting up a new home from scratch must have been a fearful strain on her. To add to her toils another son was born eight years after me. How she coped I know not. I certainly have no memory of being neglected. I do not remember being either happy or unhappy. I followed along in the wake of my sisters, apparently unnoticed which is what I liked to be. In due course, I don't know why, we moved a mile or two away to 32 Waldegrave Road, another rented Victorian house. Then my father bought a house - 228 South Norwood Hill, again not far away, which he named 'Clonyquin' after his family home in Ireland. Clonyquin, now converted into five flats, was a roomy house with a huge basement opening out into a large garden, below the level of the house. This room was left pretty well unfurnished. The girls danced in it to the gramophone and tried to teach me to do the same. I bowled at some cricket stumps which I had chalked on the wall, and while the lawn was not big enough for tennis the elder ones played badminton there.

In 1987 Helen and I visited this our home of 60 years ago. Builders were in doing the flat conversion, so we had a perfect opportunity to go through the house from top to bottom and were surprised at the gaps in our memories.

The period between our arrival in England and the return of my parents with the girls and Michael to Japan spanned seven years. In that time my elder brothers, Awdry and Austin, had been through public school and Cambridge. The girls had been educated at Sydenham High School. I went to Dulwich College Preparatory School, about four miles away, first by bus and foot and later by bicycle. The only person there I remember is the Headmaster, an impressive cheery man, with a moustache, called Leake. The school left no impression on me, but I suppose my performance cannot have been disastrous for eventually I got a scholarship to St John's School, Leatherhead.

I was inordinately pleased at winning a scholarship to St John's. I suppose it was the first publicly recorded success of my life. In the course of a family meal I succeeded (I thought subtly) in bringing it into the conversation. My eldest sister, Margo, said: 'Paul - don't fish for compliments.' You would have thought that this crushing comment would have cured me of this fault for life. But no - forty years later I was required to come on radio, after *The Archers*, for five minutes, to tell the world about the virtues of the Young Conservative movement. It was my maiden voyage on radio and the result of many hours of preparation. My daughter, Libby, was a medical student at St Thomas's Hospital at the time and living with us in Westminster at Marsham Court. I asked her to be sure to listen. When I got home I naturally asked her what she thought of my performance and equally naturally she said: 'Fine, daddy.' But then, pushing my luck too far, I said: 'But Libby, if I had to do it again, how could I improve on it?' To which she replied: 'Well it was dull, wasn't it, Daddy?'

Experience shows that if you want to fish for compliments the only way to be sure of your catch and avoid humiliation is to appeal only to people who are beholden to you or are bound to wish you well.

Ken Bean, our gardener at Park Farm, had for all his early life been the gardener at Brompton Hall and gone out shooting with Sir Kenelm Cayley as his loader. I had never had the luxury of a loader but since Ken liked a day shooting he came out with me. As the birds came over he murmured quietly: 'Bird to your right, Sir' or 'Bird to your left, Sir.' When now and then I brought down quite a high bird I would say: 'What did you think of that, Ken?' He always replied: 'Wonderful shot, Sir.'

It would be a comfort if you could go through life with somebody at your side who could be relied on to say: 'Wonderful shot' when you were in need of encouragement. Wives cannot be relied upon to fill this role.

2
School

To greet me on my arrival at St Johns I found an envelope containing a welcome poem from Mr Leake which read:

So here's to fat B
May he be merry
On his way to JL
Where may all be well.

From this you will gather that I was on the tubby side at that age, though not to the extent that I was laughed at. Like most of the other new boys I had not been away from home before, but I settled down quite contentedly and to start with kept out of trouble.

Then a problem arose with which I could not cope. A feature of all preparatory schools in those days was the honesty of the boys. The fear of God was mercilessly used to keep you on the path of righteousness. A feature of some public schools, however, was that everybody cheated, and St John's, despite all its sons of the clergy, came into this category.

I was not adaptable enough to switch from honesty to cheating in a matter of days, which put me at a disadvantage and for the first three weeks I was near the bottom of the form. Caning was a common punishment in those days at most public schools, and certainly at St John's for every sort of 'crime', from wearing the wrong uniform, to lateness and laziness. For me, a scholar, to be near the bottom of the form clearly meant that I was lazy and should therefore be caned. The housemaster, the Reverend Ingram, with his sparsely covered cranium which always reminded me of a monk, was a kindly man, but also famous for the vigour of his caning. So when he performed, a group of boys always collected outside his study door to see whether or not the victim would come out in tears.

I reported to Mr Ingram's study at the appointed hour and the usual group was outside his door, but there was nothing usual in what followed. Without the expected preamble about my laziness he gave me four strokes with his famous cane, which hurt about as much as I had expected. Then he said: 'You are padded - go out and take it out.' I was not, of course, padded. I was merely paying the price of having a fat bottom, but for some reason, which now for the life of me I cannot explain, I made no comment, went out of the door and told my expectant pals what had happened. This was drama beyond their wildest hopes and they had no advice to offer. I returned and got four more strokes and went down in history as the boy who had survived eight strokes from the dreaded Ingram without crying. Failure to cry is an over-rated virtue. There have been plenty of things in life which have made me cry but caning happens not to be one of them.

In a minor way I got my own back on the establishment, for a few months later I discovered that among my father's books there was a wide selection of English translations of the very Latin books we were required to translate. Not only was this a personal boon for me as I struggled with Caesar's Gallic wars, but I was also able to swap them for other useful helps - like a last year's physics exercise book belonging to a boy much cleverer at physics than I.

At prep school I never played any games except when my older brothers were at home and might ask me why I wasn't playing, but at St John's I went mad on cricket. In those days at a public school there was absolutely nothing interesting to do outside school hours except singing in the choir, which I much enjoyed. So every spare moment I bowled at my friend Robin Keith, son of the Vicar of Wimborne, who wanted to be the future Jack Hobbs, whilst my hero was Titch Freeman, the diminutive slow bowler who played for Kent. After hundreds of hours of bowling on any spare patch of ground in the summer and in the gym in winter, I could pitch a cricket ball on a chosen spot with amazing accuracy.

This practice had a dazzling reward, for halfway through the cricket season in my fifteenth year I became the youngest member of the First XI. I shall never forget the moment I saw my name at the bottom of the list on the First XI board. For the first and only time in my life I didn't sleep all night.

The next day was fine. Our opponents, the Grasshoppers Cricket Club, went into bat at 11am and by lunchtime I had taken three wickets for 13 runs. This could not last. My final figures were four for 40, but even that made me the hero of my age group. In the end I did not follow Titch Freeman into the English side, but passed many happy days playing both for the school and for my college at Cambridge.

I got satisfaction from singing in the choir. The choirmaster was a Doctor of Music, a Dr Reed, who drove us hard and apart from our performance in the chapel most years we tackled some light opera. To this day I can sing the greater part of the Mikardo and Carmen and many hymns verbatim as a result of the discipline imposed by Dr Reed. As I have since spent an unusually large proportion of my waking hours singing or humming, Dr Reed has had a longer influence on one of his pupils than he can have imagined.

In my varied career the only thing I think I have done really well is soldiering and it was therefore surprising that the school activity I tried to avoid like the plague was the Officer Training Corps. I did this by joining the band, and remained a drummer until the regular major in command of the Corps said it was unsuitable for the Captain of South House to be a drummer boy and made me a sergeant. I then proceeded to fail the Military Certificate A examination, the only examination I have ever failed.

Scholastically I was usually in the top quarter of my form and no doubt could have done better with stimulation from the sort of schoolmaster who did not exist at St John's, but I certainly had no complaints. Opportunities were there to be taken.

Early in my time at St John's my father took a post as a lecturer at the University in Tokyo so my parents, my three sisters and Michael went back there to live. The move to Japan was, on balance, good news for my three sisters. The social life in suburban South Norwood was fairly dull and getting more so as they got older and looked for wider horizons. Nor was there much entertainment at home, for father's whole attitude to parties and the consequent mixing of the sexes was a damper on fun. For a long time he assumed that his daughters only danced with their brothers and each other and was shocked to hear that this was not so. Margo had the best of it, for with Austin and Awdry at Cambridge she did come in on the fringe of University entertainment and sometimes went and stayed at Cambridge with our Aunt Viva Cooke, a great hostess and wife of the famous doctor, Arthur Cooke, brother of a housemaster at Fettes College where I used to stay.

Social life in Japan when they got there could not have been a greater contrast. They were all three attractive and much in demand and, within a couple of years, all married. For the first time in their lives, too, they were earning money and had plenty to spend in contrast to their lives in England, for the Bryans in Upper Norwood were uncomfortably poor.

Margo married Philip Burt, a senior executive in the Nestlé company. Sylvia married David Wevill, a Canadian accountant in Tokyo and Helen married John Hare, the Tokyo manager of the Chartered Bank of India, Australia and China.

The arrangement was that I should spend my holidays with my aunt at Weybridge, my mother's sister Kathleen Marsden who was married to a regular gunner colonel working at the War Office. The regime at the Marsdens included psalms at breakfast which was okay, but the colonel was a fitness fanatic and insisted that I came for runs with him in the evenings. More importantly he was a bore and I decided to move on.

I next sought refuge with my mother's first cousin, Harry Cook, a housemaster at Fettes College, Edinburgh, a marvellous household where I spent happy holidays. Not only had one all the sporting assets that go with a house at a public school but the family was perfect. My aunt Nora was sweetness itself, the eldest son, Michael, was just my age, then at Sedbergh. Dulcie, Theresa, Ann and Christopher, completed a merry family.

Sometimes I had short stays with schoolfriends, in particular John Owen, whose father was the vicar of Higham Ferrers. When at Cambridge I spent vacations with some other cousins, the Barbers at Winchester. He was a lawyer, the County Clerk of Hampshire and a delightful old world character. At breakfast he read the *Times* propped up on a stand, conversation above a murmur was unwelcome and provoked the comment: 'It is bourgeois to be bright at breakfast.' Freddy Barber was brilliant with his hands as was his son, Vickers. They could make chests of drawers or build additions to their cottage at Selborne to professional standards.

Over these years contact with my parents and family became more and more distant. A letter to Japan took three weeks so no reply arrived for at least six. I made all my own arrangements for holidays, had my own cheque book and so became independent.

My father was more than careful with money and we were always being accused of wastefulness. To my sister, Helen, about to waste money going to the cinema he once said: 'Remember every penny you spend is a nail in my coffin.' But now and then surprising generosity would emerge. In a letter to Japan, for lack of anything to fill the page,

I complained that the school food was bad. All boys at all schools say the food is bad, but father took my complaint seriously. Instead of writing to the authorities, however, he took a far more practical step and gave me an allowance to spend on extra food, the exact figure of which I forget. However much it was it made me, in a school full of the sons of parsons, the richest boy in the school. I used to save up this money so as to be able to go to the theatre in London on 'leave-out days.'

In retrospect I am astonished at the apparent hardiness of the boys. I and presumably many others never wore a vest or a waistcoat. Our vast 40-bed dormitory with its high arched ceiling had no heating. There was a long row of china basins in an endless washstand down the centre of the dormitory, but no running water and the two boys who were the orderlies for the day used to bring in so-called hot water in jugs from a tap in the passage. But not many people seemed to get ill, and I did not have a single day in bed in the sanitorium throughout my school career.

3
Cambridge

In the 1930s there was no difficulty whatsoever in getting into Oxford or Cambridge. The only thing you had to decide was which college you were going to, a choice largely influenced by where your father went or where your friends were going and the degree you would take. I chose Gonville and Caius because my brother, Austin, had enjoyed his time there and it had a good reputation, both academically and for games. I chose to take a degree in modern languages because I thought languages would be useful in business. This proved a bad decision, for if learning a language is your objective the Cambridge course spent far too much time on the history and literature of the country concerned and too little on the language itself. This has been put right and nowadays a language degree involves a year abroad, the course taking an extra year.

I suppose it cannot be a mere coincidence that both my masters at school and my tutors at Cambridge branded me as lazy. I would prefer to say I was easy-going. I worked sufficiently hard to get through the necessary examinations.

My standing with them was probably also affected by my lack of reverence both then and ever since for academics and teachers. The best are, of course, interesting, impressive and even entertaining, but on average I found them narrow, dull and self-satisfied.

My main interest at Cambridge was sport - rugger and cricket - which might have been justified had I been a star; a blue or an international like many of my friends. I played for my college at both these games and was a member of the Hawks club, to which all the blues belonged, but in the end I finished up by being one of the less good players in some good teams. This preoccupation with the sporting life of the university no doubt deadened the curiosity which Cambridge was supposed to stimulate in the minds of bright young undergraduates. I read serious newspapers and knew what was going on, but none of the great convulsions that were erupting in the world, such as the rise of Hitler, overfilled my mind, nor was I fired with ambition to go off to the Spanish Civil War. I took no part in politics and when I finally took my degree I still did not know where the

Union was. The only future politician among my friends was Ian McLeod, a Chancellor of the Exchequer in the Macmillan government, and my friendship with him was due to his being the scrum half in the college rugger team. Little did I imagine that 25 years later he would be Chairman of the Conservative Party Organisation with me his Vice-Chairman.

The idea that one has a moral duty to make the very best of one's ability never came my way until I met my wife Betty, who had strong views on the subject. Had somebody by some means convinced me of the validity of this concept early in my life I would have lived a very much less comfortable life both at school and at the university.

I have not found myself embarrassingly undersexed in my post graduate life, and it therefore surprises me that I and my set of friends at Cambridge led an almost entirely monastic life. Girls hardly featured in our routine at all. When May Week arrived one asked the prettiest girl one had met in the previous year to the college ball, and invariably she came. In my case it was the delightful Doreen Ram, daughter of the Vicar of Petersfield, whom I had met at a tennis party when staying with the Barbers at Winchester the previous summer.

We so enjoyed the Caius Ball, Nat Gonella was the band, that we decided to go to the Trinity Ball on the next night. We spent the intervening day in the sun, mostly in a punt on the river. As we had no tickets and gatecrashing was difficult before midnight something had to be done about dinner. This is the sort of problem which was mother's milk to the Caius College kitchen. A fantastic champagne picnic was produced, memorably presented and with this we took to a punt on a gorgeous evening and the time passed quickly until we sailed down the Backs to the ball.

My evening punt adventures were not always so successful. Next year, after I had left Cambridge, I took my future wife, Betty, to the Caius Ball. Nat Gonella again. After dinner and much wine and a little dancing I suggested a trip on the river. Conveniently a couple was just getting out of a punt and we took it over. Although I did not realise it I was a tiny bit tipsy and pushing the boat away from the bank I half overbalanced, dipping just my backside and tails in the water. Betty's downcast face showed that she was unwilling to dance the night away with a man with a wet bottom and tails and that for her the ball was over. She had under-rated her man. I remembered that my friend Robert Nelson had told me earlier in the day that he was undecided whether to come to the ball. He had no girl. So leaving Betty by the bridge I ran and walked about half a mile to his room at Caius and there he was, sleeping peacefully, with his tails actually on a hanger on the door. He was exactly the same size as me. In two minutes I was re-clothed and in 10 I was back again with Betty. Robert never stirred.

The girl I knew and liked best in my Cambridge days was my cousin, Betty Barber, who was at Somerville College, Oxford at the time. I often stayed with her family at Winchester and sometimes at Selborne, where they had a cottage. When there, if we both had some swotting to do we would read away in the attic of the vicarage. Betty was entirely unvain; for day after day she would wear exactly the same clothes, the top part being a drab old sweater. She was both factual and frank. One day she said me: 'You are so ordinary that you are extraordinary.' She went on to become a barrister and secretary of the Authors' Society, where her main preoccupation was the Bernard Shaw copyright. As the years passed by I saw very little of her, but she took a great interest in my children, who loved her.

Just as most undergraduates of today live their student lives to a background of music of a kind, we lived to a background of Cole Porter ('Night and Day,' 'You do something to me,' 'Anything goes,' 'I get a kick out of you,' 'Miss Otis regrets,' 'Begin the Beguine'), Irving Berlin ('Let's face the music and dance,' 'I've got my love to keep me warm,' 'How deep is the ocean,' 'I'm putting all my eggs in one basket'), Noel Coward ('I'll follow my secret heart,' 'Someday I'll find you,' 'I'll see you again'). We all had portable gramophones, which you wound with a handle, in our rooms. On the first day of every month we went down to the music shop to hear the latest releases and the keenest went on the 15th of the month too to hear the half-monthly releases.

One summer a New Zealander at Cambridge, Fairfax Fenwick and I went off in his bullnosed two-seater Morris Cowley and for a fortnight followed the Australian cricket team, starting at the Oval and going on to Brighton and Canterbury. At Brighton we picked up two snappily dressed Cockney-voiced girls in a dance hall. In those days not many young people had motor cars and we naturally thought that they would be rather excited at the prospect of a ride in the Morris, though it had only cost £5. They said: 'Why not come in ours?' and led us across the car park to their brand new MG.

I spent a fortnight of the summer vacation every year on the Caius College cricket tour. This was a carefree affair. We travelled in three cars through the West Country playing against good sides on the county grounds in Gloucester, Devon and Somerset.

Some modern language students were successful in getting lucrative jobs in the holidays, like guiding Americans around Paris; there was a scholastic agency called Gabbitas and Thring that made these arrangements. I went to this firm to try my luck and was interviewed in French. We agreed that my French did not actually flow, but he sent me away in hope. Days passed without any news and after three weeks a telegram arrived inviting me to conduct a tour around the Highlands of Scotland. I declined.

Drink did not feature in my life at all until I went to Cambridge. In my family it was classed as 'evil,' though father kept a private bottle of sherry exclusively for himself. I remember his holding the glass of sherry under the table when the daily came into the room. In my other holiday homes drink was not taboo to quite this extent but very little was consumed. At Cambridge beer seemed to go with rugger and people got pretty drunk at the rugger equivalent of a bump supper night but alcohol was not a heavy item in my budget.

At Cambridge I felt rather poor, but not desperately so. I remember calculating that on £300 a year you could live a good life, but on £250 which is what I had you had to be careful. By keeping an account of every single penny I spent I was able to keep up with my friends, but they were not a particularly rich lot.

I did not find keeping an account too much of a toil, for by then I had been managing my own affairs for several years, buying my clothes, arranging my holidays, and had become independent and methodical for my age.

The slowness of the letter post did not prevent my father keeping up a steady stream of advice on a wide number of aspects of my life. One letter read: 'Beware of tricky fellows and men who spend a lot of money.' Clearly, in his eyes men who spent a lot of money were tricky fellows and tricky fellows always spent a lot of money.

During term-time at Cambridge a service was held every Sunday afternoon at Great St Mary's Church, at which some notability preached. This was known as the University Sermon. Another of my father's letters advised: 'You should always go to hear the University

Sermon. Many great men have preached the University Sermon. I have preached the University Sermon.'

The greatest effect of Great St Mary's Church on my undergraduate life was one of which my father would not have approved. Its bellringers insisted on practising for an hour from 8 to 9pm every Monday evening. Many of the rooms in Caius were within a hundred yards of the Church and we maintained that work being impossible in such a noise the solution was to go to the cinema. The long term effect was good because by the time I left Cambridge I had no wish to see another film for a very long time.

Another letter said: 'Do not loiter around aerodromes.' You might have thought that to interpret this phrase was quite a challenge, but its significance suddenly flashed upon my mind when I remembered that when my elder brother, Austin, was at Caius College he had attempted to join the University Air Squadron. To do this - as he was under 21 - he had to get his parents' signature, which was not forthcoming.

Though as fathers go mine seemed markedly unfriendly to his children he was violently biased in our favour when it came to dealings with the outside world. Once, when going through my prep school report he asked why it said that I was weak at English. Dishonestly I blurted out 'But English is one of my best subjects.' He turned to my mother and said 'How can you rely on these school reports when they are so inaccurate?' Perhaps he was more cunning than I realised and knew that this attitude would stop me telling lies.

He would boast that three of his sons went to the best university in the world, without adding, of course, that none of them had particularly distinguished himself there.

In the war he would boast that I was the youngest colonel commanding a battalion in the British Army without any evidence to prove that this was so. My youngest brother, Michael, was indeed a star pilot - a Wing Commander at the age of 22 with two DFCs, but to hear father describing his exploits and almost gloating about all the Germans he had killed was somewhat unexpected from a man of God. I also had picked up a couple of decorations, DSO and MC, and he liked to think and indeed to say that we were the only two brothers in the British forces with double decorations.

4
Halifax

I do not remember much discussion amongst my friends at Cambridge about our future careers, possibly because most careers got off to a slow, if not boring, start. Nowadays you often hear of graduates earning a large amount of money within two or three years of leaving the university. In the thirties if you got a job with one of the multi-nationals, say Lever Bros. or Shell, you were paid £250 a year for three years and very dreary years they were, going 'through the mill,' in a way no modern graduate would accept. Some of my friends went into family businesses, some into the professions or the Colonial Service.

I had been to see the Cambridge University Appointments Board which undertook to place me with one of the major companies provided I got an adequate degree. However, during my last year at Cambridge I went to stay with a distant cousin, Ernest Osborn, in Halifax, Yorkshire, and he asked me if I would join his family firm, Baldwin & Walker, which made knitting wool. The secretary of the Appointments Board had never heard of this firm but was helpful in saying that if I wanted to give it a try and it did not work out I could always come back to the Appointments Board.

To my inexperienced eye it looked an attractive proposition. The pay offered was niggardly, but the prospects good. What I did not realise at the time was that it was too small a company to offer much opportunity.

So, in 1934 I took up digs in Holly Bank, an Edwardian house at the bottom of Manor Heath Road, Halifax, the residence until a few months before of a Mrs Wanklin. When she died her housemaid, Mrs Burton, turned it into lodgings. A large bow-windowed room on the ground floor, previously the dining room, was my bed sitting room. I was happy there.

It was from Mrs Burton that I learned how to tell children's stories. I forget why, but she always called me 'Lord B.' She had a dear pretty little daughter, Ann, aged three, who was always popping in to see me. Now and then Mrs Burton would fear that Ann's visits were getting too much of a good thing and she used to say to her 'Do give Lord B a little privacy.' The only result of this command was a little head coming round the door saying 'Do you want a little privacy, Lord B?'

Halifax was the home town of Bernard Ingham, Margaret Thatcher's Press Secretary. In his book *Kill the Messenger*, he writes:

> Halifax was busy working at a hundred and one or a thousand and one trades, depending on the informant's enthusiasm about its varied industrial base. Up the hill from the Hebble steam at the foot of Beacon Hill climbed a forest of mill and factory chimneys. The traveller from Leeds, bursting out of Godly Cutting, had spread before him one of the classic, fuming, industrial sites of Britain and he would invariably have the muck blown in his eyes by the prevailing south-westerly winds. The trees and vegetation on Beacon Hill fought a losing battle for life under the stream of noxious gases. No wonder Ted Hughes, now a Poet Laureate, who lived in Mytholmroyd when I was a lad, wrote of 'Black Halifax, boiled in phosphorous.'

The great difference between Halifax in the thirties and Halifax now was the smoke and the 'forest of chimneys.' Everything - houses, mills, churches, trees, hedges - was black and filthy to touch. I need hardly say that my new home town was unlike anything I had ever come across before.

My social life in Halifax got off to a good start. I arrived on a Saturday night. Going for a walk on the Sunday morning, on a common known as The Moor, a man stopped me and said: 'Is that a Hawks tie you are wearing?' He was an officer from the Halifax depot of the Duke of Wellington's Regiment. Before the day was through I had lunch with him in the Officers' Mess and a game of squash. At lunch I met Trevor Bentley who proved to be the nicest, kindest and deservedly popular bachelor in the town, who, on the Monday evening, took me up to the Rugger Club and by the following Saturday I was playing rugger for Halifax. Trevor continued to be tireless in his efforts to make sure that I was not lonesome.

My daily walk to the mill was pleasant enough - about a mile across The Moor, then down a couple of hundred yards of Mill Street, a cobbled street of back-to-back houses which served as a children's playground and place to hang the washing when the weather was fine. This was almost totally undisturbed by motor cars. When the sun came out housewives would sit in their open doors doing their knitting and keeping an eye on the children who, of course, I got to know well as I walked to and fro at the same times each day.

My two year training period before assuming some undefined managerial responsibility was to consist of six months in the wool sorting department, six months 'going through the mill' and a year selling knitting wool as a commercial traveller.

My life in the wool sorting room introduced me to an entirely new life. In those days when society was more stratified than it is today I had never before met a factory worker, but the next six months, standing for eight hours a day between two Yorkshire wool sorters, was a very thorough introduction indeed to the working man.

The foreman, Squire Ogden, came from Midgley, a small village above the Calder Valley, as did Harry and two of the other sorters whose names I forget. The fourth sorter, Norman, came from Lightcliffe, in the suburbs of Halifax. I stood at a sorting board all day on which I spread out a fleece taken from a bale of wool standing at my left side. I split the fleece into four qualities, the lowest being at the neck and the breach end and put them into four large wicker baskets, known as skips, behind me. Quality in wool means fineness of fibre, the fineness in the top qualities known as sixties or seventies was very fine indeed and it took some time for your eyes to get accustomed to the work. The apprenticeship for wool sorting was five years but I swear it could have been picked up perfectly adequately in six months and the long apprenticeship was just one more example of a craft union detering new entrants.

I stood between Harry and Norman. Harry was big, not fat and something of a braggart. On my first day he was telling me how beautiful his wife looked on their wedding day, when I said: 'Isn't she beautiful now, Harry?' He stood back from the sorting board with his hands on his hips and with a guffaw said: 'She's got an arse as big as yon bloody window' and the window was wide. Many of his reminiscences were of sexual exploits between the spinning frames in his early days in woollen mills. His most surprising boast was of the girl he 'did' in a train carriage between Halifax and Sowerby Bridge stations - a distance of about two miles.

Norman, a tall, thin, bald man was by contrast religious and was inevitably and frequently 'persecuted for righteousness' sake' in that company, especially by Squire Ogden who teased him mercilessly. I remember him one day talking of the wonders of communion wine.

Squire, who surprisingly had a religious wife, retorted: 'Balls, I have seen my wife making it in the kitchen. It's nowt but jam water.'

Two nights a week I had to go to the 'Tech' - the Halifax Technical College - to take a course on worsted spinning. On two other nights in winter I went training on the ground of the Halifax Rugby Union Club, for which I played on the Saturday. So my time was fairly exhaustingly filled in a way for which I had certainly had no preparation. I was in no way sorry for myself, but what I missed most of all was the laughter of life at Cambridge. I sorted wool for far too long, six months, and was relieved when I was moved on to the colour matching department. This presented a personal difficulty because I am colour blind. I spent a fortnight colour matching away and nobody seemed to notice anything wrong.

On my first day in the combing room I asked the foreman how long we had had the combing machine at which I was working. His reply - 'Many a bloody umpteen year.'

At the end of my year in the mill I had got very fond of West Riding people and to this day I feel more at home with them than with anyone else. Their lack of snobbishness, of deference, and the completely direct way in which an employee will talk to the boss I find unique and admirable. Years later when I was chairman of our family clothing business in Hebden Bridge I was trying on an ill-fitting sports coat which had just come out of the factory. I summoned the warehouseman, Willie Horrocks, and said 'What do you think of this?' He looked me slowly up and down and said 'By, Mr Paul, thou dost look a bugger in yon.' You cannot imagine a warehouseman in any other part of England addressing the chairman of the company in such words. Of course his whole attitude meant that he was addressing a friend.

Playing rugger for Halifax was quite unlike playing in the South. They were completely unimpressed by the opposition. It did not matter whether you were playing against a team of internationals or against Brighouse Rangers, their attitude was exactly the same. The players, again unlike the South where rugger is a middle-class game, came from all classes.

I did not accept Willie Horrocks's cheap jibe about the sports coat and duly sent it on to the customer for whom it had been made - my friend Denis Forman, assuming that in those days of clothes rationing he would be grateful. His letter of acknowledgement read 'Thank you for the sports coat. It can fit at the front and also at the back but not both at the same time. With the surplus material we are planning to make a pair of knickers for the gardener's boy.'

I met Betty Hoyle early in my time in Halifax. We seemed to fall in love in a very uncomplicated way for it was not long before we both decided that one day we would get married. Despite the modest start of my career she had no doubt of my future success, as in later years she never doubted the success of her children. This trait was complimentary but alarming.

The difference between us lay in our two interpretations of 'one day.' Being brought up on the presumption that a man did not marry until he could support a wife and family, at my then uncertain rate of progress our wedding day lay years ahead. She always maintained that in proposing I said: 'Will you marry me in 10 years time?' In the end we were officially engaged after two years and married after four, just before the outbreak of war.

As a prospective son-in-law I was clearly not much of a catch, but Jimmy and Vi Hoyle could not have been nicer and I spent many happy times at Ashfield and on the golf course with Jimmy, Betty and her younger brother, Peter, then at Marlborough.

At Christmas time in 1936 while watching the pantomime in Halifax I felt unwell. This turned out to be scarlet fever - the second and last illness I have ever had and the next morning found me in the isolation hospital at Northowram. Apart from feeling weak and generally awful, life there was dull and dominated by a big boned caricature of a hospital matron. For fear of exporting our infection, no letters were allowed, only postcards, which were baked in an oven before despatch. On one I wrote to Betty: 'I am afraid I can't say much on a postcard because the Matron reads them.' Half an hour later she came storming into my ward and said: 'You should not say this.'

One item which lightened the darkness of my boring wool-sorting was the periodical visit to the London Wool Sales in Colman Street with Mr Bentley, the wool buyer. We stayed at a temperance hotel, the Bonnington in Southampton Row, which seemed to be the wool-buyers' rendezvous. A bale of wool can contain as much as 40% of oil and other foreign matter, so much of the skill of a woolbuyer lies in his ability to gauge the actual yield of wool in a bale. Mr Bentley would thrust his arm deep into a bale to handle the wool then announce the figure - say 67% and invite me to do the same. I would then have a go at another bale and announce perhaps 70% and he would say: 'No - 72.' I could never believe that these buyers could really judge a yield with this degree of accuracy. The truth came out literally 'in the wash' for the wool was weighed before and after it was scoured.

After a year in the mill I became a commercial traveller and was given a Morris 12 motor car. My ground was the Eastern Counties, so my job was to call on the knitting wool shops in such towns as Colchester, Norwich and Bury St Edmunds. I became unpopular with our other travellers for, knowing I was only going to do this for a limited period and keen to show results, I worked much harder than they did and opened a record number of new accounts. I cannot say I enjoyed commercial travelling but the experience was of value to me in later years. I found 'reps' to be a boastful and unattractive breed, far inferior to the Yorkshiremen who had become my friends in the mill. I used to meet them in such places as the writing room in the Bell Hotel in Norwich where we gathered to write out our orders for the day. I did not meet them at lunchtime as I always had a standard picnic lunch, a sandwich and a Lyons fruit pie. This gave me more time to explore the towns for new accounts. It also enabled me to save up for Betty's engagement ring out of a generous lunch allowance.

You might have thought my defective colour sense a disadvantage when selling knitting wool. I lived with it quite easily. It was the lady in the shop who liked talking about colour and I soon worked up a plausible answering patter. Anyway I knew all the shade numbers by heart. To this day bottle green is to me 138 and Cambridge blue 222. Patons and Baldwins wools dominated the market and had I been a shopkeeper I would have stocked nothing else. Our particular speciality was our Ladyship Babyship baby wool - '2-ply for undies, 3-ply for outies' as the showcard said. This was my trump card for opening new accounts, though sometimes our leaflets for baby garments took the trick. As I drove around the countryside my castle in the air which I shared at weekends with Betty was a chain of knitting wool shops called 'Rainbow Knitting Shops' with which we were going to make our fortune.

The social hierarchy in the West Riding was and continues to be very different from that of the East and North Ridings of Yorkshire. In the latter peers and baronets abound, living in large country houses, many on considerable estates which their families have occupied for several hundred years. In Halifax there was not even a'humble knight in sight. I do not think I ever met a knight until I went into politics. The elite of Halifax were the mill-owners and their families. Most of the firms were engaged in textiles, machine tools or light engineering. The average workforce was probably under 200. The only really large firms in the town were the Halifax Building Society, the biggest in the world, Mackintosh's toffee, Patons & Baldwin's knitting wools and Crossley's, whose carpet mills were the biggest in Europe. The Crossley family were the only Halifax manufacturers who had joined the large land-owning classes - though not far away at Queensberry the famous Black Dyke Mills had certainly taken the Foster family into that category.

Those mill-owners were by no means obsessed with the modern passion for expansion. The business objective of a family firm was simple and straightforward. It was to keep the family in that state of comfort to which it had become accustomed. A number of small firms, especially those with world famous names in textiles, could have expanded had they wished but saw no particular virtue in doing so. Halifax was a town of small businesses because for the last hundred years the structure of textiles had given the small man his opportunity. If you were a bright young man in a cloth-manufacturing company the chance for you to start up on your own was evident in the fact that many others had done so. The skills required came from your present employment and from the Mechanics' Institute in the town, if you were keen enough to improve yourself. This was not an industry based on 'high tech' and universities. You did not need a lot of capital to set up with one or two looms in a shed as a commission weaver, doing work for a bigger manufacturer. Opportunities of this sort abounded in an industry where vertical integration was the exception.

The sons of the elite went to middle rank public schools, such as Sedbergh and Giggleswick in the north and Shrewsbury, Uppingham and Marlborough in the south. The Leys school at Cambridge seemed popular, probably because of its Methodist foundation. Not many went to Oxford and Cambridge. The daughters of the elite were not burdened with serious education.

Betty started at a boarding prep school, Duncombe Park in the North Riding. She was one of the original band of students at this school, to which her three daughters went in years to come. She went on to a small school in Bexhill-on-Sea run by a Miss Onslow and then on to

Brilamont, a finishing school in Switzerland. Her education was fairly typical of her contemporaries in Halifax. I do not remember any girl going to a university.

Betty always regretted not having been to university but I had no such regrets for in my experience women with brains like hers remain more interesting, attractive and original, when not put through the standard educational machine.

Males of what one might call 'the management class' converged on the Halifax Club after work where they drank and played bridge or snooker until it was time to go home for dinner.

The Territorial Army was a popular hobby. It appealed to me no more than the OTC at school, seeming a laborious way to get one's social fun and an inefficient way of training an army. In the latter I was proved wrong, for when war came the very existence of the Territorial Army, however modestly trained, saved months of valuable time in building up the wartime army.

It is hard to realise the difference that the advent of the motor car made in the West Riding over two generations. Betty's grandfather, Bentley Hoyle, was the proprietor of his firm in Hebden Bridge, employing at a guess 100 people in 1913. He employed them for 56 hours a week. They could not get rid of him at the weekend for on Sunday he was the lay preacher at the Methodist Chapel and no doubt he was there at the Sunday School in the afternoon. No private cars or buses. The train was the only escape to Halifax, Todmorden, Blackpool or Manchester and this was heavily used.

Throw yourself forward only one generation, say to 1925. By then Bentley Hoyle had retired to the Lake District. His son and successor, Jimmy, no longer lived in Hebden Bridge. He had moved to somewhere rather more pleasant, Sowerby Bridge, and came by car to work. But many other West Riding employers had moved further afield to such places as Ilkley. This movement of employers from the places where they employed to more agreeable climes altered the nature of communities. The leaders had deserted. As a Conservative candidate for the Calder Valley in 1949 I soon realised that the leaders of the community in Todmorden, splendid families like the Cockcrofts, were superior to their counterparts in Sowerby Bridge or Elland. Todmorden in the cleft of the hills on the Yorkshire/Lancashire border was too isolated to tempt any leaders to escape to Harrogate or Ilkley. The quality stayed where it was born.

Most of my new friends and acquaintances played golf. I had never done so, but as both Betty's father and brother played for the county and she played well it was not long before I was a member of the golf club.

One of the more cruel trials that I imposed upon Betty was having to come and watch me play rugger on freezing Saturday afternoons. It was not as if I was worth watching for a front row forward never shines and is usually out of sight lost in the scrum. A less than exciting Christmas present I gave her was a pair of fur-lined boots.

My employing uncle, Ernest Osborn, and his brother, Bernard, were leading lights in the Halifax Thespians, as were Denis and Nancy, Ernest's son and daughter. They pressed me to join the Thespians and, currying favour with my employers, I agreed to do so. This was unwise. I was never an actor and though in later years I had no difficulty in remembering speeches, I have never been able to remember a part. I discovered that there were other hazards. These amateur thespians were professional enough to do their own make-up. No-one offered to do mine, so I settled down at the next mirror to my cousin, Denis, and more or less copied on my face what he did to his. This was a mistake. He had a very small mouth and therefore enlarged it. I have a big mouth and when I in turn enlarged that, one could see that someone had blundered.

As few of the girls had careers they had plenty of time for coffee housing, parties, going to dances - in particular at the Queens Hotel at Harrogate - playing golf, tennis and squash, amateur theatricals and so on, and this is exactly what they did. Long distance foreign travel had not yet arrived but quite a few went skiing.

The path of love did not run particularly smooth in my two years in Halifax. Brought up in a loving family Betty was warm-hearted and used to showing her emotions. She was not over-confident but very sure of what was right and what was wrong. She liked getting things done at once and quickly. She was dynamic, effervescent and, despite her lack of formal education, clever; when she qualified as a physiotherapist she passed out top of 400 in the whole of England.

I was a different sort of person. I was self-confident but also self-centred. In my school and university years I had neither been looked after nor had to look after anyone else. I was not shy, but lazy socially and did not take as big a part in conversations as she would have liked.

Betty never thought we saw enough of each other, partly because she had time on her hands but also because she was an impatient sort of person. I, infuriatingly from her point of view, thought that possibly it was as well that we did not see too much of each other considering how long our engagement had got to survive. As a lone bachelor I was inevitably asked out a lot and as it was not generally known we were engaged I was often asked without her. It was not until after we were married that I realised how hopelessly insensitive I was at that stage. Betty told me later how desolated she was when hoping for a romantic present for her birthday I gave her a book entitled 'The Best Plays of 1936.' I once gave her a record of the song 'Smoke Gets in your Eyes' because I was hooked on the tune. She being entirely unmusical took in the words - 'When a lovely flame dies, smoke gets in your eyes,' and was upset.

She was an energetic person, played tennis well and golf very well, but her health was not robust. She often got colds, flu and the like, but more alarmingly from time to time without warning or apparent cause she would faint. Early in our friendship I won hard earned credit from her parents when I carried her up to the house from the stream below the pond at Ashfield - quite a climb. Nobody discovered the cause of this fainting which fortunately got less as she grew older; it was apparently unconnected with her later illness.

Prior to 1834 the Hoyle family were cotton merchants in the Rossendale district of Lancashire, buying pieces woven in cottages and selling them in Manchester. With the coming of the Industrial Revolution, in 1834 mills were opened in Bacup and flourished to such an extent that in 1850 John Hoyle came to live at Old Town above Hebden Bridge to establish what eventually became a prosperous concern. He rented a room in a nearby mill which was equipped for spinning and weaving and then acquired a plot of land of about an acre and built the main portion of Acre Mill. The site, 900 feet above sea level, was well chosen because of the inexhaustible supply of water from the hillside above.

The only other mill at Old Town was Mitchell Mill which, according to local newspaper reports, seemed always to be at war with Acre Mill for one reason or another, such as water rights.

Due to the shortage of cotton during the American Civil War the mill only just kept going. Raw cotton was delivered by rail to Hebden

Bridge station and thence to the mill by horse transport, a steep uphill journey of three miles.

The firm was a pioneer in the manufacture of material for the interior of bicycle and motor car tyres, the second son of the founder being the first man to see the advantages of the cord tyre. As the business progressed and the surrounding district was only sparsely populated, labour was imported from other areas and whole families were brought in from Newcastle and later from the Gargrave district. After the Boer War, when Woolwich became what would now be known as a distressed area on account of the drastic curtailment of the manufacture of armaments, a representative was sent to interview prospective operatives and many large families were transported to Old Town to work in the mill. Groups of twelve year old boys were brought to work in the mill from York Orphanages and lived with families of the employees. The cost of food and clothing was borne by the employers and each boy was given sixpence a week spending money. Rows of houses were built by the mill management to cope with this influx of workers. Quoting again from the local history:

> More than sixty years ago operatives commenced work as 'half-timers,' going to work on alternate days at the early age of ten for a wage of two shillings per week. Work began at 6am and continued until 5.30pm and from 6 - 1 on Saturdays. Doors were locked at three minutes past six every morning, anyone arriving after that time being reprimanded and losing tuppence from his wage. A hooter sounded at 5.20am and again at 5.45am.

John Hoyle was very much a family man, having 16 children, and when he died in 1870 at the age of 50 he weighed 20 stone. The mill went out of family ownership in 1921.

Betty's grandfather, Bentley, was one of the younger sons of the son of the founder. As there was no room for him in the business, he went off to Australia as a young man to seek his fortune, after first getting engaged to his future wife. After eight years he came back from Australia having, in his own eyes, failed. He got married and set up in two cottages in Hebden Bridge as a clothing manufacturer. The business prospered to the extent that while still in his 40's he was able to retire to a large house in Westmoreland in the village of Burton, where he lived until his death at the age of 84.

Bentley Hoyle was not a typical mill owner. Being well-read and musical, retirement presented no problems. He handed the firm down to his son at the earliest opportunity, before Jimmy felt he was ready for such responsibility.

Betty's father, Jimmy Hoyle, was born in a large Victorian house called Ibbotroyd in sight of the mill at Old Town and of a number of other Hoyle houses. He went to school at Aldenham and soon after leaving was caught up in the First World War. He saw a lot of fighting and trench warfare in France, which made a deep impression on him for life. Often when one was talking over the port after dinner at Ashfield the conversation would turn to the war. Those of us who saw fighting in the Second World War were less given to reminiscence, probably because our experience was less intense.

Betty's maternal grandfather was a doctor in St Albans who died early in life - no doubt that's where the doctoring strain in our family comes from.

Her mother, Vi, known to all as Mardi, was a remarkable and much loved character. She died in 1989 at the age of 100. She lived at Ashfield, within a mile of our house, White Cottage, until she was widowed in 1957 and then lived with us at Park Farm throughout the children's childhood and beyond. So she played a large part in our family life.

An assessment of Mardi is difficult. It was sometimes hard to know whether she was clever or stupid. She was a good bridge player and dynamite at racing demon well into her eighties. She read a lot but nothing serious and much of life seemed to pass her by. At some time in their teenage lives the children took her to see Marilyn Monroe, of whom she had not previously heard, in 'The Prince and the Showgirl.' When asked what she thought of Marilyn she said: 'Such a dear girl, but what a pity about her figure.'

In her book, to qualify as a 'dear boy' or a 'dear girl' you had to be a member or close friend of the family and once qualified, in general you could do no wrong.

One of my Army friends, John Wheater, stayed with her at Ashfield for three weeks when he was helping me in an election. He became a 'dear boy', and remained one even after he became one of the Great Train Robbers. Denis Forman, one of my best friends and Felicity's godfather, presented a problem. He was clearly by any standards a 'dear boy' but also a Socialist - to her a contradiction in terms.

She was kind and generous to a fault, but would persist in doing everything herself so was a menace when it came to teamwork. When she worked in a canteen in Halifax in the war much more work actually got done when she was away than when she was there. At home she could never keep out of the kitchen which was why I think she never had any good staff. At Ashfield she had two regulars, one who could not read or write and the other light fingered.

She was elegant. She was physically frail though strangely effective at games. The cup she won for the Halifax Ladies Tennis Championship sometime in the twenties stood on her TV set until her dying day. At golf she hit the ball a tiny distance but infuriatingly ended up with a good score through guile on the greens. She drove a car long after it was safe for her to do so. For some reason she insisted on a car with a twin carburettor. As these were rare among small cars she was hard to suit.

Having said all this I repeat she was greatly loved by the family, her friends and everybody who knew her.

Mardi's life included more than the usual extremes of sadness and happiness. To outlive your only son by 43 years, your husband by 28 years and your daughter by 18 years was tragic for a woman of her affections. On the other hand the joy she got from her three granddaughters was beyond measure.

She would have been touched to hear the tributes they paid to her from the pulpit at her memorial service.

As the months passed it was becoming clear to me that I had no future with Baldwin & Walker. It was typical of the family firms of the West Riding. They were run, understandably, for the benefit of the family. They employed a minimum of non-family executives, most of whom had been with their firms from boyhood and did not expect to be highly paid.

Spurred on by Betty I sought an interview with Uncle Ernest and explained that unless he could reveal prospects at present invisible to me I would have to seek my fortune elsewhere. This did not appear to unsettle him unduly. I don't think he believed me. His main comment was that nobody had left the firm of Baldwin & Walker voluntarily for the last 26 years.

5
Marriage

After I left Baldwin & Walker the Cambridge Appointments Board fixed me up with a job with a firm called Louis London & Sons, a medium sized manufacturer of men's clothing in the East End of London. This was a private firm, owned and managed by four Jews, two in their sixties, their sons in their forties. It was not a place for the easy life. Everybody seemed to work hard, but even that did not prevent a steady turnover of staff as one after another they incurred the displeasure of one of the four Londons.

The most valuable lesson I learned there was responsibility. I was put in charge of the bespoke department. On the Monday and Tuesday of each week hundreds of individual orders came through the post from shops all over the country. On Thursday and Friday these made to measure suits would be despatched. I was always there until 10 o'clock on a Friday night and sometimes until midnight, for - as I was in charge - I had to be there until the last suit had gone.

On my very first morning I was standing looking through a rack of coats which the passer had just passed. Up came Eddie, the oldest and fiercest of the Londons. For lack of anything else to say I suggested that one of the jackets was not up to scratch, to which he replied: 'All right then, what are you going to say to the passer?' and he stood over me while I gave the passer a dressing down, with all the conviction of one who had been in the trade for three hours. Working for the Londons could not be said to be agreeable since three out of the four of them were so horrid. Nevertheless my two years there were not entirely unhappy. For the first time in my working life I had people under me to order about and I found I could do this and still keep their goodwill. Judging by the efforts that the Londons made, firstly to prevent my going to the war and secondly to keep in touch with me during the war with several uncharacteristically generous cheques, I must have been successful in their eyes.

Betty had by now come to London. We celebrated our engagement, my new job and her launch into physiotherapy with an evening out at the Savoy. She found me a bed sitter in Earl's Court Square and she and Ann Henniker, a very old friend also studying physiotherapy, shared a flat in the Cromwell Road only half a mile away from my abode.

In the two years of our official engagement Betty and I saw a lot of each other. We were both working hard, but as our respective flats were so close few weeks passed without our having several meals, usually supper, together. She had a little Ford car so at weekends we visited friends and relations. My parents and brother Michael had come back from Japan and we used to go and see them at Milton Earnest in Bedfordshire where Father had become the vicar as a retiring job.

On June 17th 1939 the great day at last arrived and we were married at St John's Church, Warley, near Halifax, with my brother, Austin, taking the service. There had been a large cocktail party the night before in a marquee at Ashfield to deal with those who could not be accommodated in the church. About a hundred came back to Ashfield after the service for a sit-down lunch and Betty's great Uncle Bertie gave the usual sort of friend of family speech. There was quite a cluster of Bryans there - my mother, my half brother Arthur with his wife, Evelyn, my sister Helen with her husband John Hare, and their daughter Judy and my younger brother Michael as my best man.

The *Halifax Courier and Guardian* of the day reported 'Given away by her father the bride wore a gown of white Chantilly lace, pearl embroidered and a Tudor headdress of pearls. She carried a sheaf of white orchids, stephanotis, and lilies of the valley.'

'The bride's mother's dress was of delphinium blue with coatee trimmed with blue fox, and she wore a spray of orchids on her handbag. The bridegroom's mother wore a dress of figured blue crepe de chine and her bouquet was of red roses.'

It is interesting to see how life has treated our bridesmaids and ushers since our wedding day.

Margaret Beall, 'Muggs,' the prettiest girl at the wedding, was our closest family friend during the children's childhood, at times almost their mother during their own mother's long illness and to this day is in close touch with them. She always made their best dresses beautifully and now does the same for my grandchildren when they are bridesmaids or pages. She is Libby's godmother.

Dorothy Cunningham, as she then was, is a lovely mixture of charm and Scottish competence. She would have been the perfect wife for anyone up to the rank of Prime Minister and beyond. She was won by Jimmy Davidson, a tall handsome Irish Officer in the Duke of

Wellington's regiment. In addition to his good looks and soldierly bearing he had a secret weapon up his sleeve. Dorothy's mother, Mrs Cunningham, was a rugby football fan and, unusually for a middle-aged lady, could discuss the prospects of every club in England, Scotland, Ireland or Wales with anyone. She certainly knew the names of the Scottish team by heart. Jimmy was a great rugger player, at that time playing for the Army, so he was able to fascinate her with tales of the rugger field. He was frequently asked to the house and in due course Dorothy perceived that there was more in this big Irishman than rugby football and a loud laugh. They were married a year after us and have lived happily ever after.

The friendship between the Davidsons and the Bryans has prospered to the extent that Betty was their daughter, Diana's godmother; Dorothy is Felicity's godmother; Libby is godmother to Fiona, Diana's daughter. Despite the war and their long periods overseas our family friendship has remained close.

Francis Blackadder was a brilliant rugger player at Cambridge, an international playing for Scotland, but he was big and clumsy and I never imagined him as a pilot. Nevertheless, he won the first DSO in the Air Force in France in 1939, flying a Hurricane just above the treetops deep into enemy country. In civilian life he had a successful career as a director of Runcimans, the Newcastle shipping firm. Sadly he is now plagued with Parkinson's disease. He is Libby's godfather.

I first met Jim Gillam two years before the war. We both had digs in the same house in Halifax. His parents were great friends of my in-laws and Tom Gillam, an ex regular Army officer, spent many a winter weekend playing golf and shooting with Jimmy. Tom Gillam was head of Homfrays, his wife's family firm which manufactured carpets with great success. Jim was not only the eldest, but also the favourite son, all set to take over the family business in due course. His brother, Denys, an unruly schoolboy and certainly no scholar, was deemed less suitable for the family firm and joined the Royal Air Force before the war.

With the outbreak of war their roles were reversed and Denys became the star. He won the DSO with two bars, DFC with bar and the AFC. As Group Captain Gillam he was one of the most famous pilots in the war. By extraordinary chance my younger brother Michael was serving under him when he was shot down over France in 1944.

With the advent of peace the Gillam brothers' fortunes reversed once again. Tom Gillam died, Jim took over the company and over the next twenty five years made it into one of the most successful textile companies in Yorkshire and himself and his family very rich. He bought a lovely estate at Healaugh, near Tadcaster.

Jim Gillam married Diana Holliday at the beginning of the war. Diana was the beautiful daughter of the tough Yorkshire industrialist and well known race horse owner, Major Leo Holliday. Diana inherited his love for horses and for hunting. Part of my duty as an MP was to attend half a dozen agricultural shows every year in the East Riding and in my early days Diana was at most of them showing horses that she had bred. Her daughter, Vanessa, a friend of Libby's at Duncombe Park, is happily married in Scotland with Libby as godmother to one of her children.

Roy Smith was unique in the literal sense that I never knew anyone quite like him or faintly like him. Academically he was brilliant. He got a first at Cambridge and was Harmsworth Law Scholar of the year. Very few people were aware of this side of his character. In everyday life his brilliance came out in his wit and his sense of humour. He remains the funniest man I have ever known. It was fitting that as I gave the oration at his memorial service from the pulpit of the village church in Spennithorne, from time to time the packed congregation of his friends broke into laughter. He was a successful enough businessman but duller men have done better. What he really enjoyed was sport. I must have played a thousand rounds of golf with him. He was a good soldier and won a Military Cross in the war but on the whole he liked to avoid responsibility. In contrast his wife, Margot, carried all before her in the political world, became Dame Margot Smith and as the top Conservative lady of the year chaired a Conservative Conference at Blackpool. They were an unusual and none too peaceful a couple, but happy - their son Nick is my godson

Betty's brother, Peter, died in the war. He was captured by the Japanese at the fall of Singapore and no more was heard of him. This was not unusual in the case of prisoners of the Japanese and Jimmy and Vi were kept hoping for his return for three years when it was finally learned that he had died in an accident in the prison camp. Peter was the perfect younger brother, loving, intelligent and fun.

The youngest of the ushers, my brother Michael, was quite a happy though not outstanding schoolboy. Eight years younger than me he was the apple of my parents' eyes and his death as a fighter pilot in 1944 was as crushing a blow to them as Peter's was to Jimmy and Vi.

Dorothy Cunningham and Ann Henniker were Betty's closest friends in Halifax. Ann married John Bairstow, a golf-playing solicitor in Halifax. They had two children, Janet and Susie, with whom Bunny is particularly close. Sadly they both died early, John in his early fifties and Ann in a motor accident in Halifax.

After the wedding Betty and I took the 5.15 train from Leeds to London. In my wool-sorting days she had always teased me about staying in such a dull hotel as the Bonnington in Southampton Row when I went up to the London for the wool sales. I counter-teased her by saying that that is where we would stay for the first night of our honeymoon and to add verisimilitude to my unconvincing story I told the taxi man at Kings Cross to go to the Savoy via Southampton Row, slowing down to almost a halt as we passed the Bonington. Betty did not know whether to laugh or cry as this saga unfolded. However, all's well that ends well and she notes in her diary: 'Lovely room at Savoy, nineteen lights, thirteen mirrors, five vases of flowers.' The next day we took the 4.30 train from Victoria to Basle and on to Flims Waldhaus, a picture book village in the Swiss Alps where we spent a happy, sun-drenched honeymoon.

All honeymoons should be special, but ours seemed especially special because we had waited so long - four years. This was only made tolerable because of Betty's complete confidence in our joint future - despite the snail's pace at which my career was progressing - which continued to the end of her life. She alone was quite unsurprised at my later success in the Army and it was her confidence that made me blunder, ignorant and unprepared, into politics.

On our wedding day, June 17th, war was only ten weeks away and its threat hung over Europe, not least over little Switzerland, but as we strolled among the eidelweiss in the sun we managed to pretend it wasn't there.

In the months before our wedding we had spent a lot of time looking for somewhere to live and finally settled for a flat in a Tudor house in the High Street of Seal near Sevenoaks, with which we were highly delighted. It was so genuinely antique that in places you could see daylight between the ancient timbers - charming, but in winter, cold. Much of the furniture had been made specially for the flat by a Mr Edwards and allied to our other purchases and wedding presents it all looked perfect.

Wildernesse Golf Course was only five minutes away and the magnificent Knowle Park stretched beyond that. These first few weeks in our new house were blissfully happy, but by then overshadowed by the darkening clouds of war. We came back from our honeymoon on July 2nd and the entry in Betty's diary for July 6th reads: 'Paul went to his first drill. He is a private in the Fourth Battalion of the Royal West Kent Regiment.' With war in the air there had been a rush of volunteers for commissions in the Territorial Army with consequent delays in acceptances. I joined as a private just to save time. On July 30th I went off with the battalion to a camp at Hythe for a fortnight. Betty's diary entry on August 28th reads: 'Paul called up this evening at two hours notice. Left him at Sevenoaks Drill Hall at 8.30.'

As war broke out my family were spread around the globe: my half-brother, Arthur, was Canadian Consul in Liverpool. Awdry and Vi were in Montreal, he shortly to join the Intelligence Corps of the Canadian Army. Austin was a vicar in Hampshire, shortly to become a chaplain in the RAF. Philip and Margo were in Colombo. Helen and John were in Japan but soon she took the children to Australia and when the Japanese war broke out John was interned. My parents were at the vicarage at Milton Earnest with Michael, who was just about to leave Tonbridge School.

Part Two: War

6
The War: France

For me the war came at an ideal time in relation to my career and my age. It could hardly be said to have nipped a promising career in the bud. I had nothing material to show for my two years with Baldwin and Walker, but in those two apparently barren years I had achieved my greatest success to date - the winning of Betty.

At Louis London's I was more successful than I had been in Halifax but managerial stardom was not on the horizon. On the other hand it was there that I learned responsibility, the most important quality for an army career. Betty too had unconsciously stimulated in me a new interest in people, another necessary leadership attribute. Twenty-five was an ideal age to join an infantry battalion, old enough to be confident and young enough to be able to cope with the rigours of infantry warfare.

The outbreak of war was something of an anti-climax. I was corporal in charge of the guard at Swale Bridge in Kent. Sitting in the burning sun around our trenches at the side of the bridge, stripped to the waist ready to dig more slit trenches, we listened to the Prime Minister's statement at 11 o'clock on the radio. Almost at once we heard the air-raid sirens in London. A false alarm. The Germans were too occupied in the East overrunning Poland to spare time or forces for the West and this remained the situation until the following May - 'the phoney war.'

However, nothing could be taken for granted; all vulnerable points, VPs as they were called, had to be guarded against sabotage or possible attack from parachute troops. As the months passed this seemed less and less likely, but nevertheless the Sixth Battalion of the Queen's Own Royal West Kent Regiment was distributed in penny packets around Kent guarding aerodromes, radio stations, strategic bridges, military research stations and the like.

At that stage we had had so little training that we could hardly be called soldiers, more civilians in uniform. Our military immaturity kept becoming evident, often in dangerous ways. One night at Swale Bridge, luckily not when I was on guard, an airman cycled across the bridge in the semi-darkness. The standing order was that the soldier on guard should challenge anyone crossing the bridge and in the unlikely event of his not stopping after being called upon to halt three times, a warning shot should be fired in the air. In this case the soldier fired a warning shot through the airman's arm. Later in the winter one dark foggy night one of our men detected movement in front of him and as the mover did not react to his challenge he fired a shot. This time a cow it was that died.

During the phoney war I saw a lot of Betty. None of these VPs was far from Seal so few weeks passed without my going home for a night or her visiting me. Her first visit was to Swale Bridge where once again we were digging trenches in the sunshine. One of my soldiers hailed her in an over-familiar way. I said to him: 'Hey, that's my wife.' 'Oh, sorry, Corpie,' He replied.

At Sutton Valence, a beautiful village surrounded by orchards, there was a pleasant pub where Betty sometimes spent the night when I was guarding the radio station.

My promotion was rapid. Private soldier in July, corporal in September, sergeant in October and an officer in November. Normally if commissioned from the ranks one was sent to Sandhurst or to an OCTU (Officer Cadet Training Unit) for four months of officer training before being commissioned to a regiment. Now and then direct commissions were awarded, in which case you were a sergeant one day and an officer the next, but invariably then posted to some other battalion. For some unknown reason I got a direct commission into the same battalion in which I was a sergeant. I have never known this happen before or since. It had the strange outcome that when in Tunisia three years later I became a lieutenant-colonel, I was to command the same battalion in which I started as a private soldier and had never left.

It was then I realised that my decision, taken instinctively, to join the ranks rather than wait for a commission had paid off handsomely, for many of those who chose to wait were still waiting when I got my commission plus the valuable experience in the battalion that preceded it.

At the time of my commission we were actually guarding Detling Aerodrome and its most pleasant immediate effect was that becoming an officer I then moved into the RAF officers' mess, where life was comparatively luxurious. Within a year that officers' mess building had been destroyed by German bombers during the Battle of Britain.

I am by nature a non-diarist and a burner of files. This has had the good effect of shortening this book in that all I can write, or rather dictate, is what I actually remember.

Betty kept intermittently a five year diary which was very little more than a list of happenings. Sometimes their very curtness added poignancy when they recorded in a sentence an event which turned our lives upside down and our emotions inside out - for example:

> April lst. Sunday. Paul left with 6th RWK for France. Started from flat 7am. Travelled via Southampton and Havre. Muggs spent day with me.

Here are some of her entries up to and during the phoney war:

> August 28th. Paul called up evening at two hours notice. Left him at Sevenoaks Drillhall 8.30.

> September 3rd. War declared 11am. Air raid warning 11.15 False alarm.

> October 29th. Paul came to tea and supper from Swanley. Walked up to see puppy he is giving me. Golden Cocker Spaniel called Vim.'

> November 2nd. Paul's commission came through. Mum drove us up to town very early. Staying at Bonnington Hotel. Bought all P's kit. Had fitting, etc. Lunch Spanish Restaurant. Dinner and Dance at Savoy.

Throughout the war Betty's qualification as a physiotherapist was a great boon and she was always welcome at the hospital wherever we or she might be at the time. Her first mention of the hospital comes in her diary entry of October 31st:

> Hospital morning. Paul came back to supper from Swanley. Mum and I fetched Vim from kennels.

In March 1940 I became the battalion Intelligence Officer - in other words the colonel's PA. To become Intelligence Officer, if not a promotion in rank, was at any rate a recognition, in that a colonel does not pick the worst officer as his PA. By then I was sorry to leave Sutton Valence, the VP my platoon was guarding. I had got to know the men and the village pub had become quite a social centre.

The battalion headquarters where I was now to work was at 'The Blue Lagoon,' the public swimming baths at St Mary Cray, only a few miles away so I could live at home at Seal. My colonel, with whom I was henceforth in hourly contact, was a long-serving Territorial, aged 49, though he seemed much older to me. Lt Col Nash was the chairman and owner of W.Nash and Company, Paper Manufacturers, St Paul's Cray. He was kind, meticulous and orthodox to a degree, never surprised you in any way, successful at his paper-making but I could not then imagine him leading us into battle.

In March came the news that the battalion was to move to France in a fortnight's time. In the end we did not go for seven weeks so the feverish packing and preparation calmed down to a steady pace and we were given a week's embarkation leave.

We spent the first night with my parents at the vicarage at Milton Earnest and the rest at Betty's home at Ashfield. By good luck Peter was on leave from the Duke of Wellington's Regiment at the same time, as were Dorothy and Jimmy Davidson. Golf and parties at Ashfield and at the Majestic Hotel at Harrogate, where we met Jim Gillam and his then fiancee, Diana Holliday, were the order of the day.

We went to Betty's grandparents at Burton near Carnforth for the day and stopped at Hebden Bridge on the way to go over the works of J.B.Hoyle & Company, little thinking at the time that I would spend many years of my future working life in that very building.

We spent our last night at the Savoy, the end of a very happy leave.

On April 21st we embarked for France, a dramatic event in the life of the battalion. We could hardly be said to be 'marching as to war.' We were not ready for war. Our training had not advanced much since, nine months before, as a group of civilians, we put on uniforms and called ourselves soldiers. The original Territorial battalion, the 4th Battalion of the Queen's Own Royal West Kent Regiment, had been doubled up and we, the 6th Battalion, were its offspring.

Being divided up into small groups defending Vulnerable Points all over Kent was hardly conducive to training or the creation of a battalion spirit. We were almost devoid of modern weapons. Every man had a rifle similar to those used in the First World War and we only had one automatic weapon, a Bren gun, per platoon instead of three. Our armament against tanks consisted of one anti-tank rifle per platoon, incapable of piercing anything but an armoured car. Our intended role in our first six months in France was, therefore not to fight but to train in the mornings and to help the Pioneers unload railway wagons in the afternoons at Alizay, near Rouen.

Our journey was uneventful. We crossed the Channel in perfect sunshine and were soon accommodated comfortably enough in a tented camp.

Our life, training and unloading trucks in the sunshine was quite fun. Everybody got fit and something of a battalion spirit developed.

When serving abroad officers have to read the soldiers' letters home to make sure they contain no information useful to the enemy. As Intelligence Office I had eight soldiers in my Intelligence section. The enemy would have been surprised at the information in some of their letters, with their accounts of the way we had been bombed and suffered other hardships on our journey. One learnt what I suppose the mature know anyway, that in general people like to be admired or pitied or both.

At the beginning of May 1940 I was summoned to an Intelligence Officers' course at Forges les Eaux, 12 miles east of Rouen. There were 12 of us - one from each of the nine battalions in the division and one from each of the three brigade headquarters. We were to be there a week, spending our time listening to lectures on our duties, the state of the war and of the enemy. We were told, among other things, that the German Army after its campaigns in the East and the effects of our blockade, was showing all the signs of strain and were shown samples of their uniforms to illustrate the low quality of materials to which they were having to resort.

This all proved a little wide of the mark. That very week the German blitzkrieg exploded, their Panzer divisions broke through the 'impregnable' Maginot Line in a dozen places and in no time were racing across France. The immediate effect of these events at Forges les Eaux was a westward stream of wretched refugees, some in motor cars with all their possession on the roof, others in horse-drawn carts and the rest plodding along on foot.

We had received a message from the headquarters of our division, the 12th Division, that our battalions would each send for us. Over the next two days, cars or trucks duly arrived and picked up my 11 companions leaving me on my own in the hotel. I was at a loss to know what to do as I knew that the whole division had moved but had no idea of the whereabouts of my own battalion. Another day passed and I was wondering whether it wouldn't be wiser to join the refugees rather than to wait for the Germans when I suddenly saw a truck bearing the 12th Division markings. I rushed out and managed to stop it and got a lift back to the divisional headquarters, some miles away. In its move towards the battlefront at Doullens my own battalion was due, during the night, to pass through Forges les Eaux and the plan had been for my commanding officer, Lt-Col Nash, to pick me up en route. He had forgotten all about me which was just as well for had he remembered I - like him - would have spent the rest of the war as a guest of the Germans. In the desperate situation his untrained, semi-armed battalion, had been strung out along an impossibly wide front and was duly rounded up bit by bit by the German armoured columns, nearly all taken prisoner.

The British Army was now in full retreat, the bulk of it towards Dunkirk and its eventual evacuation from that port and by small boats from the neighbouring beaches.

The remains of the 12th Division fled westwards and we came to a halt at Nantes, on the Atlantic coast 150 miles away. I had a particularly nerve-wracking duty. Being an Intelligence Officer I was supposed to be good at map-reading so was given a little car in which to lead a convoy of lorries. I found the French maps hard to read and when now and then I got it wrong, I got it wrong together with 50 lorries behind me.

When we came to rest at Nantes it transpired that I was not the only survivor of my battalion. Lt John Carr with a party of six had managed to escape through the advancing Germans. On the way, one of the party, Sergeant Fenton, had bayonetted a German soldier so it was as well that they were not captured. The battalion rear party, numbering 16, under Lt John Culham, had not been in the battle and also turned up at Nantes. Unknown to us most of the battalion transport drivers under Lt Jack Nixon had already escaped through Boulogne.

Amid the general chaos, astonishingly and absurdly, the complete battalion post arrived at Nantes including a mountain of parcels. The parcels were nearly all full of food, the contents noted on the labels, so we feasted on a diet markedly superior to the army ration.

By now, though we did not know it, the evacuation at Dunkirk was complete. At my level we had no idea what was going to happen to us.

Then after a couple of days a string of lorries arrived. We were transported to Cherbourg, transferred into cross-channel steamers and sailed peacefully to Southampton on a calm sunny day with no German aeroplanes in sight.

Since all my 25 companions lived in Kent, not too far from Southampton, they all thought they would be home in no time. We were put in a train which hardly stopped until it got to Newcastle, 400 miles to the North. It did stop in York station long enough for me to ring up Betty who was happily flabbergasted, especially as she had just had a letter from me, indicating by our private code where I was in France. On the platform at Newcastle we were greeted by officers of the Northumberland Fusiliers as war heroes in need of comfort and rest. In truth few of us had seen a shot fired in anger or even been bombed from the air. We had spent the last days lounging about in the sun, overeating and waiting for something to happen. However, we did not want to spoil their plan which was to give us a week's perfect rest staying in a good hotel with them looking after our troops.

Betty came up the next day and we had an uproariously happy evening together. The day after, she got 'flu.

The following weeks were very different. We camped on the moors near the village of Wark, about eight miles from Hexham. Our battalion still numbered three officers and 24 men, the officers in order of seniority being John Carr, myself and Culham.

The battalion Transport Officer, Jack Nixon, arrived with 50 of his drivers. Then a message came from the War Office that 200 men would be coming. We had not got nearly enough tents for that number so we went round the local farms arranging shelter for the rest. Twenty officers arrived. By now cheerful chaos reigned. It was all so unmilitary as to be hilarious. But not for long. We were brought down to earth by the news that a lieutenant-colonel, a commanding officer, was on his way.

I said to John Carr: 'Before he comes we had better decide what jobs we want. Whatever we tell him we are, we are likely to be.' John Carr said: 'I would like to be the adjutant.' Culham and I said we would like to be company commanders.

So when the great man arrived we introduced ourselves to him in these various roles which he naturally did not question. Two years later when we landed on the shores of Algeria I was still commanding D Company which I had chosen for myself.

This was the first and last time I took any liberties with Lieutenant-Colonel 'Swifty' Howlett, so nicknamed because he played cricket for Kent as a fast bowler. He was a magnificent soldier, the best trainer of men and in particular officers that I came across throughout the war. In the two years before we next went into action in North Africa he trained us up into what must have been one of the best battalions in the Army. Swifty was also an admirable fighting soldier. After the Tunisian campaign he became a brigadier and was just about to be made a general when he was killed in Italy.

Twenty-nine months passed between our escape from France and our landing in Algeria for the North African campaign. We were first stationed in the Malvern area, allegedly a mobile reserve, ready to be rushed to any point threatened by German landings. Our mobility consisted of a fleet of Corona fruit-drink vans, our armament, a few Bren guns and a rifle and 50 rounds of ammunition per man. The majority of the battalion had never fired a rifle and as only five rounds were available for practice, in the heat of battle I imagine we would have been as dangerous to each other as to the Germans. However, under the iron hand of Swifty Howlett, as a disciplined body we were improving by leaps and bounds.

Betty joined me there, our quarters being the Club House of the Malvern Golf Club. Dick and Bridget Allen shared our house, the start of a long family friendship. It was at that time that the Germans launched their bombing campaign on our big cities and we could hear, night after night, the bombs falling on Coventry.

Swifty Howlett believed in training the battalion on a competitive basis. My company, D Company, won most of the competitions mainly because I was blessed with a brilliant team, the leading lights being John Sibree, later to become a distinguished staff officer, and as company-sergeant-major, Landman, a future battalion quartermaster.

In November 1940 we moved on to Haverfordwest, a rundown market town in Wales, where again we shared a house, 'Camelot,' with the Allens, this time a council house. Life continued at a hectic exhausting rate with long marches and endless cross-country exercises. Our sister battalion in the brigade, the Buffs, operated under a far milder commanding officer and with more time on their hands romance flourished and a number of their officers got married. We were far too busy for that sort of thing. At Haverfordwest Bridget Allen gave birth to Jane, destined to be Betty's godchild and our, as yet unborn, Libby's best friend for many years to come.

At about this time there were all the signs that we were going to be sent off to the Middle East. We were actually issued with tropical kit. I still have a photograph of me looking ridiculous in a solar topee. This turned out to be a false alarm but not before we had enjoyed a delightful embarkation leave with the Allens at Branksome Towers Hotel, a pleasant place near Bournemouth.

Among our preparations for active service was the widespread making of wills which we were all strongly advised to do. Frank Taylor, whose finances were notoriously shaky had just put himself further into debt with yet another bet, this time on an obviously unreliable horse called Hasty Shot. As he signed his will he said: 'What a surprise for Mum.'

In August 1941 we moved to a more attractive area, Inverary, in the highlands of Scotland, where we lived in Nissen huts in the grounds of Inverary Castle. There we practised assault landings on Loch Fyne, and then from an assault landing ship in the Hebrides, at one point landing on the beach at Tarbet, made famous by the film *Whisky Galore*. We then reboarded the *Winchester Castle* and sailed down to Glasgow to another Nissen-hutted camp in a dreary suburb called Pollock.

Training now rose to a new crescendo. The training grounds were to the south of the city on the road to Stewarton and around the village of Eaglesham. So a routine training day involved the march of eight to 10 miles, quite apart from the distances covered across country in the course of training. To add to our toil, the battalion generally carried the full loads of ammunition and equipment laid down for assault landings.

Several large exercises stand out in my memory. One of these consisted of a march of about 30 miles from Greenock through Inverskip, Largs, Kilburnie, Loch Winnock and back to Glasgow. After many hours marching in bitter cold weather and having had nothing to eat all day the battalion halted between Largs and Kilburnie and was given a large hot meal at about midnight. Despite the intense cold, some of the men decided to snatch a little sleep before we were due to move on again at about four in the morning. But the warmth engendered by the hot meal was deceptive and before an hour was passed those who had attempted to sleep were desperately trying to restore the circulation to limbs chilled by 14 degrees of frost. Needless to say, no-one had any rest that night. Before dawn we resumed our weary marching until the scheme closed in the mid-afternoon and we all trudged back to the camp in Glasgow. Our trials were still not quite over, for a mile from camp we were met by the battalion band and required to march to attention with arms sloped, just to prove to ourselves that we were not as finished as we thought.

On another exercise, jokingly called 'Exercise Dryshod,' we set out one cold wintry afternoon across the hills between Stewarton and Strathavon - an area of bleak moors nearly one 1000 feet high with few and rough roads. As the evening wore on it grew cold and began to snow heavily. On the higher ground we had to force our way through drifts of snow.

In the early hours of the morning the brigade deployed for an attack across country. The unfortunate leading companies of our neighbouring battalion walked on to the frozen surface of a reservoir which in the half light looked like a level snow-covered piece of ground. The ice gave way and many of the men were immersed waist deep in water. By the end of this exercise some of the men were losing consciousness and had to be carried on stretchers which, through the snowdrifts, was no easy task.

By now we were fantastically fit and no-one was surprised when ordered to our next station, Crieff in Perthshire, that Swifty Howlett had decided that we should march there, which we duly did - 60 miles in three days, packs on backs. As usual, as we were approaching Crieff, footsore and weary, we were greeted by the battalion band and had to march at attention the last mile to the Crieff Hydro, a mammoth hotel which was to be our next home.

At just about this time there was a fundamental change in infantry training which had a profound effect on the battalion. Hitherto training had been based on the development of fire power and infantry attack, much as at the end of the 1914-18 war. Henceforth, the individual was to be regarded as the smallest tactical unit in battle, and the development of battle-drill - the constant practice of fire and movement on the parade ground, taught each man his role as an individual in the various phases of battle. At the same time officers and men were sent to Battle Schools intended to reproduce the physical conditions and the mental terrors of war. The novelty and individuality of this type of training was a welcome release to junior officers and NCOs. Officers returning from the Battle Schools understood the new form of training better than their seniors and since the new ideas had, under pressure from the War Office, to be adopted quickly, these officers were often able to take the initiative. From now on there was much independent company and platoon training.

Once we were in Crieff wives were not allowed and Betty stayed at Ashfield. This was sad but made tolerable by the great news that the long-awaited Libby was on the way. She was born to our great joy on May 13th 1942. The timing was perfect for four months later the battalion embarked for North Africa.

Leaving Betty was hard but knowing she had Libby made it much less so.

7
Djebel Abiod

In October 1942 Rommel had been defeated at El Alamein and his army was in the long retreat towards his base at Tripoli. The allied plan with which we were concerned was to land an army at Algiers and race along the coast to Tunis and thence to Tripoli from the West. The unknown factor was the French army in Algeria. The French were deeply offended at Churchill's sinking of their fleet in Oran harbour and might well have decided to resist our landings, a great snag considering the lightness of our forces.

None of this did we know as we embarked in the *Marnix*, a Dutch liner, at Gourock, but as we steamed out of the Clyde into the open sea we soon saw that we were part of a large convoy.

As it sailed through the Bay of Biscay it grew in size as additional passenger ships joined us from various quarters and four great battleships joined our accompanying destroyers.

On November 1st our commanding officer, Swifty Howlett, put us in the picture. Our battalion was to be part of the reserve during the initial landings at Algiers and as soon as this had been achieved we were to sail on to do an assault landing at Bougie, a port further up the coast.

Despite the cramped conditions on board we prepared and overprepared for our landing. Maps were studied again and again; every officer and man knew his role in the coming battle. Weapons were cleaned, ammunition checked. Physical exercises were done endlessly. Our crew-cut heads made us look like Americans. We eventually sailed blacked out through the Straits of Gibraltar, the land dark, the town below the rock blacked out, but lights twinkling on the opposite Moroccan coast.

At 1.15 on the morning of the 8th November 1942, the invasion of Algeria was launched with the 5th Battalion of the Northamptonshire Regiment of the 11th Brigade, which was also on our ship, being the first troops to land. It was hoped that the French would not resist, in which case we in reserve would not disembark. In the event there was some resistance at the airfield at Blida and for 24 hours the situation was sufficiently confused for us to be ordered ashore.

Our landing was something of an anti-climax, more like our exercises at Inverary than a real battle. As we clambered down the side of the ship in the darkness into our assault craft we heard no noises of battle and, not for the last time in action, wondered what was happening. It was as well that we did not have an enemy to cope with for in the darkness the navy managed to land my company on the wrong beach, though the naval officer in charge of my particular craft was reluctant to admit it.

During the next morning it transpired that the French had capitulated, and we were ordered back on to our ship. This was easier said than done for by now the sea had become positively rough and a number of our assault landing craft (ALCs) overturned, fortunately without casualties. We had to board larger replacement motor landing craft which meant wading up to our waists through the waves.

We then re-prepared ourselves for our main role as the leading troops landing on the beach at Bougie. This was more exciting. As we clambered down the nets on the side of our ship we could see the naval ships looming up in the semi-darkness. Despite their bulk they were manoeuvred with great skill. Just as we were coming up to the beach at dawn one could see the two massive sixteen inch guns of the monitor *Roberts* pointing menacingly over our heads at the shore defences. I almost wished that the French would show a wee bit of resistance so one could see the guns in action, but we were unopposed and before long we were marching into the town, finishing up in defensive positions on the high ground overlooking the port of Bougie, though the cunningly sited pillbox commanding the beach had been an unpleasant reminder of what we would have had to face had the French chosen to fight.

All was peace and sunshine until the afternoon when three evil great lumbering Italian bombers came over and dropped their bombs only to be shot down by our destroyers as they banked away. They were followed at intervals by waves of German JU88 dive bombers which hit a cruiser and sank two of the three troopships, the *Cathay* and the *Karanja*. All through the night the blazing hulk of the *Cathay*, a beautiful P&O liner, lay on the surface of the water, whilst every few minutes the roar of exploding ammunition resounded across the harbour. There was something terrifying, awesome and sad as just before dawn with a hiss of steam this great ship slipped to the bottom. Our old friend, the *Marnix*, though bracketed by bombs, managed to

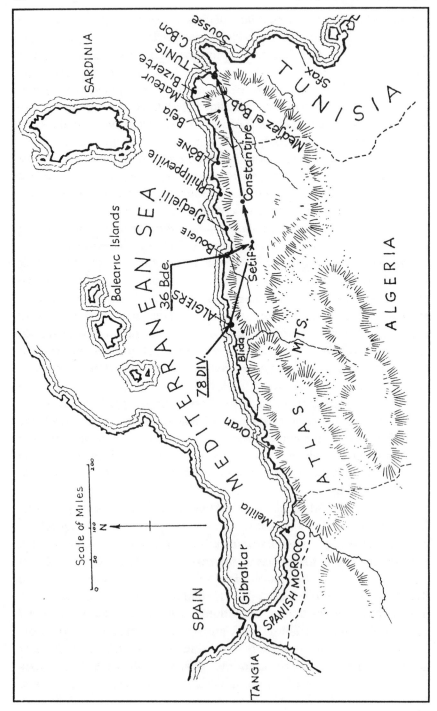

sail away to Algiers unharmed and I believe survived the war, having previously been the last ship out of Singapore.

Though we did not realise it at the time, the sinking of the *Cathay* was to have a very personal effect on each of us during the coming months. For with it went our overcoats, which meant that we were faced with living *al fresco* for the next two months of a Tunisian winter with no protection from the elements except a shirt, a vest, a sweater, denim trousers and a gas cape.

The next day the four rifle companies boarded two destroyers and sailed east up the coast to the port of Bone. As dawn broke and we were entering the harbour a German JU88 appeared overhead, not a welcome sight when we were all crowded on the decks waiting to land. Mercifully its first two bombs landed in the harbour, by which time our ship had reached the quay and we had scrambled ashore hardly waiting for the ship to be tied up. It came over once more and this time the ship's anti-aircraft guns brought it crashing down onto a warehouse in the docks, to our deafening cheers.

We then marched 25 kilometres to Lake Fetzara, where we took up defensive positions and waited for the rest of the battalion, which was coming up by road from Bougie. Eleven French charcoal-burning lorries and several similarly propelled buses were commandeered to complete the transport of the battalion. They were smelly and difficult to start, but enabled us to motor up the coast for another eighty miles to Tabarka. There were still no signs of any enemy on the ground, but at this point it became clear that they had complete air superiority. We had still to see an allied plane. From now on we were dive-bombed by JU88s or straffed by fighter planes several times a day. So far our casualties were only two trucks destroyed and several men wounded.

These early attacks were a salutary lesson in concealment from the air. When not actually on the move we tried to make ourselves invisible in woods. This was not totally effective because the enemy pilots would often know which woods we were likely to be in and machine-gunned them at random, although this did not actually cause many casualties. The enemy pilot was in a position similar to a sportsman shooting at a covey of partridges, who imagines that by shooting into the middle of the covey some bird is bound to fall. This proves not to be so. You have to pick an individual bird to get any result.

The first time we were machine-gunned in a wood was a truly terrifying experience with machine-gun bullets tearing through the trees all around us, the process being repeated a few minutes later when the plane returned to give us another dose. But when it was all over we found that nobody had been hit.

One of the bravest acts I came across in our early days in Tunisia took place on the all-important bridge at Tabarka. A Royal Engineers truck loaded with explosives was attacked from the air and set on fire as it was crossing the bridge. The driver, guessing that it would soon blow up, made a dash for it. Stephen Fletcher, a gunner officer from Halifax, seeing that if the truck blew up the bridge would be destroyed, calmly walked onto the bridge, got into the truck and drove it off into some waste land where in due course it did blow up. Though his hands were badly burnt Stephen Fletcher refused to be evacuated and he went on to fresh acts of bravery a few days later in the battle of Djebel Abiod and later in Sicily. He was awarded the DSO.

Although the allied landings in Algeria had taken the enemy by surprise, their reaction was swift. The German airforce occupied the airfield at Tunis only a day after our landings and German and Italian troops began to arrive in large numbers in Tunisia by air and sea within a week.

At last we came to the event for which we had been so vigorously training for the last two and a half years - a battle with the Germans. They had been hurrying westwards along the coast road from Tunis as fast as we had been hurrying eastwards. We were destined finally to clash at the village of Djebel Abiod, twenty one miles to the east of Tabarka at the junction of the roads south to Beja and east to Bizerta.

The march was along a main road, twisting through the hills, where cork oaks afforded good cover from enemy aircraft which dropped flares overhead during the night. Djebel Abiod proved to be a collection of no more than thirty to forty houses scattered round the road junction and a battalion headquarters was set up in the telephone exchange.

The position was not an easy one to defend. The road from Tabarka approached the village round the spur of a large hill, meandering gently down the slopes to the road junction in the village, where the road to Beja took a sharp left turn over a modern concrete suspension bridge under the lea of a small hill. The other road, straight on through the village, entered a narrow defile on the way to Beja. The three

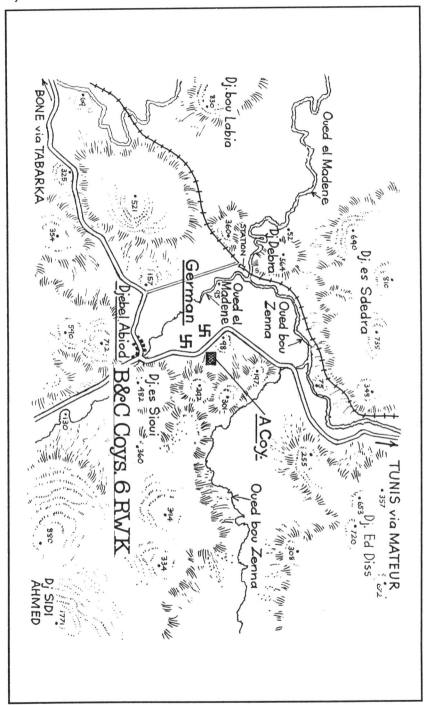

company commanders (my company had been left behind at Tabarka to defend brigade headquarters) had to reconnoitre their positions in the darkness and adjust them as best they could in the light of dawn. A Company was stationed to the right of the village covering the bridge over the *oued* (river) with one platoon forward and on the other side of the river. B Company were well to the left and C were immediately in and around the village. The battalion's six two-pounder anti-tank guns, which had only arrived in Algiers the day before, were placed in positions covering the bridge over the river and the road as well as the valley leading to Beja.

During the rest of the morning the battalion dug in with a skill born of long training. At a quarter past two in the afternoon, C Squadron of 56 Reconnaisance Unit, which had pushed forward in armoured cars along the road to Bizerta, reported that an enemy column of tanks with motorised infantry was on its way. Fifteen minutes later eleven enemy tanks (Mark IIIs and Mark IVs) from the Afrika Korps, and a company of motorised infantry from a Parachute Engineer battalion, appeared on the main road leading to the bridge over the *oued*. Meanwhile a troop of 25-pounder guns from 138 Field Regiment had just arrived from Algiers and immediately took up positions to open fire on the tanks with solid shot at short range, firing over open sights.

When the enemy were within two hundred and fifty yards and had passed the forward platoon of A Company our 2-pounder anti-tank guns and the field artillery opened fire and within a few seconds had knocked out five tanks including the leading one in which the officer was still looking out of the open turret. As the crew climbed out of the damaged tank they were killed by our Bren gunners. This action by our field gunners, led by Stephen Fletcher of Tabarka bridge fame, was immensely brave. Field guns, having no protection, are normally sited in some convenient valley behind the infantry out of sight of the enemy and have their fire directed by radio by a forward observation officer. Stephen's guns went into action at short range in full view of the enemy tanks with devastating effect, but with inevitable casualties of which he was one.

Meanwhile, Lance Corporal Roberts, a bricklayer from Tunbridge Wells who was a Bren gunner in the forward platoon of A Company, commanded by Lt John Maling, whose father won the VC in the first world war, was given the opportunity to use his weapon to full effect. This platoon was dug in about 300 yards ahead of the rest of the battalion just to the right of the Mateur road. Not only had they dug their slit trenches with great efficiency but had camouflaged them so well with the local brushwood that the German tank crews had not seen them as they rumbled by en route for the battle just described. This was exciting enough for Roberts as he peered through his cover, but imagine his emotions when, a few minutes later, three lorry loads of infantry drew up straight in front of the platoon's position and started debussing. The men held their fire with admirable discipline until about half the Germans had got out of their buses. Then John Maling gave the order; Roberts squeezed the trigger of his Bren gun and with a deafening clatter emptied an entire magazine into a cluster of milling Germans, not more than fifty yards away. The other two Bren gunners and the riflemen of the platoon followed suit and in the following carnage fifty Germans must have been killed. The rest ran away and escaped out of sight into some lower ground where they were later joined by the surviving tanks. As dusk fell German stretcher parties could be seen gathering their dead and wounded.

John Maling now decided to withdraw his men and the main body of A Company in the village. Now that the position of his platoon had been exposed by their fire it would have been untenable against any counter-attack with tanks and they had more than done their duty. To have gone straight back down the road to the village in the semi darkness would have been asking for trouble for they might well have been taken for Germans by our men. John therefore took his platoon by a circuitous route across country and around the mountain which dominated the crossroads, actually rejoining the battalion many hours later.

Despite their casualties the enemy tanks and infantry re-grouped and made a desultory attack, this time trying to cross the shallow waters of the *oued* instead of the bridge, but B Company were not to be moved.

To add to the confusion one of the battalion's ammunition trucks, which was attempting to reach the village, was hit and caught fire. The crackle of exploding bullets and the louder bangs of exploding mortar bombs made it appear that B Company were heavily engaged whereas in fact no enemy reached within striking distance of their positions.

Intermittent firing continued until dusk, when the enemy troops withdrew leaving behind five disabled tanks and a number of dead.

They no doubt took away more dead and wounded. Another tank was later discovered abandoned in the river bed, stuck in the loose sand.

In this first battle the battalion learnt a number of valuable lessons. Firstly, battle is always confused. Those neat arrows on television screens and newspaper maps depicting definite victories or defeats do not look like that on the ground. Only at the end of the day did the battalion realise that they had imposed a humiliating defeat on veterans of the Afrika Korps. Their discipline under fire, acquired through months of hard training, had worked. This was to give them enormous confidence which they were to need in the rough times ahead. Our casualties turned out to be relatively light. No officer had been killed or wounded and the number of casualties among the other ranks was small.

Meanwhile D Company, my command, was 20 miles back, positioned to defend brigade headquarters. During the fighting at Djebel Abiod every sort of rumour came back to us, all implying that the Germans had broken through and would soon be in sight - yet another lesson of war - that rumours are always alarmist and nearly always wrong.

We spent all day preparing our positions to defend brigade headquarters, which was situated in a cork factory near Tabarka. During the night a troop of 40mm light anti-aircraft guns arrived from Algiers. The next attack by enemy aircraft was therefore awaited with more than interest, but to the company's disappointment no attack came until just before lunch and even then the enemy fighters disappeared as soon as the guns started firing.

Nothing more spectacular occurred until the late afternoon when, hearing the noise of engines above the clouds, everyone stood by for the expected attack. Suddenly a single fighter dived almost vertically out of the clouds followed by two other planes, whereupon the Bofors guns at once opened fire and knocked the tail off the leading plane, which crashed to the ground. The men were cock-a-hoop at this success and I at once sent an officer, Ronnie Palmer, to identify the plane. When he returned the look of horror on his face told its story. The plane was in fact a Hurricane, a British plane which had been on reconnaisance until spotted by the enemy and forced down through the clouds. The pilot had lost his head and legs in the crash and could not be identified.

The brigadier then ordered me to take D Company up to Djebel Abiod in preparation for an attack expected next morning. We mounted the charcoal-burning lorries, arrived at midnight and took up positions in the houses on the edge of a village, with the exception of Shaun Stewart's platoon which was sent to take up a hill position on the right flank and forward of the battalion. From dawn onwards the village was intermittently shelled, we presumed in preparation for an attack, but no tanks or infantry showed themselves.

At midday the enemy moved a self-propelled gun to a hull- down position behind the embankment of the road about 1000 yards away, from which it was able to fire high-velocity solid shot and high-explosive shells directly at the houses in the village. This was an unnerving experience for those occupying these buildings and the battalion headquarters was compelled to move several times. Our own gunners did their best to silence this gun, but every time shells got too close for comfort the gun - the crew protected by a shield of armour plate - moved away again.

In the early afternoon we were bombed and machine-gunned by Messerschmit 109F fighter bombers. By now the troop of light anti-aircraft guns which had defended us at Tabarka had arrived and been sited in and around the village. As soon as they opened fire at the enemy aircraft the village was heavily shelled. Nevertheless, the crews continued to fire at the aircraft as they leisurely circled the village before deciding where to drop their bombs. Before the day was through two out of the four guns had been put out of action. During that raid the battalion suffered its first officer casualty when Lt Norman H.Edden was killed by a bomb which landed close to the bridge over the *oued*.

The exposed defensive position at Djebel Abiod was held by the battalion for nine days, between the 17th November and the night of the 26th-27th. We were then relieved by 8 Argyll and Sutherland Highlanders, apart from my company which remained with the Argylls until the night of the 29th. During this period casualties were not heavy, but persistent and accurate shelling added to frequent bombing attacks put a strain on the men. More demoralising perhaps was the lack of any opportunity to hit back at the enemy in the face of the superior range and firepower of his mortars and machine-guns and the dominance of their airforce.

On most days we had to endure at least two attacks by fighter bombers. When these took place everyone crouched at the bottom of his trench, hoping it wasn't his turn to be singled out for attention. The bombs did not matter so much because we could judge from the direction in which the plane was flying whether or not the bomb slowly parting company with the aircraft was likely to fall in the immediate vicinity. Straffing, however, was quite another matter. The aircraft changed direction so quickly and the bullets had so wide a cone of fire that it was impossible to be sure that one was not in danger of being hit, and when the tail of the plane was in line with the centre of the propeller-boss one could only hope the pilot was not pressing the firing button at that moment.

On the morning of the 20th the battalion was greatly encouraged when the usual squadron of aircraft turned out to be Spitfires and not Messerschmit 109s. The men watched with glee as the British planes circled the village and the German positions for about five minutes. At last, they thought, the enemy would get a taste of his own medicine and we should have the satisfaction of knowing that we could hit back. Imagine the disappointment when the squadron flew away without firing a shot.

On the 22nd November Lance Corporal Donnelly of 18 Platoon in my company volunteered to take two men, Privates Clews and Kench, along the bed of the *oued* to the flank of the German positions, to see what was doing. Late in the afternoon they returned to say they had found a Mark IV tank abandoned by the edge of the river and no sign of any enemy. With the agreement of the Argylls' battalion headquarters I decided to send out a fighting patrol under Lt. Shaun Stewart with instructions to destroy the tank with an anti-tank grenade fired from a cup discharger. As soon as it was dark the patrol, Shaun, three men with Thompson sub-machine guns, two men with rifles and a Bren gunner, entered the *oued* by the road bridge. As usual in North Africa, the river, which at this time of the year was little more than a series of interconnected pools, had scoured a deep gash across the plain. Making use of the small willow-like bushes growing near the water and under the shadow of the twenty-foot bank of the river, the patrol advanced in short bounds. The moon was rising and visibility extended to about one hundred and fifty yards. About half way to the objective Lance Corporal Donnelly, who was leading the way, gave the warning of the approach of a German patrol about three hundred yards ahead. The patrol immediately halted and took up positions among the bushes by the edge of the river, but strain as they might the rest of the patrol could not see them. Nevertheless Donnelly's remarkable eyesight had not failed him and very shortly they all saw the patrol of about eight Germans pushing their way in single file along a stretch of sand on the far side of the water, followed by another six about five yards behind. When the leading Germans were less than one hundred yards away Shaun Stewart gave the order to fire. Two of the Tommy guns were jammed with mud and would not fire, but the other weapons released a hail of bullets which struck down at least two of the leading file of the enemy patrol. As soon as the magazines were empty Shaun gave the order to withdraw to a position five hundred yards back. As they retired a Spandau light machine gun fired tracer bullets hysterically into the air above their heads.

Although the enemy tank had not been destroyed the Commanding Officer of the Argylls was well satisfied with the patrol. Not so Lance Corporal Donnelly. The next morning the small, mild looking, soft spoken ex-railway booking clerk and his two comrades volunteered to make another attempt to destroy the enemy tank - this time by daylight using a sticky grenade (rather like a toffee apple). Some long time after the trio had departed, half a dozen fighter bombers made one of their usual attacks on the village and on this occasion the light anti-aircraft guns were firing very close to one of the enemy planes as it dived down and disappeared from sight, low in the distance. At that very moment a great column of black smoke rose up into the air and in jubilation the gunners claimed their first success.

Meanwhile there was no news of Lance Corporal Donnelly and his patrol until just as they were about to be given up as lost, at about dusk, they returned very tired to say that the tank had been destroyed. They had reached their objective without much difficulty, but the grenade had rolled off the side of the tank and fallen into the water, failing to explode. Undeterred the patrol cast round for some other means of achieving their object. Fortunately the enemy had left some four gallon cans of petrol and a camouflage net beside the tank. The net was put in the locker of the tank and soaked with petrol. With the addition of some British and German grenades and a rag dipped in petrol as an ignition cord, this recipe made a fine conflagration. It was this we had seen immediately after the air raid. For these exploits Lance Corporal Donnelly later received the Military Medal.

Just after dawn on the following day, the 24th, the enemy made an abortive attack on the Argylls positions on the side of the hill immediately above the village. The attack was not preceded by an artillery bombardment, nor was there any supporting fire from the main German positions in the valley. Indeed there was at first a great deal of argument as to whether or not the dark blue uniforms of the advancing troops, numbering between eighty and a hundred, belonged to our French allies, and for a time no-one was allowed to open fire. The defences were meanwhile fully manned in case the approaching troops turned out to be hostile. When some Argylls on the extreme right seemed to have been taken prisoner all doubts were removed.

In the action which followed, Shaun Stewart's platoon of my company played by far the largest part. By lucky chance the courtyard of the large house in which they were stationed (along with the Argylls' battalion headquarters) looked out across the front of the village and had a clear field of fire to where the enemy troops were clustered in the scrub on the hillside about 600 yards away. The courtyard was surrounded by a large wall some eight feet high and 18 inches thick. With the aid of bales of straw to stand on, this made a perfect fire position for the platoon's four Bren guns (an extra gun had been found by the patrol along the river bed) and was used to devastating effect. With three loaded magazines lying beside each gun the platoon commander was able to give a classic fire order using a large white rock on the hillside as a reference point.

The crowded ranks of the enemy were an easy target and many were hit in the opening burst of fire. Those who survived took cover in the scrub and tried to return the fire but their blue uniforms and white faces showed up clearly against the dark green background and attracted a hail of bullets every time they moved. A few spent bullets from the enemy's 9mm Birretta sub-machine guns lodged themselves in the woodwork in the side of the barn, but without any damage to any of our own troops. After some 10 minutes of this one-sided action the enemy showed the white flag and 30-40 of them, including one officer, surrendered.

After this action I took D company to rejoin the rest of the battalion at Tabarka, but after two days of 'rest' in the pouring rain we were warned to be prepared to take part in a brigade attack on enemy positions which were reported on the high ground astride the road north of Djebel Abiod. The next two days were spent in resting and in clearing the approach to our main objectives of any enemy outposts, in the course of which D company killed three Italian parachutists and captured 14 more.

The 26th November was spent in our concentration area digging positions and quietly resting after the exertions of the last few days. But even on 'quiet' days tragedy can strike and on that day the battalion quartermaster, Lt Huskisson, was killed in an air raid.

8
Green and Bald Hills

The advance towards Mateur was resumed at 1am on the 28th November. Three hours later the battalion halted in a wood west of Sedjenane to allow the 8th Argylls and the 5th Buffs to pass through in that order. We then brought up the rear of the brigade. After another hours march the battalion reached the village of Sedjenane, where D Company was detached from the main body and ordered to advance by a secondary road northwards towards Cap Serrat in an attempt to link up with 1 Commando, who were to make a landing on the coast that night.

The brigade meanwhile continued to advance along the main road with the Argylls as advance guard. As the sun rose the day grew warm, and for the first time our aircraft were to be seen patrolling the sky overhead. For the rest of the day almost continuous air cover was provided by two squadrons of Spitfires. After a few miles the road plunged into a narrow defile leading through the hills to the plains north of Mateur. On the northern side of the defile Djebel Azzag rose for 600 feet above the level of the road and to the south Djebel Ajred towered for more than 1000 feet, these features came to be known as Green Hill and Bald Hill.

The position was perfect for defence and it might have been expected that the hills on either side of the road would have been cleared before the leading battalions advanced into the defile. But the brigade had orders to press on to Bizerta with all speed and there was no time to waste in reconnoitring hills. Accordingly the Argylls moved into the mouth of the pass in the middle of the afternoon of 28th November with a company spread out in single file on either side of the road, interspersed with the Bren gun carriers of their carrier platoon.

At half past three, when the leading companies were in the middle of the pass, the Germans opened up with scores of light and heavy machine-guns; the road and the bare open valley floor on either side of it were swept with bullets from perfectly sited positions and the effect was devastating. Within minutes all of the Bren gun carriers were shattered and for months afterwards the wrecks of eight of them could be seen spaced out evenly along the road. Within 10 minutes the battalion had lost about 150 men, killed or missing, including all but six men of the leading company.

As a fighting unit the Argylls were temporarily out of action. Three out of four company commanders had been wounded and the battalion decimated.

Clearly no progress could be made until the two dominating features were cleared of enemy and the next day was spent in preparation for an attack by the whole brigade on the 30th November. The plan was for 6 RWK to capture Bald Hill at first light whilst 6 Commando attacked Green Hill, the Buffs being held in reserve ready to exploit our success.

At one o'clock in the morning the companies formed up ready for the attack and moved off along the axis of the railway line. Then the going got really tough, for Green Hill was 1000 feet high and carrying weapons and ammunition up the steep, rough hillside in the dark was exhausting. While it was still dark the battalion made good progress against enemy machine-guns firing on fixed lines in the light of flares put up by the enemy infantry. But as soon as it was light the leading companies were caught in devastating cross-fire from machine-guns firing from the top of Bald Hill and from the reverse slopes of Green Hill. In spite of heavy losses the companies continued to advance, but owing to the width of the front effective contact between the companies and battalion headquarters broke down and it is not possible to say exactly what eventually happened.

On the right flank A Company lost all its officers. Lt Kerr of this company is known to have wiped out two German machine-gun posts before he was killed. Both Capt Crook, the company commander, and Lt Akehurst were never heard of again and were almost certainly killed in action. The only surviving officer of the company, John Maling, was wounded in the arm. The left flank of C Company got within 300 yards of their objective when the company commander, Capt R.W.Murphy, had half his jaw shot away and his stomach riddled by machine-gun bullets, but miraculously survived. His second-in-command, Capt Harvey, was last seen leading the company into a final attack before being killed. Lt Guy Weymouth was later reported to be a prisoner of war and by a strange coincidence met the battalion again in Italy when escaping through the enemy lines.

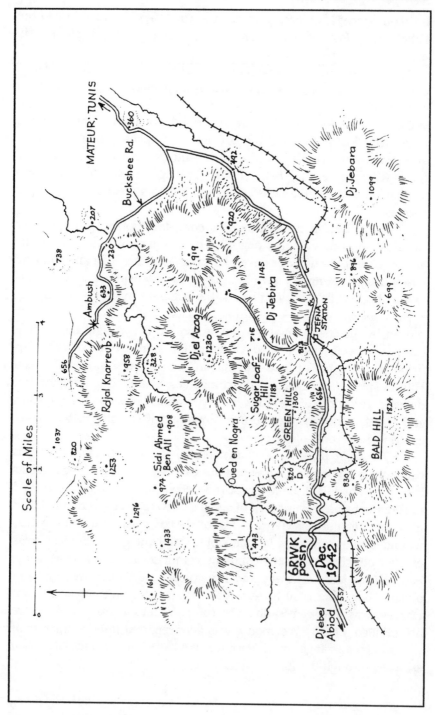

On the right flank B Company tried to outflank the enemy positions at the top of the hill, but were themselves pinned down by enemy fire and suffered heavy casualties including Lt Atkins and Lt W.J.Palmer, both killed, and Lt Gale wounded by a bullet through the foot.

By three o'clock in the afternoon the attack had come to a standstill. The three leading companies were precariously established and the attack on Green Hill had also failed, leaving our left flank entirely exposed. At five o'clock orders were received to withdraw, and to add to our misery heavy rain broke out.

Whilst directing the fire of the mortars onto the enemy positions, Lt Brian Goodenough was wounded in the arm and had to be evacuated. At about the same time the commanding officer, Lt Col Swifty Howlett, was hit in the leg, but with some skilful attention on the part of the doctor he was able to remain with the battalion.

Very few men were known to have fallen alive into enemy hands. Many who were not killed outright had to be left behind in no-mans-land, where they died of their wounds. In a day the battalion had lost a quarter of its best men. I was new to casualties on this scale and kept on thinking of the tragic news soon to be delivered to wives and mothers in towns and villages all over Kent.

Our casualties had been heavy, with 11 officers and 150 other ranks killed, wounded or missing - more than half those engaged in the action.

To put our losses into perspective I should perhaps set out the numerical strength of the battalion. At full strength a battalion consists of about 800 officers and men. There are four rifle companies, each with five officers and 120 men, which provide the main fighting force. The rest of the battalion, comprising something over 300 officers and men, includes the battalion headquarters (commanding officer, adjutant, intelligence officer and intelligence section) and the headquarters company (transport, pioneers, signals, medical section, and anti-tank platoons). In battle the commanding officer will have a battery of the Royal Artillery under his command and maybe a squadron of tanks.

In England during our training we never gave enough, or indeed any, thought to the burial of the dead. In North Africa we initially buried our casualties as soon as possible in the most convenient spot and marked the name on a rough wooden cross, but soon discovered that this was woefully inadequate when we came across German graves with their beautifully made and inscribed metal crosses. The troops felt very strongly about this and I got our pioneer platoon to design a wooden cross with the regimental crest of which we could all be proud.

It was now evident that the Germans were in too strong a position for our brigade to have any hope of dislodging them until reinforcements arrived. Moreover the troops were weary. We had lived in holes in the ground for the last month, had no proper sleep, existed on emergency rations and had rarely had a chance even to take off our boots. It was decided, therefore, to hold the ground already won and to take up a hedgehog position with all round defence astride the main road. The troops dug deep trenches in small hills at the entrance to the valley. In them they warmed up their 'compo' rations and found some protection from the heavy rain. The Germans, like us, were awaiting reinforcements in great discomfort for another six weeks.

During this time our first reinforcements, six officers and 150 other ranks arrived. Four of the officers - Capt R.L.Clark, Lts J.Eason, J.D.Magneen, R.W.Gardiner - we knew well for they had been with the battalion when we were stationed at Crieff.

Welcome stores like razor blades came up with the rations. An effort was made to give the troops some rest and parties were sent back to Sedjenane, where there was a rest centre situated in the long low building of the tobacco factory in the centre of the village, for 48 hours at a time. With the aid of palliases provided by the quartermaster the men were able to enjoy two good nights rest as well as a shower bath and a change of clothing. The village was nothing more than a railway station and a collection of houses plus the tobacco factory so there was nothing whatever for the troops to do during the daytime - not that anyone wished to do anything but sleep, write letters home and talk to men from the other companies.

As the front line was at least a dozen miles away, the only reminder of war and death was the occasional ambulance carrying wounded into the main dressing station, which was also situated in the tobacco factory.

One day this peace was shattered by the roar of diving aircraft, followed almost immediately by the harsh clatter of an Oerlikon anti-aircraft cannon firing from the floor of a roofless house. A second later the distinctive whistle of falling bombs could be heard and everybody dived to the floor as two large explosions shook the buildings. Of the building from which the Oerliken gun had been firing there was nothing to be seen but a gigantic cloud of dust from the shattered walls. As the dust cleared an officer rushed across calling for stretcher-bearers and organised the work of digging out the bodies of the dead. The bomb had fallen right in the centre of the room and had killed outright all but three of the 14 men who had been inside. Of the three survivors, the sergeant in charge was suffering only from shock and a small cut across the face, but the other two were badly hurt and both died in the dressing station a few hours later. Everyone was silent and thoughtful for the rest of that day.

On the 16th December Swifty Howlett was promoted to take command of our brigade. The second-in-command, Henry Lovell, assumed temporary command of the battalion and I became second in command, saying goodbye to my beloved D Company which, of course, in my view, I had created, starting from that moment two and a half years before when I introduced myself to the newly arrived Howlett as the officer commanding a then non-existent D Company.

On December 17th the battalion took over the defence of the forward positions from the 5th Buffs, where we remained until the brigade left the northern sector a month later.

On Christmas Day the first mail arrived, also the special Christmas ration of a tin of pork and a bottle of beer. They were not appetising when consumed huddled up in a gas cape in pouring rain, but the effort was appreciated. Although we were only holding the ground, life was not entirely peaceful. The Germans gradually acquired more artillery, with which they shelled us intermittently, and we never knew when enemy aircraft would be over. Every night patrols were sent out to keep an eye on enemy movement. It might be thought that patrolling, with its inherent dangers, would have been unwelcome to the troops, but in fact it tended to raise their spirits for it gave them a feeling of superiority over the enemy.

Apart from the patrols, the shelling, and days of heavy rain, life became a routine of eating, sleeping, digging and sentry duty. The days dragged slowly by without any mail from home, nothing to read, and no extra rations from the NAAFI; each man had only the daily ration of seven cigarettes and a bar of plain chocolate provided in the boxes of 'compo' rations.

Men who did not smoke were able to secure a high premium for their goodwill and were able to get not less than a bar of chocolate for their ration of cigarettes. The rate of exchange was so firm that no man is known to have secured two bars of chocolate for one lot of cigarettes, indeed convention largely prevented this from happening. Frequently cigarettes had been extracted from the ration boxes on their way up to the front line, which caused a great deal of bitterness.

Cooking was the main occupation of almost everyone. Unfortunately the tins of pre-cooked foodstuffs allowed little scope for initiative, but there was a certain sense of anticipation and interest in tending the fire and waiting for the water to boil and heat the food in the tins. The fires were generally in a perforated half biscuit tin filled with earth soaked with petrol, which gave off heat without too much smoke. Breakfast offered more in originality than any other meal. A skilful cook could make a good porridge out of hard biscuits soaked in water overnight and cooked slowly, which when mixed with soya-link sausages was quite an appetising dish. After breakfast most sections would boil a biscuit tin full of water in order to wash and shave, a routine which could last most of the morning, and occasionally the more ambitious would indulge in a biscuit tin bath. Fortunately the rations contained a good supply of tea/milk powder, sufficient to provide four or five pint mugs a day per head. All this did a great deal to pass the time, and the rest of the day was spent improving the dugouts used as sleeping quarters to make them shellproof, and more important, weatherproof. A few branches, sandbags and a rubber ground sheet would serve to keep the rain out on most occasions and it was generally only the careless or lazy who got wet.

A couple of hours after 'stand down' in the evening the companies would turn in for the night, which was often broken by one, if not two spells of two-hour sentry duty. Some nights would be dry and fine. When the moon rose the great hills would tower above the battalion positions and give the impression that the enemy was able to observe every movement made in the dead of night. On other nights the weather could be terrible; the rain would lash the ground and turn it to mud with the aid of passing feet. On such occasions most people felt they would rather be dead than alive, especially if it was their turn to carry the water and rations from the road up to the company positions.

Most nights the company commanders reported to battalion headquarters, 'The Grosvenor' - a structure half hut, half dug-out, built by the engineers out of railway sleepers, corrugated iron and sandbags. The approach lay up a steep bank by the side of the road and many a hard word was uttered by those who fell down in the squelching mud. Once inside the candlelit room spirits rose again with a tot of rum and the interchange of news with the other company commanders. These brief occasions were our only opportunity of getting news of events in the world outside our own valley.

One night at the end of December our intelligence services reported that 300 of the enemy had established themselves south of what was known as the 'Buckshee Road' to the north-east of Sidi Ahmed ben Ali, a white mosque situated on a spur to the north of the Oued en Nogra and easily visible from the battalion's positions. If this report were true the enemy would be able to observe any attack on Green Hill and in view of the urgency of the situation, just before midnight an officer of D Company was ordered to take a fighting patrol to the area in question to find out what was happening there. The plan was to proceed during darkness to a vantage point from which the suspected area could be surveyed in daylight; this would be done from a ridge to the northwest of Sidi Ahmed ben Ali, about a mile from the reported enemy positions.

The moon was full and the night was fine when Shaun Stewart's patrol set out. The men were divided into three groups of three, each group under an NCO and armed with a Bren gun, a Tommy gun and a rifle. They moved across the country in a box formation with 15 yards between each man so that the patrol would not suffer too many casualties if it came under enemy fire. After finding an easy way across the Nogra the patrol plodded across a broad stretch of ploughed ground between the riverbed and the hills bounding the north of the valley. As they did so the sky became overcast and by the time the patrol reached the foot of the deep gully leading into the hills the storm broke with a deluge of rain and hail. Fortunately the storm did not last long and at about 3am the patrol was able to continue, though cold, wet and miserable. The gully they had to follow was filled with scrub, juniper and occasional cactus hedges, and progress was made even more difficult by the number of small ravines. Halfway up the gully the patrol passed between a couple of Arab farms and, as was usually the trouble in this campaign, set all the dogs barking frantically in the still night.

About an hour before dawn the patrol reached the summit of the hill from which it hoped to observe the area where the enemy were thought to be. It was now very cold and no amount of movement would make the men any warmer. Before daybreak Shaun took up a position on the summit of the hill and placed his sub-groups on three sides to give all round defence.

It was soon clear that there were no enemy in the area in which they had been reported, nor was there much else to be seen. About an hour after dawn a vehicle drove north-westwards along the Buckshee Road in the valley immediately to the north of the ridge. This gave Shaun the idea of ambushing an enemy vehicle. Accompanied by Sergeant Donnelly (of Djebel Abiod fame) and Private Kench with the Bren gun, he descended to the road some 450 feet below after leaving instructions to the senior corporal to tell the other Bren gun groups what was happening. The road at this point was flanked by tall bushes on either side and ran straight for about 300 yards. The Bren gun was at once placed to catch any car coming downhill from the direction of Mateur, but no sooner was this done and the other two were in the middle of laying out their Tommy gun magazines and grenades in preparation for the ambush, than a motorcycle was heard coming up the hill from the opposite direction. A few seconds later a motorcycle combination rounded the bend in the road 200 yards away with two men on board. Unfortunately Private Kench was unable to see the enemy from his position until he stood up, whereupon he shouted: 'I've got him, Sir' and opened fire with the machine gun from the hip at about 30 yards range. Shaun and Donnelly immediately stepped into the road in time to see the machine veering into the ditch as the Germans tried to dismount, loosing off a whole magazine from their Thompson machine-guns, most of which in the excitement was well off the target because of the 'swing' which these weapons develop if they are not firmly gripped. Realising they were out of ammunition the two rushed back into the bushes where their spare magazines and grenades had been left. They re-loaded their guns and ran around to the rear of the enemy in time to see them dismounting. The man who had been in the sidecar had jumped clear of the machine and dived under the cover of the bank at the side of the road, but the other was not so fortunate and this time Shaun killed him with another burst of fire from his Tommy gun.

Once under cover of the bank the surviving enemy soldier drew his pistol and started firing. Kench, who was standing up on the opposite bank demanding to know what had happened, was ordered by Shaun to take cover while he threw a German egg grenade in the direction of the remaining German, who was a paratrooper. Unfortunately the firing mechanism of the grenade would not work and there was some further delay while he prepared a special plastic high-explosive grenade, made of a kind of Semtex, which he had acquired from the Commandos. This fell between the enemy soldier and the motorcycle combination, the force of the explosion blowing the machine sideways. At that moment a machine-gun opened fire from the ridge from which they had just come down, the bullets splattering the road about 10 yards away.

After a moment's hesitation Shaun realised that the fire came from one of our own Bren guns left behind on the top of the hill and assumed that the shots were fired to give moral support, but the original objective having been achieved and not knowing the whereabouts of the remaining enemy soldier, Shaun decided to take no further risks by withdrawing. On rejoining the main body of the patrol, the three were more than a little take aback to hear that the Bren gun had been fired in earnest by the gunner, who complained that he had not been told of the expedition down to the main road. When he had heard the explosion of the grenade he had realised something was amiss and stopped firing. Such is war!

The whole patrol now started for home as quickly as it could before the enemy had an opportunity to retaliate. Unfortunately the Nogra had swollen with rain overnight and the river had to be followed some way back towards its source before a crossing could be made. They finally reached battalion headquarters safely in the late afternoon. Two nights later Shaun rounded the operation off by returning to the Buckshee Road with two men to lay anti-vehicle mines and to set booby traps on the telephone cables at the side of the road.

The second attack on Green Hill, this time by the Buffs, for which Shaun Stewart's patrol prepared the way, took place shortly afterwards as planned, supported by a complete regiment of 24 25-pounders, two huge American 155mm 'Long Toms,' a battery of four 5.5" medium guns, a battery of mountain artillery and a company of 4.2" mortars. This was the heaviest volume of artillery support yet used in the campaign, though a minor effort compared with the 400-800 gun barrages experienced later in Tunisia and again in Sicily and Italy.

Zero hour was at 0100 hours on the 5th January, when the whole valley was immediately lit by innumerable gun flashes. The shells passing over the heads of D Company on the left of the road were so close that the noise was like a shriek of railway-brakes. Indeed shells began to fall into the back of the hill to the right of D Company and knocked out one of the heavy mortars. The firing was immediately stopped to check the laying of the guns and when the barrage was resumed a few minutes later the error had been corrected.

A barrage is meant to saturate the enemy positions with high explosive and lift just as the attacking troops arrive at their objective and before the enemy recovers. Unfortunately, in their case the barrage was useless because the men were quite unable to keep to the timetable laid down for the attack. The night was dark and the pouring rain made the ground so heavy and slippery that the troops made slow progress. Nothing like enough time had been allowed for the Buffs to reach their objective, with the result that there was a long pause between the end of the barrage and the arrival there of the leading companies. Furthermore, Green Hill had by now become a legend which sapped the morale of the attacking troops. Like a later nightmare (Longstop Hill) the hill was riddled with deep caves said to be the workings of Phoenician ironmines.

When daylight came the Buffs were still on the lower slopes of Green Hill and making little progress. Enemy machine-guns from the southern flank of Green Hill were also harassing the battalion area. D Company in particular were worried by 'tired' bullets fired at long range among their positions on the reverse slope of the hill. The faint hiss of the bullets and the soft plop as they hit the damp earth was disconcerting. One attack from the north on Green Hill by two companies of the 2 Paratroop battalion succeeded in gaining their objective at midday, only to lose it again to a counter-attack by German troops in the late afternoon. This time 6 Commando were on Sugar Loaf Hill, repulsing an enemy counter-attack with heavy losses to the enemy with the aid of the 6 RWK Vickers machine-gun section, which distinguished itself and accounted for a large proportion of the enemy's casualties. In the end one of the two guns had to be destroyed, but the other was brought back safely. For his part in the action Sergeant Kendal, who commanded the section, was awarded the Distinguished Conduct Medal.

By the afternoon of the 6th January it was clear that the second attack on Green Hill had failed. The men were so exhausted that there was no alternative but to withdraw. Unfortunately wireless communications with the Commandos had broken down, so Lt 'Bolo'

Howard of my old company was ordered to make his way with one other rank to Sugar Loaf Hill to let the Commandos know that withdrawal was to commence at midnight. The most direct route lay through the forward companies of the Buffs at the foot of Green Hill and then through the enemy positions facing the Commandos. At the bottom of Sugar Loaf Hill they bumped into an enemy patrol and before they could escape were blown over the side of the bank by enemy grenades. They were not badly hurt and after extracting themselves from the bushes pressed on until they were suddenly challenged by a German sentry. Before they could escape the sentry opened fire, whereupon Bolo Howard pretended that he had been hit in the leg; this made the German hesitate and before he could make up his mind what to do Bolo jumped to his feet and disappeared into the darkness. His companion also escaped in the confusion and returned to the battalion. Shortly afterwards Bolo found the Commandos in position at the top of Sugar Loaf Hill and was able to pass on the brigadier's order. On the return journey he felt so exhausted that he lay down by the banks of the Oued en Nogra and fell asleep until mid-afternoon the following day. For this exploit Bolo Howard was awarded the Military Cross.

A few days later the company commanders, assembled in 'The Grosvenor,' heard a dramatized account of the Battle of Green Hill on the BBC programme 'Radio Newsreel.' The account of the fighting was nauseatingly inaccurate and engendered a good deal of cynicism among us. After the equivalent of a fanfare of trumpets and a roll of drums, the commentators declared: 'Once again we shall be on top of the green hill that looks down on the road to Bizerta.' The truth was to be that Green Hill was never wrested from the enemy by force of arms.

It was during these first few months of the Tunisian campaign that I first realised the fighting qualities of one of my officers - the 20 year old Shaun Stewart, who went on to win three Military Crosses as well as the Distinguished Service Cross of the United States, the highest military award short of the Congressional Medal of Honour, while the battalion was serving with the 5th US Army in Italy. He succeeded me in command of D Company when I moved on to become second-in-command of the battalion. Shaun led a number of important patrols and as company commander was the inspiration of others. Whenever I gave him an order he always carried it out and a lot more besides - for example the occasion when his patrol shot up the two

Germans on the motorcycle combination on the Buckshee Road. His orders were merely to find out whether the area was occupied by the enemy, but having done this his patrol went on to create what must have been alarm and despondency among the Germans who can have had no idea that they were in danger.

Typical of the patrols carried out by the battalion were two exploits by Bolo Howard and Lt Peter Beall. Bolo Howard took 15 men of my old company on a patrol with orders to kill a group of enemy in a large French farmhouse at the foot of Sugar Loaf Hill. The patrol set off at half past six in the evening, following the line of Oued en Nogra as far as the lower slopes of Sidi Ahmed ben Ali and then south-eastwards towards Sugar Loaf Hill. In fact the men never reached the farmhouse because they were fired on from enemy positions about 200 yards short of the objective. Nevertheless, they pressed home their attack and inflicted a number of casualties on the enemy before withdrawing under cover of a concentration of artillery brought down by our guns at a pre-arranged signal. After this success the patrol rejoined the battalion just before midnight with one man wounded in the stomach and another slightly in the left foot.

On the other side of the valley Peter Beall of B Company was leading an equally successful foray into the enemy lines. This patrol started out just before midnight and followed the railway line for a couple of miles to a point on the north-east spur of Bald Hill. There he placed a group of eight men with three Bren guns in position to give covering fire to the rest of the patrol. The assault group then moved north-east in the direction of Jefna station and after a brisk engagement with three or four small enemy positions returned safely to the battalion without any casualties. Unfortunately the Bren groups were fired on from higher up the hill as they returned along the railway line and in the ensuing engagement two men out of the eight were killed by enemy machine-gun fire.

9
Longstop

The patrolling was part of a general increase in activity intended to distract the attention of the enemy while preparations were made for the brigade to be relieved by 139 Brigade of the 46th Infantry Division. Ever since the second battle of Green Hill we had been led to believe that we would soon be taken out of the line for a period to rest and refit, and as day succeeded day without news of the relieving troops they came to be known as the Phantom Brigade. But in the afternoon of January 16th our dreams came true when the commanding officer and other officers of the Sherwood Foresters from the newly arrived 46 Division were seen walking along the main road towards battalion headquarters with their shining map cases flashing in the bright sun. Experience had by now made us sensitive to anything or any activity that stood out against the natural background and we watched with horrified fascination as the four officers marched along the road in full view of the enemy, but by happy chance the stillness was unbroken by the silk-tearing whistle of enemy shells and the reconnaissance party reached battalion headquarters apparently unnoticed.

On 17th January the company commanders of the two relieving battalions reconnoitred the positions they were due to take over from us the following night. The additional movements soon attracted the enemy's attention and his guns were active during most of the day. The area of D Company was heavily shelled for the first time and the company commander and his opposite number from the 2/5 Sherwood Foresters had a narrow escape whilst observing the enemy from the crest of the ridge.

At eight o'clock in the evening of 18th January the relieving troops deployed from the main road in brilliant moonlight and made their way up the hillside to the forward company positions. After a wearisome half hour of impatience the relief was finally completed and the men shouldered their heavy packs, weapons and blankets and trudged down the hill to the main road. From here the battalion had to march three miles to the troop-carrying vehicles which were to take us to a rest area north of Beja. It seemed strange to be leaving Green Hill after what seemed a lifetime, but the exhausted troops were in no mood or condition for philosophical rumination and soon fell asleep as the lorries droned on through the night.

Eleven weeks had passed since our landing on the beach at Algiers. During that time we had been in almost continual contact with the enemy. I have described this period of the battalion's history in some detail because it was a period of high adventure, far removed from the battles of attrition which were to come later and because both the fighting and the terrain were typical of the North African campaign and of those in Sicily and Italy.

The background was always mountains, not always craggy but always either high, steep, commanding or all three. When not steep or high the slopes were either covered with dense thorny scrub or cluttered with boulders or loose stones, hostile to trench digging. On the plus side there was usually a crevice, a gulley, a valley or the vertical banks of a dry river, or wadi, in which you could hide yourself from enemy view.

These mountains and hills were intersected by *oueds*, rivers and streams which at times were merely interconnected pools but given a spell of heavy rain could turn into a raging torrent higher up and an impassable river lower down.

The weather was our most unpleasant surprise, it was appalling. Not only did it always seem to be raining, but the rain was so heavy and in an area so sparsely populated, even Arab huts, made from branches and mud, were few and far between. As warfare involves, we had discovered, a high proportion of your time waiting about, it seemed wretched luck that we should have to do this in the open in that weather.

On 19th January 1943 we moved south to an area near Beja where for three days we rested and there was much cleaning of weapons, washing of kit, repairing and replacing uniforms and even hot baths.

The Germans had no intention of allowing the allies to re-organise in peace. On January 18th newly landed German troops supported by Mark VI Tiger tanks swung in from Tunis to drive a wedge between the British and the French at Robaa. The French were overrun and reinforcements had to be found to go to their assistance, so our rest at Beja was cut short.

On the evening of January 22nd we were placed at one hour's notice to proceed to Robaa, arriving there the next day to take up defensive positions. As second-in-command I was in charge of the administration of the battalion, my chief preoccupation being to get supplies of all sorts, mainly food and ammunition, to our companies, spread over several miles of wild hilly country. Frequently vehicles could not reach their positions so I had to resort to a company of mules led by Arab muleteers who took a lot of persuading that risking their lives and those of their mules for the cause of foreign invaders was their bounden duty. My sympathy was with them but it did not make them any less infuriating to deal with. One was often operating by night under fire, if only intermittent fire, but the explosion of one shell a 100 yards away is enough to scatter the laboriously mobilised train of mules and the process has to start all over again. I remember one night taking mules along a railway track. They would keep getting their legs trapped between the sleepers on the little bridges that went across drains, needing at least three muleteers to extract each mule from his predicament. My association with mules and muleteers was a long one, for even after Tunisia we were back to mule transport in the hills around Mount Etna in the Sicilian campaign and later in Italy at Cassino, but by then I was commanding the battalion and had passed mule-care to my second-in-command with my very best wishes.

In the Robaa area we came in contact with the Italian enemy for the first time and quickly learned to prefer them to the Germans. It remains a mystery to me why a nation who, 2000 years ago, were the warriors of the world, in modern times have lost all stomach for the fight. They excelled themselves in the Abyssinian campaign when British troops arriving in a village found that the Italians had not only built themselves a prisoner-of-war cage but got into it to make absolutely sure that it was recognised that they had surrendered.

After our successful brush with the Italians, the Germans and their tanks arrived 10 days later and overran the French on our right. My old D Company, with the aid of three Churchill tanks, counter-attacked, drove the enemy back and captured a large number of prisoners. After this the Germans switched their attacks to the North and for the month of February there was not much activity among our hills.

The French were now our neighbours and we made our first acquaintance with their equivalent of our Gurkhas, the Morrocan Goums. These formidable and wild colonial soldiers put terror into the hearts of the Germans. You would see them sometimes coming back at dawn from a patrol riding ponies with German prisoners walking painfully barefoot at their sides. Depriving them of their boots was the simple device by which they made sure that prisoners did not escape. They were said to collect the ears of those they had killed as evidence of their successes.

The speciality of the Goums is mountain fighting. They wear the Arab 'burnous,' and although they will consent to carry rifles they prefer their knives. They are organised in 'goums,' groups of about 70, under French officers. Their uncanny gift for moving silently through trackless mountain country brought them fame in the following year in the final battle of Cassino, when 12,000 of these doughty characters were unloosed in the mountains to the west of Liri valley, assumed by the Germans to be impassable, and, threatening the enemy rear, had a decisive effect on the battle.

Spring had now broken through and the news from Libya was good, General Montgomery's Eighth Army was chasing Rommel across the desert towards Tunis. The First Army, to which we belonged, started local operations which were to lead up to a major assault on Tunis and Bizerta from the West.

Local operations turned into a main battle, for the Germans decided to take us on in strength among the craggy hills which dominated the main road running through the Medjerja Valley from Medjez el Bab to Tunis. Many an old soldier will have tales to tell about such places as Djebel Diss, Chaouach, Longstop Hill and Banana Ridge. The first signs of the impending weight of the German attack appeared on 31st January. The German tanks led an attack down the main road on the position of 5 Buffs. Eight of these tanks were put out of action by our six-lbr anti-tank guns, including two of the new Mark VI Tiger tanks. Two hours later German infantry attacked the 6 RWK right flank without success and D Company took a number of prisoners who turned out to be Austrian Alpine troops, whose cap badge was an eidelweiss.

Prisoners were always searched for documents and the most memorable possessions of these Austrians were their wallets which contained lots of jolly photographs of pretty girls and beer drinking parties, something of a contrast to the contents of the average British soldier's wallet which would typically contain a rather solemn photo of mum and dad.

After some preliminary skirmishing around the village of Chaouach our first really serious fighting was on a large and horrible craggy hill called Djebel bou Diss which the enemy held in strength. Artillery is not very effective in mountainous country and most of the fighting took place at short range and even hand-to-hand in small groups. The attack was followed by a fierce counter-attack, but after three days bou Diss was ours with many prisoners taken. We handed it over to the Argylls and moved back in reserve for a rest.

A week later we were in action again; the task of capturing the dreaded Longstop Hill which dominates the Medjerda Valley was allotted to 36 Brigade. Our companies were so reduced by casualties that we had to bring up the cooks and storemen. Even then the rifle companies were only at just over half strength.

After 400 guns had bombarded the enemy positions we and the Buffs attacked by night, impeded by barbed wire and booby traps. By dawn we had been brought to a halt and the Argylls, who had been kept in reserve, put in a fierce and heroic attack supported by the tanks of the North Irish Horse and reached the crest of Longstop, only to find that there was a second crest some 800 yards further on. One of their company commanders, Jack Anderson, who had already won the DSO as a captain, was awarded the VC. He was killed in Italy. The Germans had never imagined that tanks could get up that hill but Churchill tanks are versatile and found a way. By now the casualties of the battalion had been so severe that we took no further part in the attack, though holding on to what we had taken was costly enough, for the Germans continued to saturate the area with mortar and artillery fire.

I spent each night of this battle supervising the evacuation of the wounded and persuading the mules to take food and ammunition up to the troops. Every time I assembled a train of mules, got them loaded and the muleteers in some sort of order, all in the semi-darkness, a shell would land among us and mules and muleteers would scatter in all directions. The whole thing was a nightmare. I was awarded the Military Cross. My friends derisively called it 'the Mule Cross.'

An attack by the Buffs, well supported by tanks, finally clinched the battle by taking the second crest and 300 Germans surrendered. During the battle Lt Col Heygate who had taken over at Robaa two months previously, received a slight shrapnel wound and so Henry Lovell was once again in command of the battalion and was promoted to lieutenant-colonel.

The remnants of the battalion marched back to Chassart Teffana where we were able to rest and re-fit. Two hundred reinforcements arrived and we organised ourselves for further action. The back of the German defence had been broken; supported by massive concentrations of artillery the 6th Armoured Division swept through the valley and on its way to Tunis.

The regimental history says that the battalion had no further serious fighting in this campaign. This is not quite how it appeared to those required to capture the start line for the leading elements of the 6th Armoured Division! This involved advancing across some flat cornfields and although the bursts of enemy machine-gun fire were few and far between they took the heads off the corn through which we were walking, which I found alarming. We had got used to fighting in mountains, where this sort of thing did not happen.

As we were waiting to set off on this 'minor action,' Gordon Defrates and I were sitting side by side on the ground leaning up against the bank which formed the boundary of a field. Our heads must have been about four feet apart. Precisely through this gap arrived an enemy shell which exploded in the bank within a foot or two of our heads. But as all the explosive force went forward we were untouched although not unmoved. Gordon, one of the best officers bred by the battalion, survived many other perils of war, winning the DSO and the MC and Bar, going on to command the battalion for the last 18 months of the war.

By now the position of the Germans was hopeless. In the south, Rommel was being battered by the Eighth Army under Monty at Mareth coming up from the south and by the American Army from the south-west. We in the First Army were giving von Arnim no peace in the west. There were certainly no signs of surrender and there was plenty of fighting to be done before Tunis and Bizerta were captured by the First Army on May 6th. By then there was a vast army of 250,000 Germans and Italians trapped in the small area around Tunis and Bizerta. They had no hope of evacuation *à la* Dunkirk, which anyway Hitler had forbidden, because the British had complete command of the air and the sea.

Soldiers toiling through the mud and mountains of Tunisia or the sands of the desert little realised how much we owed to the Royal Navy and the RAF who were slowly strangling the enemy. Our submarines from Malta were playing havoc with their supply ships so that between 20th April and 4th May only a single enemy merchant ship managed to cross the channel between Sicily and Africa. The air offensive supplemented the naval blockade became even more important when the Germans began to sneak troop and cargo planes through our defences.

In Churchill's *Second World War* he writes:

> The relentless blockade by sea and air was fully established. Enemy movement over the sea was at a standstill, their air effort ended. To quote from a subsequent German report: 'The Anglo-American Air Forces played a decisive role in the enemy operational success which led to the destruction of the German/Italian bridgehead in Tunisia. They took part in the ground fighting to an extent never before attempted.'
> Day and night destroyers and coastal craft, together with the RAF, continued the ruthless work. In all 879 men surrendered to the Navy, and only 653 are known to have escaped, mostly by air and at night. Our casualties were negligable.

The result was that the axis supply situation became desperate. They were so short of petrol that by the end of the campaign von Arnim was incapable of manoeuvre. The long and stubborn defence of the Germans suddenly collapsed and the final breakthrough came with astonishing speed, such speed that when the Derbyshire Yeomanry burst into Tunis they found German officers sitting outside the cafes with their girlfriends sipping gin. To quote Churchill again:

> No one could doubt the magnitude of the victory of Tunis. It held its own with Stalingrad. Africa was cleared of our foes. One continent had been redeemed. In London there was, for the first time in the war, a real lifting of spirits. Parliament received the ministers with regard and enthusiasm and recorded its thanks in the warmest terms to the commanders. I had asked that the bells of all the churches should be rung. I was sorry not to hear their chimes but I had more important work to do on the other side of the Atlantic.

May 8th 1943 was a great day for 6 RWK. Passing thousands of Germans and Italians, many of whom were driving their own vehicles to the prison cages, we drove into Tunis in lorries at about midday. The population gave us a wonderful welcome, waving flags and giving flowers and wine to the troops. Billets were allotted in the town and many of us had the joy of sleeping under a roof for the first time for six months. The following day we moved out of Tunis and on the 11th settled down at a pleasant seaside resort, La Marsa, where we relaxed, re-formed and re-equipped ourselves for the invasion of Sicily which took place two months later.

10
Tunis

During our period in Tunis Henry Lovell, of whom we were all very fond, was posted away and I succeeded him in command of the battalion. This did not come as a surprise to me nor, I think, to my fellow officers, but it did surprise our neighbours for I did not look like a lieutenant-colonel. A gunner officer, visiting our mess, asked who was going to take over the battalion. One of my officers answered: 'Paul.' The gunner said: 'Yes, I know, but when are you getting a proper colonel?'

On the other hand, after the war an officer from the Buffs writing to Denis Forman said: 'Paul was obviously a great soldier but I found him too glittering to be at ease with' - so it seems that in time, and I hope only to outsiders, I began to look almost too colonel-like.

Our two months rest gave me time to ruminate on the strange experience through which we had passed over the last six months. Four years before, the men in my battalion were factory workers, farm labourers, clerks, shop assistants, insurance salesmen, bank managers, clothing factory managers, university students, who can never have imagined that the time would come when they would spend six months living like foxes in burrows and killing their fellow human beings whenever the opportunity presented itself. The adaptability of the human body seemed to know no bounds. The frail, pale factory worker from Gravesend put on a stone on the much-maligned army food within months of joining the army. By now he had become incredibly tough, with always something in reserve. At times when you felt exhausted and wet through and incapable of further effort all that was forgotten when a shell fell beside you and you became as lively as ever.

Through all these trials people remained healthy. In the early months after our overcoats and our blankets had sunk in Bougie harbour we had nothing but gas capes for protection and at least part of one's body was often soaked through to the skin and remained so with only the passage of time to dry one out. But we got no more colds than usual. On the rare occasions when we came out of the line for a day or two the sick list immediately rocketed. People did not go sick in the line.

I have come to the conclusion that the secret of good health is planned excess. If you live on a perfect diet and never over-exert yourself you build up no natural resistance against illness. This is a comfortable theory for it justifies regular over-indulgence to harden your constitution against the diet it will have to face on an Indian holiday.

I became interested in the subject of courage. Why are men willing to fight at all? Why were the men of the 4th Indian Division willing to fight so bravely, so far from home, for an alien monarch?

I believe in the theory propounded by Lord Moran, Churchill's doctor, and a regimental doctor in the First World War, that each of us has a capital of courage upon which we draw and therefore expend. It is never easy to be brave but it is easier your first time into action and gets harder and harder as the campaign goes on. That is why, when recommending men and officers for decorations, I never recommended anybody on the strength of his performance in his first battle. I tended more to chose people who had been at it for a long time and deserved some recognition.

Moran's contention regarding the anatomy of courage was born out by the performance of military units in the Italian campaign. I never wanted to be supported by tank regiments which had fought in the desert. They had gone through such a bloody experience there that they were too cautious for my liking and more so than the North Irish Horse who had been with us all through North Africa and only suffered moderate casualties.

It is easier for officers and warrant officers to be brave than for men. When you are leading troops in action your mind is so full of your own responsibilities and worries, for example: how your men are going to fight; when the hell are they going to start the barrage; what on earth has happened to No. 2 Platoon? Why can't I find this place on my map? What shall I do about that wounded corporal? All this preoccupation makes you less concerned about the shells that are falling about you than the private soldier who has nothing to think about but going over the top in a few minutes time.

Fear of shame is a stimulus to courage. At the beginning of the North African campaign most of us had been together for the last two years training in England. We knew each other very well. We nearly all came from the county of Kent, so in some cases knew each other's families. No-one wanted to behave in a way which would bring the scorn of his friends. This is one of the virtues of the regimental system by which the whole of a battalion will come from the same part of the country.

An individual's courage can vary in varying circumstances. When well led, among old friends, pride and self-confidence can make him brave. Thrown into battle after being newly posted to a poorly led unit in which he knows no-one, he could emerge a less robust character, especially in the face of surprise.

Surprise is the most devastating weapon of war at all levels. An army can surrender to a comparative handful of troops if surprised, as happened when the great fortress of Singapore fell to a small force of Japanese appearing from nowhere. At a lower level a platoon in our division surrendered without a fight at all when caught having breakfast in the snow in an Italian mountain village by German ski troops.

Courage, or at any rate the attitude to battle, differs between the Army, Navy and Air Force. The fighter pilot, judging by my brother, seemed always keen to 'get at' the enemy. When my brother was on leave as a squadron leader, if he heard that his squadron was going out on a mission he would come back from leave to go with them on the mission, then go on leave again. I found that most of the men of an infantry battalion were willing to do their duty and more in battle but were not disappointed if on some particular occasion their unit was not included in the battle.

The position of a fighter pilot was of course unique. He appeared to the general public as a lone champion but he was in fact the champion of quite a team of fitters and others who not only kept him in the air but maintained the weapons upon which his life depended.

The most praiseworthy courage in wartime is to be found in the civilian populations - mainly unrecorded and unsung - especially those suffering under enemy occupation. I often wondered whether I could stand up to torture under the Gestapo and came to the conclusion that perhaps I could manage it, but would collapse the minute I was called upon to see my family tortured, a horribly common practice.

The way the London population withstood the long drawn-out misery of the bombing followed by the doodlebug, sleeping week after week in air raid shelters after losing their homes called for as much courage - if of a different sort - as their menfolk were called upon to show in the campaigns abroad. The theatres in London never closed throughout the war and the only reaction to an air raid warning was somebody appearing on the stage asking those wishing to go to the shelter to do so quickly so that the show could go on. What a contrast in the recent Gulf War when American companies forbade their staff to travel by air for fear of terrorists and some of their companies abroad were told to take down their American signs. How Saddam Hussein must have smiled.

The rest period at La Marsa also gave me time to think about myself. Not that one was actually short of time during the campaign. One often stayed in the same place for a week or more, but the fact that the Germans were only a few hundred yards away, that they could attack at any time and that they kept you reminded of their presence by lobbing shells at you from time to time, produced rather a tense background, especially if you were in command.

Looking back on my childhood, school and university, I seemed to have used what brains I had to secure myself a stressless life rather than to excel. Once launched on a career I had tried very hard indeed but with modest results.

Compared with the pedestrian start of my commercial career my military career had been, at least on paper, brilliant. I was at that moment one of the youngest battalion commanders in the British Army, certainly the only one of my age to be a lieutenant-colonel commanding the battalion in which he had been a private soldier. This was admittedly largely due to a charmed life. Out of the 30 officers in my battalion who went to France in 1940 only four came back and I was one of them. Of the 30 officers who had landed with the battalion in Algeria, a year later I was the only one who hadn't been killed, wounded or left the battalion for some other reason. Some of the wounded, of course, recovered and came back.

Another major reason for my success was my original training in the UK by Swifty Howlett and my continued training in battle under him as my battalion commander and later as my brigadier. As I was his product he was violently biased in my favour - hence my early promotion during the period I was under his command.

Remaining unkilled and unwounded gave me continuous battle experience which made me confident. The fact that when in battle I sometimes had up to a 1000 men under my command did not worry me at all. Another, perhaps less attractive, trait of my character was that the horrific parts of my duties did not affect my performance. It was obviously grim ordering your friends into actions in which they were positively likely to be killed or wounded. It was shattering when they were. But I did not find that it affected my judgement.

My temperamental makeup turned out to be suited for war. Fear has different effects on different people. Some raise their voices. Some talk a lot. Some burst out into feverish activity. Some start blaming others. Some start justifying their own blunders. When I was terrified my instinct was to say nothing and do nothing. I thus got a reputation for calmness.

I also have a 'Lord, take this cup from me' trait in my character which wishfully pretends that the worst is not happening or at any rate that it will soon go away. When I hit the ball into a gorse bush at golf I cannot believe it has really happened and certainly not that my next shot could be as bad.

I also did not find it difficult to make decisions and if they proved wrong it did not weigh on my mind for long. In infantry fighting, if the tide is running against you any decision however sensible at the time can turn out to be wrong.

In the war many people, including myself, felt more at peace with themselves than in times of peace. In war your conscience is clear. You know you are doing the right thing. If you are in the infantry you cannot be doing anything much more dangerous. In peace you are lucky if you are confident that you are living to the best of your ability.

In war your pride is at rest. You never chose to be a soldier. If you happen to be a good one, *tant mieux*. If you aren't, well you never chose to do this anyway. In peacetime whatever occupation you pursue is the area in which you presume to excel. So if you turn out to be a bad architect or lawyer or wool sorter it is shaming and it is hard to know what to do about it.

The whole apparatus of the army is designed to support your weaknesses. For instance as a battalion commander I was quite uninterested in anything to do with the parade ground - arms drill, marching etc., but there were plenty of sergeant-majors who were mad on it, so the battalion did not suffer. Similarly, though vehicle maintenance has never fascinated me I could always rest assured that the 6 RWK Transport would be the best in the division because Jack Nixon MC, who had been our Transport Officer ever since he brought our drivers home through Boulogne in 1940, looked upon our every truck as his own beloved child. At a more personal level, if you are haunted by an inability to get up in the morning, the army attended to that little weakness.

I was actually happiest in my role as battalion commander because for the first time I seemed to be in complete charge. I had, of course, a brigadier above me but he seemed more distant than a battalion commander did when I was second-in-command or a company commander.

The experience of commanding troops on active service actually makes you a nicer person. Cut off from their families, their homes and all outside interests, your men were so dependent on you that you in turn became more concerned about them and became what is nowadays called 'a caring person.'

In Denis Forman's book *To Reason Why* he attributes to me the 'memory of an elephant.' I myself do not think much of my memory as a general purpose instrument but I do seem to have a good memory for people, what they do and have done. My fellow officers were amused at the way I quizzed any newcomer to the battalion about what he did in civvy street. It never ceased to fascinate me that the smooth assistant in Burtons, the tailors in Maidstone, had become a rough tough sergeant in C Company, or a former joiner looked ready for a commission. As a member of parliament I was no better at remembering names than anyone else but when a constituent accosted me at the Driffield Show I could usually remember where he came from, what he did and maybe even that his son was in the army in Germany.

When I was abroad in the war I used to write to Betty every day. I found this an easy and comforting thing to do. I never knew she kept my letters but when she died I found a trunkful of them. I threw them away, which I now regret.

At one point in Italy, the Army mail services had become so sophisticated that at very small cost you were able to send a telegram home every week. A series of numbered standard phrases were offered: 'Lovely to get your letter, love to Mum and Dad, fit and well and longing to see you.' So all you had to write on the form were half a dozen figures and quite a long telegram arrived at your home within days. Having started sending such telegrams to Betty I suddenly realised how ghastly it would be if I forgot one week for she would then think I was dead. I therefore said to my orderly room sergeant: 'You have to send returns in to the brigade headquarters every week. When you do this please send my wife the following telegram.' I knew he would never forget so my mind was at rest. However, when I got back to England Betty said: 'It was nice getting those telegrams, but why did you use exactly the same words every week?' Unguardedly and stupidly I said 'Which telegrams?' I had quite forgotten that I had set this process in motion.

In addition to writing to Betty daily during the campaign I amused myself writing a different sort of letter. I got interested in the contrast between real warfare and the training for warfare that we had received in England. So I wrote a number of 'letters' from an officer serving at the front to his colleague at a training establishment in UK, not disparaging of the training in England but putting it in perspective. I got these illustrated by our intelligence sergeant Bill Baker, who was a talented caricaturist. Then I gave them to Brian Valentine, one of my officers, also an England cricketer, who was going home and asked him to present them at the War Office to see what happened. They were rather a success and appeared as a regular feature in the War Office publication 'Notes from the Theatres of War' which came out every month. In fact when they had run out of the letters actually composed by me the series continued under the title 'Dear Paul' and some of the contents would certainly not have met with my approval.

In the First World War both the public and the troops were, on the whole, critical of the generals; the apparently pointless carnage of trench warfare having convinced people that there must be some better way of winning a war. Despite such debacles as Dunkirk and Singapore, by the end of the Second World War the prestige of our generals was high, partly due to the fact that the great bulk of our forces did not go into action until the third year of the war. By then a nucleus had had battle experience and there had been time for the rest, like my battalion, to be properly trained, in contrast to 1914-15 when thousands of British troops were thrown untrained into battle and to their deaths. Our war did also produce a number of generals - Montgomery, Wavell, Alexander, Mountbatten - who commanded universal respect.

11
Sicily and Termoli

Two months after the fall of Tunis, Sicily was invaded by three divisions of British and American troops. Our division, the 78th, remained in reserve at Sousse on the North African coast for a fortnight and then made a peaceful crossing by tank landing ship on a sunlit Sicilian afternoon, disembarking on a beach south of Syracuse.

We moved 40 miles over rough roads to our concentration area, through olive groves, vineyards and steep mountain tracks, through steamy, dusty heat. Every man's throat was parched by the heat and the slight sulphur fumes from Etna, some miles away. The dust was the worst trial of all - a heavy white dust that clung to the skin, whitened hair and moustaches and yet was fine enough to penetrate the handkerchiefs of officers and men.

The first task given to the 78th Division in Sicily was the capture of Centuripe, a village in an impregnable position high up in the foothills of Etna. The Germans had been ordered by their high command to hold it at all costs. Centuripe was guarded by smaller but very steep terraced hills which could be easily defended. A machine-gun perched on one of these could keep a whole company at bay.

Our attack on the first of these hills was a comfort for my battalion but nerve-wracking for me. I had been ordered to capture a hill, which we duly did without any resistance. When we got to the top my gunner officer said to me 'Sir, we have captured the wrong hill.' This was not an absurd suggestion as the contours on the Italian map of the area with which I had been supplied looked like a pile of worms and I could easily have read the map wrongly. What is more, gunner officers are usually good map readers. I retired under an olive tree, put my head in my hands and gazed intently at the map and finally said to the gunner 'We bloody well haven't' - and we hadn't. Had we done so, we would have been in real danger of being shelled by our own artillery.

A history of the 78th Division reads 'The vast Centuripe feature occupying a width of five miles or so was defended by what General Alexander later described in his dispatch as 'fanatical vigour' by the best German troops in Sicily. It was approached by a narrow corkscrew road that ran for a couple of miles along the flank of one of the precipitous ridges jutting out from the main mountain mass. Every yard of this road was commanded from steep slopes above; the slopes were deathtraps to men, mules and vehicles. The road had been mined, breached and blown and its hairpin bends were made for ambush. The village itself had been built on the steep edge of the final slopes. Immediately around the town the slopes were terraced for cultivation in six foot steps; farther away there were dizzy angles of coarse slippery grass or loose crumbling stone. 'The strongest mountain position I have seen' cabled a correspondent who had seen the worst that Tunisia could show.'

I won't attempt to give a blow-by-blow account of this battle except to say that my battalion was in the thick of it for the next three days. In addition to the fighting and the casualties the conditions were awful; it was desperately hot; the sulphurous fumes from Mount Etna made the troops agonisingly thirsty and you would see men drawing water from farm wells and drinking it by the bucketful. The jumble of rocks and ravines made it impossible country for vehicles so the men were overloaded and the mules as infuriating as ever.

Montgomery's Chief of Staff, General de Guingand, had watched the attack from a hilltop to the south and recorded in his book that; 'It appeared too much to ask any troops to undertake, yet this fine division climbed the heights. It was an imposing sight and will forever spell valour in the records of the 78th.'

Once Centuripe had fallen the capture of the rest of Sicily was just a matter of time. To the Germans it was a planned withdrawal and the other little towns around the base of Etna: Adrano, Bronte and Randazo fell without heavy casualties.

My battalion had one more serious and bloody battle on Monte Rivoglia when I lost two close friends, Stephen Fletcher, the gunner officer from Halifax who was so brave at Djebel Abiod and Ken Scott, an Oxford Blue at both golf and cricket. He had the distinction of having bowled Bradman.

In the attack on Monte Rivoglia Stephen Fletcher was walking up the mountain at my side, his large gunner's radio set carried by a mule. A burst of fire and down the mule went. I told two soldiers from a passing platoon to carry the set and we moved off again. Another couple of hundred yards, another burst of machine-gun fire, this time through Stephen Fletcher's legs. Badly wounded he nevertheless survived and in fact recovered very well. I saw quite a lot of him in

Halifax after the war. Ken Scott was killed commanding my old company, D Company.

After the battles of Centuripe and Rivoglia I was awarded the DSO, not because I had done anything that most of my fellow officers would not have done but presumably in recognition of the fact that by then I had seen a lot of fighting.

Rivoglia was a foretaste of the many attacks we were going to have to carry out on hills as we slogged our way up Italy. It was not held by a large number of Germans; the reward of victory was not hundreds of prisoners. The natural strength of the position meant that a small number of men with a large number of machine-guns would force us to deploy a whole battalion on which they could inflict heavy casualties before themselves making a planned retreat. Once you had captured the hill, that was not the end of your casualties for the German artillery, knowing exactly where you were, would shower you with shells before you had got properly dug in. The whole strategy of the Germans before Cassino was a slow retreat up Italy to inflict the maximum casualties on the allies at the minimum cost to themselves, and the mountainous Italian countryside was perfectly suited to their purpose.

Over the centuries armies have often lived like locusts off the land they were conquering. Motivation for marshal and soldier alike was provided by the hope of loot. This did not apply in poverty-stricken Tunisia where the most that could be squeezed out of the wretched Arabs was eggs in return for 'once-used tea.'

The first time I came across the loot problem was after we had captured the small and completely deserted town of Adrano on the slopes of Mount Etna. Nothing untoward seemed to happen but it was noticeable that after that most of the troops had trinkets of one sort or another in their kitbags. The battalion headquarters and company offices were suddenly well equipped with typewriters and the officers' mess better provided with cutlery and china. This did not occur seriously again. It never fell to our lot to capture another completely deserted town and looting of occupied houses seldom happened.

The Sicilian campaign had been short for us - only just over a fortnight - but intense. Morale was much higher than it was at the end of the long slog of the Tunisian campaign, mainly because we could always see the end in sight.

My memories of the next six weeks are of sun, sea and bathing as we got up steam for the Italian campaign. I acquired a delightful villa belonging to an Italian naval officer with the beach at the end of the garden where I entertained in style. One hundred and twenty reinforcements joined us while the battalion was still in a rest camp near Patti on the north coast of the island and must have got rather an erroneous impression of the Mediterranean campaign.

I have disturbing memories of that rest camp, brainchild of a newly arrived regular second-in-command, Major Winky Benyon. I had not seen the site for myself but he was full of enthusiasm for the idea of sending the companies in turn to this idyllic spot. When the first company came back I asked one of the men what it was like and got the answer: 'OK, sir, except for the mosquitoes.' We were on a strict malaria routine and I ordered the camp to be evacuated forthwith, not a minute too soon, for cases of malaria soon started popping up. The brigadier, a demon regarding malarial discipline, said he would like to come and see me next day and I knew exactly why, but he never turned up. Mercifully he himself had gone down with malaria.

The large number of casualties the battalion suffered in North Africa and Sicily raises the question of what happens to the spirit and the working and fighting efficiency of a unit which has gone through such traumas. This was an experience for which one was quite unprepared by training in England, when it was presumed that every battalion, company, platoon and section would always be up to strength. This was never in fact the case except at the very beginning of a campaign.

When a battalion has heavy casualties, in due course, and certainly not at once, reinforcements come up. From a reinforcement squad of, say, 120, 20 may be former members of the battalion who have been ill or wounded. The remaining 100 may or may not be members of the same regiment. I remember when we were halfway up Italy and the strength of the rifle companies was below 300. A reinforcement squad of 120 arrived, all belonging to the Somerset Light Infantry. The last thing they wanted to do was to join the Queen's Own Royal West Kent Regiment, but this they had to do and were actually fighting wearing their unwelcome new cap badges within a week.

We landed in Italy at Taranto on September 24th; the port was clogged with the ships of the surrendered Italian fleet. Typically, their battleships and cruisers did not look like ours or the Germans; less business-like, more graceful, more like large yachts.

During the next few days we moved via Trani to the port of Barletta where we were due to board infantry landing craft, sail up the coast during the night and land behind the Germans at Termoli.

As I was standing on the quay watching my troops embark a flag-carrying jeep drove up and out stepped the great General Montgomery, invariably known as Monty. Then followed an extraordinary conversation with this extraordinary man. After a few preliminaries he said: 'You have been promoted seven times in the war. Most people have only been promoted three or four times in the war. You have done very well.' We talked about not very much, he continuing with his short staccato sentences. For some reason he was impressive, and he had clearly taken a lot of trouble to know all about me. He seemed to have time on his hands.

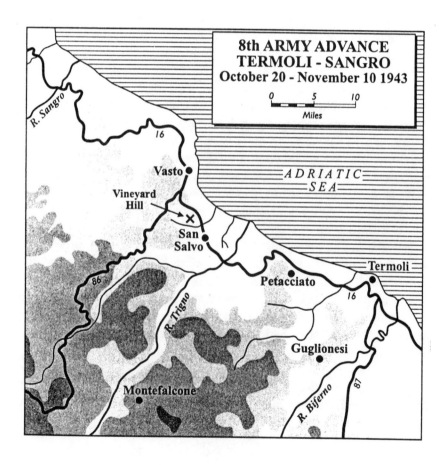

8th ARMY ADVANCE
TERMOLI - SANGRO
October 20 - November 10 1943

Our voyage up the coast went smoothly enough. The Commandos had already landed at Termoli, taking 100 German prisoners, so we were unopposed. There followed a successful day for my battalion. We were given a number of objectives to capture and this we did before nightfall after some fierce fighting with not too many casualties. For the first time I came across the Germans using light anti-aircraft guns in an anti-infantry role. These were less likely to hit you than their standard machine-guns, but when they did they caused nasty wounds.

As night fell the battalion took up defensive positions awaiting the arrival of our supporting tanks which had been held up by the destruction of a bridge over the Biferno River, which was in full flood and could not be forded. I had faith that these would not be long delayed, for the Royal Engineers were brilliant in the speed they could put up a Bailey bridge, a Lego-type contraption which they always seemed to have available. The arrival of the tanks was particularly important to me as, owing to the continuous rain and boggy ground, our own anti-tank guns had not been able to get up to our positions.

During the night I sent out patrols. Two farms in front of us were found to be clear of any enemy but, more seriously, the patrols heard the sound of German tanks. Fortunately my brigadier, Swifty Howlett, realised my predicament and came to see me at dawn. I asked him the straight question: 'What do I do if we are overrun by tanks?' He said: 'You will have to get out.' I dreaded this prospect. Given the open nature of the land around us it would be almost impossible to retreat in any sort of order under fire from tanks. I made a plan to retreat behind a wood several hundred yards away, but was far from happy.

At 10.30am the worst happened. German tanks arrived in some numbers. The next half hour was the worst 30 minutes of my war and indeed of my life. If we had been insanely brave we could have stood our ground, in which case the Germans need not have bothered even to shoot us - they could have run us over. With permission from the Brigadier to 'Get out' - that is what we did. With all my battle experience I had never actually had to run away before. Here I was in full flight with machine-gun bullets from the tanks whistling round my ears and my battalion scattering like rabbits at speed down the slopes all around me. As we ran my intelligence officer beside me, Peter Peerless, was killed - his leg blown off by a shell from the tanks. There died one of the nicest men I have ever known. As the rout went on I remember no great feeling of fear - not through gallantry on my part but because my brain was completely overwhelmed by the disaster of losing all control over the several hundred men I presumed to command.

By the evening we had gathered together again in some sort of order on the outskirts of Termoli and that night the Brigade intelligence officer reported in his daily situation report that: '6 RWK had retreated from one map reference to another.' He was firmly reprimanded on the grounds that the British army never retreats. It only withdraws!

I discovered that the battalion had not been in total rout. Peter Beall, aged 19, whom I would place among the dozen bravest officers I have met, put up a wonderful defence of our battalion headquarters with the anti-tank guns on the lower ground. In the process he was badly wounded and only survived thanks to the bravery of Sergeant Peter Obbard, who carried him back in full view of the German tanks. Pete Obbard became the most decorated of all our warrant officers.

Peter Beall had to have his leg amputated - a terrible blow at any age but at 19 somehow even sadder. I have read the letters he wrote home from hospital making light of his wounds - he had been hit in the arms and body as well - they were very moving. This is an extract from Peter Beall's first letter to his parents after he was wounded:

6 October 1943

My dear Mother and Father
I am wondering how long it is since you got the telegram from the War Office informing you that I had been getting in the way of bullets, etc. again and... I hope you have not been too worried. I must admit I made a more complete job of it than my effort in Tunisia but I am extremely well in myself, reading, eating or drinking all day long.

I am still not quite sure what hit me, you see, we were playing against tanks and they carry quite a lot of nasty weapons and probably the tank let fly with them all. Anyway it made rather a mess of my right leg. I could see that my right arm was bleeding a bit and a bit out of shape and bruised and the left arm was as I had seen it twice before - I could see I had completed the hat trick in breaking it.

Unfortunately on the 7th they decided they couldn't save my leg and they amputated it above the knee...

You must realise that I am getting very well. I haven't any pain at all and am in an excellent base hospital. You must realise that the loss of a leg is very little handicap and nowadays it is even possible to play tennis with an artificial one. I suppose it will mean Blighty but how soon I don't know. Please don't worry any more. I shall be glad to hear from you so write here in case I am here for a bit.

Love to you all, P

The other two battalions of the brigade had not fared very much better at the hands of the tanks and had retreated towards the town. By then the army engineers had put up a Bailey bridge across the Biferno river, the British tanks were with us and the crisis was over.

No doubt the history books will record Termoli as a victory, maybe a battle honour, but did not feel like that to me. Considering the precarious situation in which we found ourselves the brigade got away comparatively lightly. The 16th Panzer Division had served in Russia and was being reformed in France when it was rushed down to the Italian front. Had they been fully trained and experienced, catching us undefended in open country like that, they should have been able to inflict far more serious casualties and taken prisoners.

It was at about this time that two potentially famous men came into my life. Denis Forman became famous. Lionel Wigram would certainly have done so had he lived.

Lionel Wigram was a brilliant, tireless Jew with an original mind and the gift of leadership. He had challenged the long-established methods of infantry training in the British army with his development of 'battle drill' so successfully at the Battle School he created at Barnard Castle that it was officially re-named 'The School of Infantry.'

The one weakness behind his achievement was that he had never himself been in a battle. This he decided to put right and got himself attached to the Buffs in our brigade for the Sicilian campaign.

I quote from Denis Forman's book *To Reason Why*:

He had been in at the start of the Sicilian campaign. He saw every important action on the east side of the island. Although starting as an observer he became so trusted by battalion commanders that they allowed him to take command of

platoons, sections and companies, and finally at Rivoglia he had
been appointed to command a battalion action. It had been an
exciting experience and an eye opener. Some of what he had
taught at the battle school had been absolutely right but a great
deal was hopelessly wrong. He made notes throughout the
campaign. He had discussed them with a wide cross-section of
officers from brigade staff down to ex-Barnard Castle students
commanding companies. He had taken immense pains to ensure
that his views were endorsed by the majority of officers in the
field, he had written his report carefully and been sent back to
Barnard Castle to deliver it and to adjust the syllabus and
methods of training in accordance with his experience in battle.'

So far so good, but General Montgomery, the hero of the Desert War
and now commanding the British army in Italy received accounts from
his own officers who had heard Lionel's report. He was displeased.
When Lionel arrived in Italy, ostensibly to become second-in-command
of a battalion, he was summoned into the presence, given no chance to
defend himself and demoted to company commander.

My brigadier, Swifty Howlett, apologised to me. 'I am so sorry,' he
said; 'as senior battalion commander I am afraid you will have to take
on this tiresome fellow.' I was delighted. I couldn't lose. If he was a
nuisance, with the reputation he had acquired I could get rid of him in
the morning. The chances were that he would be a star, and he was.

When he reported I let him do all the talking, which went on for a
long time. To show the scale of his humiliation I quote again from
Denis Forman:

> I sat bemused. Lionel in disgrace. That meant the Battle School
> movement in disgrace. All the work of the past two years would
> be under threat. And Lionel himself? He was proud, he was
> passionate, he knew he was right, he was much more than a
> lieutenant-colonel in charge of a training school - he was a leader
> whose word was law to many hundreds of disciples, some of
> them the best officers in the infantry. It was almost as if the
> Almighty had deposed Moses just as he was leading the
> Israelites out of the Dead Sea.'

He was outraged that Monty had 'not even listened to me.'

He certainly could not have made that charge against me. After I had listened to his lament without comment for a very long time, I explained that there was nothing novel in this situation. Successful generals do not tolerate post mortems on their campaigns, especially by amateur strangers. Monty would not have it - period. The only way for him to get reinstated was, by his performance, to put me in a position to be able to report favourably on him to those above. My words had not the slightest effect on him and he was still nursing his humiliation when he was killed three months later.

In the meantime he was certainly the most brilliant officer that ever served in my battalion. He transformed the morale and the fighting performance of the company he commanded, but for obvious reasons he was not a favourite with some of my less gifted officers.

Denis Forman was reluctant to join my battalion due to his natural desire to stay in his own regiment: he was an Argyll & Sutherland Highlander and had come all the way to Italy to join their 8th battalion in our brigade. They had too many majors so he was wished onto me.

Again I couldn't lose. Denis had been commandant of a Battle School. He was tall, athletic (a Cambridge running blue), musical (he later wrote a book on Mozart and became Deputy Chairman of Covent Garden), creative (he later became chairman of Granada Television) - and over the next 50 years he was to become one of my best friends and godfather to my daughter Felicity.

I already had some very experienced company commanders and with the addition of Forman and Wigram I would guess that at that time I had the best team in the British army.

***

Our winter toil up Italy continued with yet another river crossing - the Trigno. The Buffs had led the advance and we followed them, wading across the river thigh-deep in the pouring rain under sporadic shellfire. We waited around in the rain all day until about 5pm until the San Salvo feature ahead of us was said to be securely held.

The brigadier then sent for me. It seemed that we were going to be asked to do a belated attack on a feature beyond San Salvo known as Vineyard Hill. I told Lionel and Denis to have a look at the approaches to Vineyard Hill while there was still light as I did not savour an advance across unknown country in the dark. While this was going on a dozen German tanks, the rearguard of the retreating enemy, elected to attack and dislodge the battalion on the San Salvo feature but then retired, apparently to rejoin their main force.

I came back from the brigadier with a very unattractive proposition. The normal routine for a battalion attack on a feature is to form up on a start line which has been secured by some other troops and then at a set hour advance into the attack under cover of as much artillery fire as is available. Before setting off on this venture the battalion commander will have taken his company commanders as far forward as is safe to show them the ground and explain the plan. Time, the general confusion and the nearness of the tank battle, made all this impossible. Quoting from Forman's book:

> Back in San Salvo as darkness fell, as Sergeant-Majors collected and counted their men and Quartermasters attempted a hot meal, Paul collected his O group in a convenient stable, Lionel and I told them of the difficulties and tried to make the map come alive with vivid descriptions of steep slopes covered with vines, deep ditches, wire fences and thickets. Paul formulated a plan and we were to set out from San Salvo at 2200 hrs with my company in the van. It would take about two hours to reach the forming up position. I could not absolutely swear to it but my recollection is that the first two soldiers in the advance up the main road from San Salvo to the next major town, Vasto, were Paul and myself.

Forman's recollection is correct. By going in front I did at least know where the battalion was. One had to assume that the enemy had retreated a good distance, otherwise, in the dark and in those conditions the task was impossible.

All of a sudden all hell broke loose. In the dark we had stumbled on the enemy tanks which had done the dusk attack on San Salvo and were now waiting for dawn to rejoin the main force. They fired their machine-guns at random, red and green tracer zipping through the trees. Denis's company in the lead exchanged some fire with the tanks but in the darkness it was impossible to control the battalion. I got back to my headquarters and sent messages to the companies to re-group on the village of San Salvo.

In the course of our somewhat chaotic re-grouping in the darkness towards San Salvo, blundering through the undergrowth I fell into a tank trap - a large, deep, smooth concrete ditch. Ridiculously I could not get out. Each time I climbed up the side I came sliding down again. I had shaming visions of a patrol being sent out from San Salvo to find the commanding officer. My time in the tank trap was probably five minutes. It seemed like half an hour before, with the aid of knees and fingernails, I scrambled to the top and to self-respect once again.

In San Salvo I managed to get the battalion into some sort of order again and persuaded the brigadier that there was no point in moving before dawn.

There then followed a very successful day for the battalion, and in particular for Lionel Wigram's company which in the course of our operation against Vineyard Hill carried out three separate successful attacks. This day was perhaps the highlight of Lionel's career with the battalion.

On the next day Denis's company took the lead and after one successful set piece attack we went on, with resistance lessening all the time, until we reached Torino di Sangro.

The last few days had been an extraordinary experience for Denis and Lionel. They had spent two years together at the School of Infantry at Barnard Castle, studying and teaching modern infantry tactics. A few months later chance had thrown them together again to practise on the battle field what they had taught at the school. From what I saw of the practise they could be well pleased with the teaching. I could imagine the post-battle discussions that went on and on.

12
The Sangro

The rapid advance of the Division, with Wigram and Forman in the van, ended at the Sangro River. All the signs were that this was to be the Germans' next line of defence. They had destroyed both the bridges in the area, leaving the river as a formidable obstacle. It was formidable enough in its width but even more so in its eccentric habits, ankle deep at one time and shoulder high at others - all dependent upon the fall of snow in the mountains.

As my battalion had done most of the fighting in the approach up to the river we were absolved of a main role in the final attack. Our task was to patrol a section of the north bank of the Sangro in preparation for the corps attack. We were to identify enemy positions, sweep the approaches clear of mines, harry the German forward troops, force them back from the top of the escarpment which dominated the river.

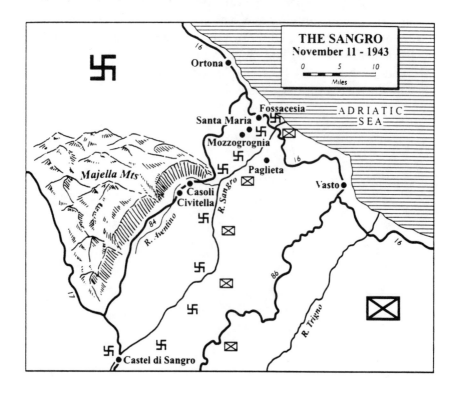

As a commander the plans you make can be governed as much by personalities as they are by conditions. The routine way to carry out my orders would have been to allot various patrolling tasks to the four rifle companies, but in Denis Forman, now my second-in-command, I knew I had a personality who could take charge of the whole operation with thoroughness and inspiration.

He set himself up with headquarters in a farmhouse overlooking the river. I quote from his book:

> Swifty Howlett and Paul Bryan treated me like a patient about to go in for an operation, probably terminal. Nothing was too good for the patrolling force. I was to have an adjutant, a briefing officer, a sergeant and three men from Intelligence, permanent staff to run the OP, signallers, cooks, batmen, one regiment of twenty-five pounders and one Medium regiment on call. Nothing however could alleviate the heavy weight I carried in the pit of my stomach which was the weight of fear, fear not of the Germans but of my failing to do what everybody expected me to do.

> As the operation got under way, however, fear gave way to tension. As each patrol slipped over the brow of the hill I wondered - would it do what it was meant to do? Would it find out if the red house was occupied? How many casualties? Would it come back on time? Would it come back at all? For ten days from November 10th I sent out from four to seven patrols each night - in all usually between fifty and one hundred men. At first the reconnaissance of enemy positions ranked in equal priority with the search for crossing places for tanks and mine-sweeping on the approach routes for the company attack. But then another hazard threatened the whole operation. It rained continuously on the 14th and 15th November and the Sangro began to rise and to cause casualties.

He goes on to quote the official report of a patrol by Sergeant Knight and Lance Corporal Lingham which ended with Lingham being drowned on the homeward crossing. It was a venture hard to equal for intelligence, courage and perseverance:

Patrol "HOPE"

Composition: Sgt Knight, L/Cpl Lingham, R.

Date: 14 Nov 43

Task: To answer question "Do the Germans use MT (motor transport) on the SANTA MARIA - PAGLIETA rd to supply outpost line on the escarpment?"

Briefed: 0900 hrs 14 Nov 43

Time out: 1900 hrs 14 Nov 43

Time in: 0730 hrs 16 Nov 43

The patrol was sent out in company with two other small patrols. All were to cross the road below the escarpment. Each patrol was then to carry out a separate task.

The river was crossed without incident, but, just as the patrols reached the point at which they were to disperse, they were fired on by a hitherto unlocated gun from the top of the escarpment, immediately opposite them. All patrols withdrew some 200 yds and after 20 mins wait the other two patrols proceeded on their routes.

Sgt Knight struck the escarpment about 150 yds to the left of the position from which the gun had fired. He scrambled to the top of the bank, and, as he poked his head over the crest, he saw a German sentry a few yards away. The sentry heard him and lay down. No action was taken by either side. After a few minutes Sgt Knight slipped down the escarpment and tried again between the sentry and the gun position. This time he succeeded in penetrating up the stream without being observed.

He followed the line of the stream for about 400 yards and then struck SOUTH WEST, on his prearranged route, towards the SANTA MARIA road. At one point on the route on scrambling up a wooded bank Sgt Knight found himself looking into a German MG pit which was manned by a sentry. The sentry raised the alarm and grenades were thrown down the bank, not

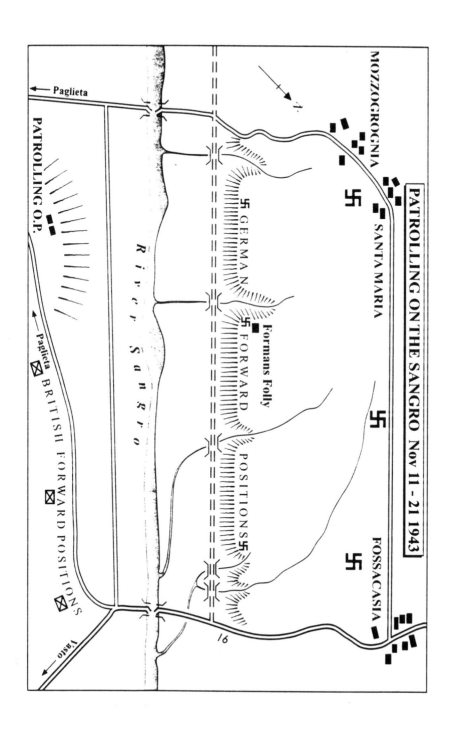

PATROLLING ON THE SANGRO Nov 11 – 21 1943

near enough however to wound Sgt Knight or L/Cpl Lingham.,
When the alarm had died down he continued until he reached
the gully running parallel with the SANTA MARIA rd.

In his search for a good OP Sgt Knight again found himself
looking into a German MG position, in which the gunner was
asleep. He proceeded NW up the road for some 400 yards and
lay up until dawn. He then went to a lying up area which had
been previously selected, and throughout the hours of daylight
he, and L/Cpl Lingham lay in a bank of brambles.

No enemy movement was heard during the day except for the
practice firing of some weapons in the area of the main defences.

At nightfall the patrol again moved to within earshot of the road
and listened for some five hours. Nothing was heard.

On the return journey, which followed approximately the same
route, a German MG position was being relieved, and the patrol
watched the relief march in and take over, and the party relieved
march out towards a farm house. The remainder of the journey
to the bank of the SANGRO was without incident.

During the patrol there had been a heavy fall of rain and the
river had risen about two feet. Sgt Knight and L/Cpl Lingham
attempted to cross in two places and failed. On the third attempt,
when they had nearly reached the home bank, L/Cpl Lingham
was swept off his feet, and, as the current was too strong to
make swimming possible, he was drowned. Sgt Knight was
swept off his feet also, but was luckily cast upon the home bank,
where he lay for some time in a state of exhaustion.

He reached patrol headquarters at about 0730 hrs on the 16 Nov
43, having achieved his object and gained certain information
that the SANTA MARIA road was not used by German MT, and
was therefore almost certainly demolished and mined.

Throughout this patrol there had been continuous rain, and
although the NCOs had taken some food with them they had
been too cold to eat anything except one or two biscuits.

Sgt Knight carried a revolver only, and L/Cpl Lingham a Tommy gun. Both men wore gym shoes although the distance covered was between six and seven miles. They carried great coats and wore them when lying up. These they discarded before attempting to cross the river on the return journey.

Sgt Knight, after this astonishing display of stamina, was unable to give coherent identification of the positions he had encountered on his first day back. During his de-briefing his eyes turned dull and after a time he could no longer answer questions, rolling his head slowly from side to side and crying out for Corporal Lingham. He was placed ceremoniously in a shed a few hundred yards from my OP where medical orderlies ministered to his needs. He went to sleep about noon and the MO insisted I should not wake him up for 24 hours. When at last he was in a fit state to be questioned, it took us three days, de-briefing him in short spells of two hours at a time, in order fully to identify his route on the map and on the ground with any certainty. This is one of the hazards of patrol life: the information about the MG positions was desperately needed to brief patrols going out that night, and in this case I was to be the person most seriously affected.

The patrolling period ended with Denis himself leading a force of 81 men across the swollen river to wipe out an enemy position known as Red Farm. The combination of the river, the rain, the darkness, and the strength of the enemy position made it a fearsome exploit. Denis could never forgive himself that he lost 20 of his men killed or wounded but this is a harsh self-judgment. I had been at war long enough to know that however intelligent and careful the preparation you make - and no-one could excel Denis in that department - luck good or bad can play a large part in the outcome, and there wasn't much good luck on our side that night. At the end of the day, or rather the night, let us just remember that the objective was achieved. The Germans abandoned Red Farm for good.

My personal disappointment was my failure to get Denis a decoration of any sort for his patrolling work. To make sure he was recognised I put him in for the DSO, a very unusual honour for a major, in the hope that this would ensure he got a Military Cross. Possibly I was being too clever by half for he got nothing. I think this was not unconnected with the fact that my brigadier, Swifty Howlett, was killed shortly afterwards. I am sure he would have intervened to put this right.

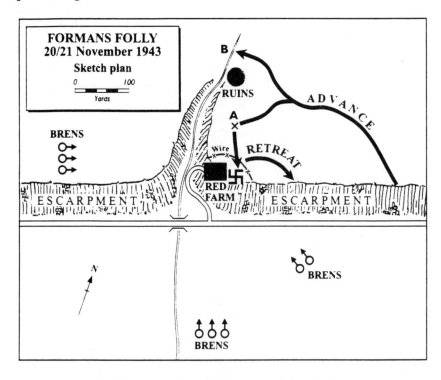

Among the patrolling casualties on the Sangro River was one of my closest friends, Dick Allen. He and Bridget shared houses with us as we moved around England in the training period before we came abroad.

Dick was a charming, intelligent, modest, reliable person with a sense of humour whom nobody could fail to like and respect. He was a good athlete and I always remember how gracefully he sped across a rugger field, gliding like a gazelle. Grace is not a normal attribute of rugger players but I mention it because Jane in her teens was a very good ballet dancer and I am sure she inherited her grace of movement from her father.

Though I knew him so well in England I saw little of him through the North Africa and Sicily campaigns because he had become intelligence officer to Swifty Howlett at brigade headquarters. He came back to the battalion in Italy and at the time of his death was second-in-command of D Company.

I happened to be with Dick in a farmhouse on the river bank while he was waiting for the appointed hour at which he would cross the river with his patrol. We lay on a bed chatting about the past, I suppose to take our minds off the immediate future. We talked about Betty and Bridget, Libby and Jane, and the times when we had shared the Golf Club House at Malvern and the council house in Haverfordwest.

He set off with his patrol in the darkness, wading across the wide river. After what seemed a long time I heard and saw explosions on the far bank. The patrol had walked into a minefield; Dick and five of his men were killed.

All this came back to me when in the summer of 1990 I watched his beautiful granddaughter being married in Worcester cathedral with my granddaughters, Alice and Elizabeth, as bridesmaids and my grandson, Max a page.

Our patrols were successful in forcing the Germans back onto the escarpment and the night before the main attack I took two companies of the battalion across the river to secure the far bank as a forming up area for the main assault. When patrolling in the dark, we used a different password each night to identify friend from foe. On that night the challenge was 'Wilfred Wooler' and the answer was 'Cardiff and Wales.' This combination had the necessary virtue that no German was likely to ever heard of Wilfred Wooler, nor to know that he was a rugger player who played for Cardiff and Wales. It had the disadvantage that Wilfred Wooler, said quickly and in a gruff voice, sounded very German. When I was wandering in the dark on the far bank of the Sangro a figure jumped up from behind a bush pointing a gun at me shouting 'Wilfred Wooler,' and for a split second I thought he was a German. My heart dropped, then with relief I realised what he was saying, murmured 'Cardiff and Wales' and all was well. Had I known that the figure in the darkness was Sergeant Obbard, the fiercest and most decorated warrant officer in the battalion, whom the reader has already met rescuing the wounded Peter Beall at Termoli, my heart would have fallen even further.

Traditionally generals have been secretive. The number of people who know the plan for a battle in advance is kept to the absolute minimum in case the information gets to the enemy, but General Montgomery took the opposite view. He maintained that unless every single soldier going into action knew the battle plan he could have no enthusiasm for the fight. Monty used other methods to deceive the enemy about his intentions.

To this end, whilst my battalion was patrolling the Sangro River, I was summoned back to a cinema in Vasto where the general was to brief the likes of me and above with his plans for overcoming the enemy defences on the Sangro River.

Monty started by saying that he expected everything he told us to be in the knowledge of every soldier in the division by the time he was asked to take part in the attack, the inference being woe betide the commanding officer who had not taken the trouble to impart this information to his troops.

He then proceeded to explain at length his plans for the battle. He impressed me for the following reasons:

> 1. He was actually up-to-date on the reports of our own battalion patrolling on the Sangro.

> 2. The details and thought that had gone into his plan, all of which seemed to me sensible.

> 3. The huge scale of the support from bombers and artillery, was impressive. I felt quite sorry for the Germans.

> 4. He was sufficiently confident and detached from the urgencies of the situation to be able to give us quite separately a lecture on how to do our jobs in our various commands.

He started: 'I, as an army commander, have only eight essentials in my job.' Down came a great screen with his eight essentials. Number one was 'Winning the air battle' - I forget the rest.

He continued: 'Every morning I look at the items on that list. If I am doing everything I can about each of them I have a free day. I can visit the troops.' He turned on us and said: 'You are not army commanders. There will be less than eight essentials in your job. Think out what they are and check on them every day.' This simple theme was well ahead of its time. Today it is taught in far more high-faluting jargon in modern business schools.

The simplicity of it captured me straight away. In later, complicated days when I found myself with an ailing family business to run in Hebden Bridge, an invalid wife, three lively children to follow, a large country constituency to look after, an allegedly full-time job as a government whip, a money-losing farm to deplore and a score of other worries or temptations to pursue, I found the Monty system invaluable. Even in my semi-retired life of today, every Monday morning I look at my eight points, which always start with the family, and as a result feel more at ease with myself, whether or not it does any good to anyone else.

Monty's confidence at the confernece at Vasto was justified. Supported by 400 guns and a vast number of aircraft, 78 Division crossed the Sangro, swept through the German winter line and by the time the division had reached the town of Fossacesia, had captured 1000 prisoners and inflicted heavy losses on the enemy without suffering too many ourselves. My battalion had more casualties in our 10 days of patrolling the river than any other battalion in the main battle.

It was at this point that my brigadier and former commanding officer, Swifty Howlett, was killed as he rode up to one of our forward companeis on a horse. This was a blow to the brigade for, as I have repeatedly said, he was a brilliant commander. It was a personal loss to me for he had taught me almost everything I knew about soldiering, originally in the training period in England and then by example in battle. I could feel his influence in the decisions I took and later in the gospel I preached to the cadets when I was commanding an OCTU (Officer Cadet Training Unit).

When he died he was just due to be promoted to major-general to command a division in the Normandy landings. I think he would probably have taken me with him.

His speciality was officer responsibility. If there was a job to do which was dangerous, difficult or boring he would expect an officer to be in charge. A dangerous patrol was always an officer patrol. If battalions were required to send fatigue parties for some tiresome task like unloading baggage from a ship, my battalion would tend to have an officer in charge, whilst the others would have a sergeant.

At all times in his eyes somebody had to be 'in charge.' If he saw two soldiers talking together he might easily say: 'Who's in charge?' He would expect one of them to jump to attention and say: 'Me, sir.' The reasoning behind this was that if ever the enemy were to catch you unawares somebody would instinctively take command.

Long service under Swifty embedded in your mind the habit of examining your own conscience before blaming others for misfortunes. If a company got lost in battle I automatically asked myself such questions as 'Were my orders clear? Was the manoeuvre too complicated to succeed anyway?' Not that I spent life in one long guilty self-recrimination. I was quite generous to myself in my judgements. It was a useful training for civilian life, especially business where passing on the blame is a chronic condition. Swifty was never one for 'if onlys' or 'might have beens.'

Part of Swifty's inspiration as a leader came from his high expectancy. He always talked as if he really expected you and those under your command to perform well above what they actually thought possible. When you had been fighting for a number of days and the troops were exhausted, he still assumed that you were itching to get at the enemy, whereas deep down you were praying that they would disappear and give you a rest. He always talked as if yours was the best battalion in the division and in so doing shamed you into making sure it was.

Swifty would have been proud of his son, Geoffrey, also a regular soldier, who rose to the rank of lieutenant-general, was knighted and won an MC to boot.

13
Majdalany

After the crossing of the Sangro the battalion collected itself in the village of Paglietta for a much needed wash and brush up. The division had been in battle continuously since the landing at Termoli in October, and my battalion in particular had had a hard time, being in the van all the way and losing more men on the Sangro than any other. Hot showers, clean clothes, six itinerant barbers and three hot meals a day worked wonders in a short time. Paglietta was just a staging post before we moved further up into the mountains to a village called Baranello. Here the battalion settled contentedly into a period of rest and recuperation, a little square bashing, gentle field exercises, lectures on current affairs and 12 hour passes to Campobasso where there was an army cinema and feminine attractions.

The second-in-command of a battalion is by tradition in charge of administration, so Denis Forman came into his own. He conceived the idea of an officers' ball, which by his own judgement was a total disaster. Every young lady invited brought her mother with her. Every mother brought a large handbag, some almost the size of a small sack. When supper was announced, within two minutes all the carefully prepared food was swept into the sacks and not long after the ball was over.

Lionel Wigram had been away ill with jaundice and was now back but in a fairly depressed state. He perked up no end when I asked him to run a two-week course for NCOs. He was back in his Battle School element.

Just before Christmas our general decided that while the division was at rest one of the commanding officers and a major should make a tour of the hospitals and reinforcement camps in Italy, Sicily, Malta and North Africa to check up on the welfare of our wounded. I was the chosen lieutenant-colonel and my companion was to be Major Fred Majdalany, MC, of the Lancashire Fusiliers, whom I did not know.

When we met in our respective jeeps at divisional headquarters he did not look particularly impressive - short, fat, dark, bespectacled and bald. This facade hid a brilliant mind. He had been the *Daily Mail* theatre critic and had written the lyrics of a musical which was only thwarted by the war. He was the best conversationalist *à deux* I have ever known. I have endless memories of talking with him deep into the night as he stood in front of the fire, a cigarette between his fingers and a glass of whisky in his other hand with time passing unnoticed. He played the piano marvellously and without music. Many nights on our months tour ended up in an officers' club with him quietly taking over the piano, to everyone's astonished delight for, as I have suggested, he did not look that sort of person.

As a fellow visitor of the wounded he was admirable, but when we went around meeting generals, staff officers, doctors, etc., I had to do most of the talking. Once we were back in the staff car together he scintillated. Nothing had missed his journalist's eye. His verbal caricatures of everyone we met were hilarious.

In Tunis, our first port of call, we reported to the officers' hotel where we got moderate accommodation and a tepid welcome. After that we always looked up the local general, bearing the compliments of our own General Eveleigh. These former warriors were always delighted to see somebody 'from the front' and treated us like kings.

Our hospital visiting was a success. A soldier's family, when serving abroad, is his battalion. He feels at sea in the impersonal surroundings of a hospital or a transit camp. Once in North Africa I sent a truck back to a base hospital to collect three of our recovered wounded. It came back with 15; the extra 12 were all convalescing, heard the truck was there, and were off. They knew they were unlikely to be punished for deserting *to* the battle. As Maj and I came from different brigades in the division we were able to bring the men direct news of their battalions and take any letters they wanted delivered to their friends.

We spent Christmas Day in Tunis, Boxing Day in Philippeville and by New Year's Day we were in Algiers. Someone in Tunis had given us an introduction to a family in Algiers and we were duly asked to lunch on Jour de l'An, a day of particular celebration for the French. In Tunis we had drawn our standard army Christmas ration, a diminutive Christmas pudding and a tin of turkey. Imagining that our hosts would be short of food and appreciate such delicacies we approached their house, rations in hand. On arrival, seeing the magnificence of this large white house, we rather doubted whether they would be short of anything and felt a little awkward with our Christmas puddings. We thought we had solved the problem by giving them to the dainty maid who opened the door. The puddings were not to be so easily dismissed. When the time came to sit down to lunch, in the smartest possible company, the table groaning with goodies, there were our two little puddings, cold and looking out of their class. No-one mentioned them. The meal was a feast. Conversation sparkled, although not much to my advantage for my French was rusty and Maj's rustier still. The meal was enlivened by the arrival of the police at the coffee stage to arrest one of the guests. Once he had gone conversation got even more frenzied. I never discovered his alleged crime.

In Malta we were subjected to an even more testing sort of entertainment. One of the regular battalions of the Lancashire Fusiliers, Maj's regiment, had been stationed there all the war. They were regular soldiers and their officers' mess had all the traditions and habits of a peacetime battalion, including that ghastly ritual known as mess night. On such a night the officers dress up in their mess kit and after a variety of ceremonies people get drunk and traditionally get up to all sorts of manly party games.

Our visit happened to coincide with one of these mess nights and as guests we were expected to take our humiliating part in the party games. At the expected hour, by general demand, the commanding officer stepped forward to do his particular trick.

This looked to me impossible. There was a small strong table about half the size of a card table. He lay across it, his head and legs dangling on either side. He then proceeded to wriggle under the table and over and back into his original position without upsetting the table or touching the floor. Prolonged applause followed by demands that I should do the same. There was no escape. I went through the same ridiculous motions and to my amazement with the same result. I suppose God gave me a big bottom especially to give me the right weight balance to do this sort of thing.

Then a junior lieutenant with the shape and look of a gorilla hung on the picture rail. He travelled hand over hand along the rail around the room with cheers rising to a crescendo. At last, exhausted, he reached his starting point.

Now came the demand that the visiting major should do the same. There was, to my mind, no question of the unathletic Majdalany attempting such a thing. But at that time I was not to know that Maj was a strong swimmer, so had strong arms. His piano playing gave him strong hands. Never mind why, he equalled the feat of the gorilla subaltern to slightly less than enthusiastic applause.

We had had so much drink poured down our throats that as we went to bed it was clear to me that Maj was drunk. I therefore challenged him for a pound to a game of ping pong on the table which happened to be outside our room. He fell into my trap and it was not long before I was surging towards victory. But then I discovered yet another of his qualities - doggedness. Crouching down with his nose nearly touching the table, time and again he poked back my most brilliant shots. We reached 20 all, then he won. I gave him his pound, he went to the loo and I went to bed. When I woke up in the morning no signs of Maj. He had gone to sleep on the loo.

We went back via beautiful Taormina where I found one of my company commanders, Dick Clarke, convalescing.

In my copy of a book Maj wrote about Cassino, published in 1946, is inscribed:

> To Paul, in happy recollection of fried chicken in Foggia, Christmas in Tunis, Boxing Day in Philippeville, Jour de l'An in Algiers, Omelette in Constantine, red coat for Elizabeth in Taormina, lace in Malta, high society in Catania, brawls in Bari, squalor in Napoli, peace in Positano and laughs and Lacrima Christi everywhere - and to Betty, who so patiently bears with these recollections - Maj - January 1946.

Red coat for Elizabeth is self-explanatory and was her smartest and proudest garment until long after she grew out of it. At the same time I remember buying at least 200 buttons, picturesque and various, which were a great success at home and kept on appearing on the childrens' clothes over the years. Maj was uncomplimentary about the lace in Malta only because we spent too much money on it. Our lack of money curbed our shopping later and each time he was frustrated he would say: 'If only we hadn't bought that bloody lace in Malta.'

Throughout our trip we kept coming across old friends. When resting in the Tunis area after the North African campaign we got to know what seemed at the time a bright lively prosperous little section of local French Society. When we captured Tunis the French were buoyant. They had only been under the German heel for six months, but were all ready to bubble when released. Nevertheless, in a letter written after our trip to one of my wounded ex-officers in the UK I see that I wrote:

Our Tunis friends I found a little deflated. Raoul, strange to say, has become married to a beauty called Maud and looks a tired man. Daisy is with child, Edmond, a private soldier scrubbing lavatories in the French Army at Cairo, Elise the same as ever, and the seven Sherry sisters I just could not face visiting.

We took Christmas with Bill Heygate and Rumbold (Heygate was the colonel I succeeded). They are both astonishingly good hosts. John Maling was there, not looking very well I thought and at Constantine we had lunch with Algie Heber-Percy - his crowd are a bit bored with life but I should say a good unit. At Algiers we found Colonel Mack at the 95th with his arm in a sling but very ready for a party and it was chiefly under his influence that two or three hospital visits took up five days. Guy Oliver is down there too as second in command of one of their other battalions and O.C. an Irish nurse. This African journey was all done in an immense Lincoln Zephyr with the General's driver at the wheel. This sumptuous equipment we found greatly increased our entertainment value and so did the fact that Fred Majdalany is a magnificent pianist.

Of the characters mentioned, John Maling won the first Military Cross in our battalion at Djebel Abiod, a doctor now. Algie Heber-Percy was the commanding officer of the 3rd Grenadier Guards, a battalion we had got to know in Africa. Colonel Mack was my fellow commanding officer in the brigade, commanding the Buffs and was wounded on the Trigno. Guy Oliver was a Buffs Major we all knew.

Whilst Fred Majdalany and I had been sharing our Christmas rations with the French in Algiers, my battalion had remained at rest at Baranello, where turkey and plum pudding were issued - very different from Christmas the year before spent in the pouring rain in the hills of Tunisia.

By the time I returned from my travels the battalion was in contact with the enemy once again - this time in the foothills of the Apennines, widely scattered in the villages of Casoli, Roccascalegna and Gessopalena. The weather was cold, snow fell intermittently, the few roads were often blocked.

The Germans faced us from similar villages of various sizes, each perched on the top of a mountain with wide open and very difficult country between. The distance as the crow flies between two villages

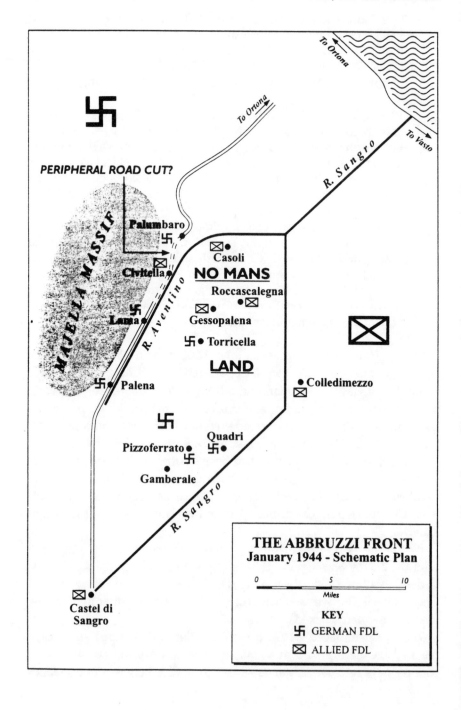

PERIPHERAL ROAD CUT?

MAJELLA MASSIF

To Ortona

To Vasto

R. Sangro

Palumbaro

Civitella

Lama

R. Aventino

Casoli

NO MANS

Roccascalegna

Gessopalena

Torricella

LAND

Colledimezzo

Palena

Pizzoferrato

Quadri

Gamberale

R. Sangro

Castel di
Sangro

THE ABBRUZZI FRONT
January 1944 - Schematic Plan

0   5   10

Miles

KEY

卐 GERMAN FDL

⊠ ALLIED FDL

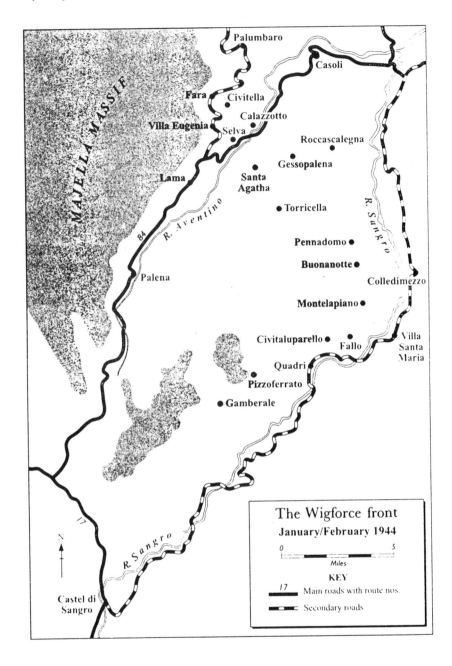

The Wigforce front
January/February 1944

could be a couple of miles and by road 12 miles, negotiating steep slopes and hairpin bends covered with snow.

One surprise was the brutal behaviour of the Germans to the local peasants, a surprise because their conduct towards our troops was usually extremely correct. Later at Cassino our stretcher bearers carried the wounded under the Red Cross flag in some places within 50 yards of the German front line, confident they would not be fired upon. In his book Denis Forman, referring to the lot of solitary farms, says:

> But if they were really unlucky they would fall prey to a German foraging party, an NCO and four men, who would approach a hamlet or a farm, open fire, drive out the inhabitants, loot every article of value, kill all the animals and set the buildings on fire. Sometimes the men would be shot as they ran away, sometimes the women captured and raped. In our area alone several dozen men had been shot, some by putting a rifle in their mouths and discharging it so that it scattered their brains over the walls and the roof of the room where the atrocity was committed.

Not surprisingly, this had provoked the rise of a guerilla force which Lionel Wigram was particularly keen to co-opt and arm. The question then arose as to what our policy should be - should we follow that of the battalion from whom we had taken over and live in comparative peace, if not comfort, by leaving well alone or should we mobilise the guerillas and harass the enemy villages with some really aggressive patrolling?

Sanction, indeed enthusiasm, for the second option came from above, with personal visits from the divisional and corps commanders to cheer the battalion on its way.

When I rejoined the battalion the patrol reports made fascinating reading. Lionel Wigram made an ideal commander of the guerilla force, now called Wigforce, which he had built up to the strength of seven platoons, based in the forward villages on our front. Beyond them he had a network of standing patrols spreading between and behind the nearest German strongpoints. Beyond these again he had single sentries in listening posts and in German occupied villages, ready to send a runner back with news of any movement.

Night after night, joint battalion and guerilla patrols went out in snowy, mountainous country, sometimes for 10 hours at a time, giving the Germans no peace. In time Lionel's area of operation with his guerillas extended well outside the battalion's front and it was decided that he should come under the command of Corps headquarters.

Though Denis had actually recommended this logical change in the command structure, it was a bitter pill for him to swallow. Denis and Lionel were ideal military partners; they had developed Wigforce together; their minds worked in the same way. Denis was probably the necessary restraining influence on Lionel when he too quickly and too enthusiastically adopted venturesome plans of action.

The foreboding which seems to underlie that last statement was justified. Lionel's patrolling, whilst still successful, got bigger and bolder. He was finally killed leading a 100 strong mixed patrol of British troops and guerillas in a night attack on Pizzoferrato on February 3rd 1944. There were about 35 other casualties in his force. This was a sad day for the battalion, but in particular for Denis Forman for they were the closest of friends.

During my month away from the battalion it had been in good hands. Patrolling had been the order of the day and his intense experience on the Sangro had made Denis Forman a master of the art. If there was a world-wide competition for the best patrolling carried out by any battalion in the British Army in World War II, I would confidently submit the war diaries of the Royal West Kent Regiment covering our patrolling on the Sangro and in the Appennines in the winter of 1943/44. If in this imaginary contest Forman was permitted to give the presentation no other battalion would have a chance.

14
Cassino

What none of us had bargained for, from GHQ downwards, was the severity of the winter weather in the mountains of Italy.

I do not remember a single military operation which was not seriously affected. Our battalion disaster at Termoli was entirely due to the rain which turned the low ground into a bog and prevented our having any anti-tank guns. The same rain flooded the River Biferno and delayed the arrival of our tanks. Our patrolling on the Sangro was halted when torrential rains made the river impassable, sweeping away anyone trying to cross it, like Sergeant Knight and Corporal Lingham. My most enduring memory of the bloodbath of Cassino is of trucks and guns stuck in the mud and troops perished by the rain and the cold. Among the unsung heroes in all our battles were the Royal Engineers who strove day and night, often under shellfire, to replace blown bridges or establish crossings with amazing speed.

Cassino was to be our next trial. This description is taken from Fred Majdalany's book, *The Monastery*:

> From the crest above the village we could look down over the whole of the Cassino battlefield. Even at a distance, and to eyes not unused to destruction, the ruins of Cassino were awe-inspiring. This was indeed a stricken town. Not a single whole building remained, only fragments of walls and heaps of rubble. Those jagged fragments of buildings had a ghostly, slightly obscene quality, that is hard to describe; it was like a forest of stalagmites. Cassino in destruction was different from all the other places.

> Away to the left ran the thin streak of the Rapido river, stretched like a steel cord across the entrance to the Liri valley. The fortifications on its far bank linked up with the mountain range which began behind Cassino, and became higher as it went east till it culminated in the towering peak Monte Cairo, over five thousand feet high and the anchor of the Cassino defence system.

Stark and clear now was the one that was the most important of them all, because it was the key to all the others - Monastery Hill. Having seen the country we could properly understand now the difficulties of this battle that had already been going on for nearly four months. The Monastery converted into a fortress and securely planted on the crest of the precipitous rocky slopes of Monastery Hill, commanded a perfect view of every single approach to the Liri Valley, through which an army marching on Rome must pass. This amazing viewpoint - from which the German artillery was so accurately directed for so long - was protected on its eastern side by the mountains and to the west by the narrow, but fast-flowing Rapido, and the steel and concrete defences behind it. It was obvious now why the Monastery had become the bogey of every operation.

If you were on the move anywhere within 10 miles of Cassino, and looked up, there was the Monastery always looking down upon you. Theoretically Cassino could have been held without any troops, just plenty of artillery observers sitting in the Monastery directing hundreds of shells at you. This is not how the Germans operated.

Far from depending on an artillery defence the Germans used parachute troops in large numbers and by means of well-prepared gullies and ancient tunnels they were able to reinforce their troops from the monastery to the town and to the mountain positions with ease. The obvious question to arise is why such a fortress should be attacked in the impossible conditions of an Italian winter. This is explained by events far away on the eastern coast of Italy at Anzio, where after the landings our forces had failed to break out of their bridgehead and were in danger of being swept back into the sea if some of the German forces were not diverted to another front. To this end, on the 17th January, 10 Corps tried and failed to make a crossing of the Garigliano river. On January 24th the Second US Corps tried and failed to cross the Rapido with heavy losses. On the 20th February a second attempt was made and failed.

On the 10th February the Americans made the first attack on Cassino, without success. A week later the New Zealand division together with the 4th Indian Division met the same fate.

When the 78th Division joined the 4th Indian and the New Zealand Division for the third attack on Cassino the allies were probably represented by, at that time, the three most famous divisions in the

British army. Nor had we unworthy opponents. In January Hitler had deemed the defence of Cassino sufficiently vital to issue a special directive in which he declared that even if no military purposes were served it was necessary on political grounds to hold to the death this key bastion. Such a drastic dictum drew to the defences the elite of fanatical Nazi manhood. In the German military hierarchy No 1 Parachute Division stood at the top. At the end of February this *corps d'élite,* one of the greatest fighting formations ever to take the field, relieved 15th Panzer Grenadier Division on the Cassino sector.

As a variation on their strategy in the Sicilian campaign and the Italian campaign thus far there was no question of retreat. Cassino was where the Germans chose to make their main defensive effort. For three months the 14th Panzer Corps had worked at the defences and to help them they had a large detachment of the TOD Labour Organisation. The town was heavily fortified. Buildings were turned into strongpoints. Cellars and ground floors were reinforced. Tanks were concealed inside some of the larger buildings. Tunnels and connecting trenches were constructed between a cellar strongpoint on one side of the road and a shelter on the other. Many buildings, strong in themselves, were made stronger by the inclusion of a bunker or pillbox inside.

In contrast, the attackers were either struggling up mountainsides, littered with boulders in full view of the enemy or trying to winkle out machine gun nests buried deep in the ruins of the town and manned as soon as the bombardment finished.

Fred Majdalany sums up:

> This was Cassino - the hard core of what the Germans called The Gustav Line - a natural mountain barrier made infinitely stronger by the ingenuity of military engineers; a natural river barrier made infinitely stronger by steel and concrete fortifications and artificial flooding of the wide valley approaches.

The plan now was that the New Zealand and the 4th Indian Divisions should take the monastery and the town and the 78th Division would then follow through on to the road to the north, crossing the Rapido and drive on towards Rome.

As usual the weather was ghastly. The scheduled day for the attack was February 24th, when the New Zealand Division stood ready but at this juncture the weather broke completely. The assault was postponed for three weeks while winter gales, driving snow and freezing rain pelted on the exposed infantry. The 4th Indian Division, in range of the enemy, dourly waited, enduring an average daily toll of 40 to 50 casualties. Meanwhile 78 Division in reserve trained and exercised in a dreary landscape of pools and semi-liquid quagmires.

On March 15th, which dawned bright and dry, the long-awaited new attack on the monastery began with a tremendous onslaught from the air. At eight o'clock in the morning we could see the first wave of bombers flying high above Cassino looking like lazy silver insects and soon the ground shook with the fury of the bombardment. In the next three and a half hours, 514 heavy and medium bombers crashed 1100 tons of bombs on the monastery and the town. After the war there was quite a debate as to whether the allies should ever have bombed that holy place. I am bound to confess that such doubts did not enter my mind as I hoped that this treatment would put the brake on the flow of shells landing on us. As we waited I took the opportunity to reorganise my battalion. We were low in numbers and I expected casualties in the weeks ahead so I reduced the number of rifle companies from four to three and kept the surplus NCOs in reserve. Hardly had I done this before we were on the move. With their heavy casualties the 4th Indian Division were running short of infantry and my battalion was to be lent to them for the immediate attack on Cassino. By now the attack had been going on for three days with heavy casualties. One would have thought that no living thing could have survived the aerial bombardment, but once this was over the defence came to life with a vengeance and merely became harder to dislodge as all the newly created rubble prevented the use of our tanks.

On the morning of March 19 my battalion moved to the village of San Michele while I and the company commanders went forward to the mountainside overlooking Castle Hill. We were to take over this feature from a battalion of the Essex Regiment in the 4th Indian Division. As we neared the battalion headquarters I left my company commanders behind in the shelter of a hollow and climbed up the craggy slope to find the Essex CO, who had established himself under the cover of an overhanging rock. After brief greetings he got down to the business of describing the situation and we stepped out onto a ledge to survey the scene. As we stood there together looking at his map I heard a sharp crack, he fell at my side - yet another victim for yet another German sniper. Fortunately he was only hit in the arm but that was certainly the end of this battle for him.

I scrambled down the scree and re-joined my company commanders, but during the long rough walk back to the battalion we were under constant shellfire. Captain Weatherley was killed and Captain Birch was wounded and was to die later. Despite these disasters, as dusk fell, the men of the battalion made their way up the mountain track and during the night got into their new positions.

Our layout could not have been more bizarre. By far our most important duty was to occupy and hold the ruined Cassino castle. This consisted merely of a strong ruined tower and a courtyard which was surrounded by a thick wall, part of it ruined, some 10 feet high. Perched on its rocky crag behind and 300 feet above the German held parts of Cassino town, some of the enemy positions to the west and south were within 100 yards of the wall. Moreover, the Germans looked down straight into the courtyard from Cassino monastery so movement was virtually impossible in daylight. The castle commanded a valley which led from Cassino town up towards the monastery, the most natural line of progress for any attack on Monastery Hill.

The plan was to devote one company to the defence of Castle Hill and the rest of the battalion would be round about a certain point 165 which was on the hillside immediately opposite, where I established my battalion headquarters. In view of the importance of Castle Hill I put my second-in-command, Denis Forman, in charge there.

While the battalion was getting into position, Brigadier Bateman, to whom I was reporting, arrived to introduce himself - a charming man for whom during the next week I acquired a great respect. He told me that the divisional general wished one of my companies to do an attack that very night on a certain position known as Yellow House. It did not take me very long to persuade him that this was not a possibility. The troops had not even yet come into place. They had never seen their surroundings by day, let alone the objective they were meant to capture. The terrain they were asked to cross, a steep hill with a savage surface of rough boulders, rocky outcrops and stony escarpments would be hard enough to tackle after proper reconnoitring and in daylight.

The general himself arrived in due course and Donald Bateman passed on to him my reasons why the attack was out of the question. He was less easily convinced and after a frosty exchange with Bateman the conversation ended with his words: 'I would not like to be in your position if Yellow House has not been captured by tomorrow morning.' To his eternal credit Bateman did not turn a hair.

For the last two years the 4th Indian Division had enjoyed the command of General Gertie Tuker, much-loved, much-respected, almost a hero figure. He had fallen ill and the general now commanding was his substitute.

Next night D Company had to carry out the fearsome attack. Owing to minefields and other hazards the only way to deploy a company on to the side of the hill preparatory to an attack was for the men to emerge in single file through the castle gate. Needless to say the enemy had a fixed-line machine-gun on the gate and no doubt an artillery registration too. If they had any idea we were coming they would stop us before we started.

Our men finally got assembled on the hillside but they had not been climbing long when there was a most enormous explosion - mines. There were many casualties. Alerted, the enemy brought down heavy artillery fire. In the end the attack had to be abandoned.

On the next day things went better for us. It was clear to me that as the capture of the castle was one of the few allied successes there was bound to be a counter-attack. I therefore had the two most obvious approaches carefully registered by the guns of the corps.

On the code word 'Ginger Rogers' 600 guns would shower their shells in one area. On the code word 'Fred Astaire' on another. Sergeant-Major Dixon from our side of the valley had his machine-gun platoon with their guns on fixed lines ready to back up the artillery.

It all worked like a charm. At dawn the signal came that an attack was imminent. I gave the code word - I can't remember which. All hell broke loose. It was too much even for the famous parachutists and 40 of them came up to the castle with their hands above their heads. We were in need of that sort of tonic.

After we had been in the Castle Hill area for a week the planned attack was abandoned. The monastery held out until the 18th May, after yet another bloody attack - this time by the Poles. Our casualties in this grim week were 11 officers and 120 men. Denis Forman was one of them.

One of the more tiresome aspects of life in Cassino Castle was the constant falling of canisters from our own smoke shells. A smoke shell which is fired for the specific purpose of creating smoke to blind the enemy contains three canisters, each weighing 10 pounds which fall away when the thing explodes. Hundreds of these shells were fired at the monastery to unsight the observation posts. Our own troops were the unwilling recipients of the canisters which seldom did any harm as they did not explode, but could fall with a frightening thud at your side. Denis writes:

> On the morning of 23rd March I was leading a counter attack onto the castle against a German force only about sixty yards away when I saw a smoke canister from a supporting New Zealand battery land in a shell hole. 'Lightning never strikes twice in the same place' - I yelled to my batman, Rutherford. 'Let's get in there.' But we were no sooner in than lightning did strike again in the shape of a second smoke canister which landed on and shattered my lower left leg. By impressing some stretcher bearer members of the neighbouring Indian division, Rutherford managed that night to lower me, still woozy from a heavy intake of morphine - down the precipitous cliff to the town below. But every time a shell fell the bearers dispersed and poor Rutherford had to recruit a fresh squad. Later I was told that my leg was amputated in an Indian field hospital at the base of the rock. I had fleeting memories of a seemingly endless nightmare trip in a field ambulance with five other wounded men, all of us screaming for water of which there was none.

Thus did he acquire a cross which he has borne with great bravery for the rest of his life and the battalion lost one of the best officers it had seen throughout the war.

Heavy as were the battalion casualties I had not the slightest doubt that those we inflicted on our enemy were heavier. In addition to the prisoners we took, the volume of artillery we were able to direct on the German battalion which made the attack on the Castle must have caused a massacre as they formed up in a very confined space to make the attack. The casualties of most battalions in the 4th Indian Division and the New Zealand Division were even worse than ours.

The Indians were aiming to capture the monastery from the mountainous area north of their objective. This involved hand-to-hand battles over the rocky mountainside with the Germans in pre-prepared concrete positions. They were unable to dig-in owing to the hardness of the ground. Their supplies had to come seven miles by mule, the route overlooked by the Germans by day and shelled by night. In the fortnight or so over which the main attack was delayed owing to snow and rain, the wretched Indians had to sit soaked through in their positions under a mounting toll of casualties from enemy shellfire. In all, the 4th Indian Division suffered 3000.

In the same situation on the outskirts of Cassino town, three battalions of the 6th New Zealand Brigade lost 263 men without even carrying out an attack. When the area was being cleared of mines after the fourth and final successful attack, half a million mines were lifted, most of them devastating SCHU mines which were difficult to detect, being in wooden boxes, which blew off your foot if you trod on them. These took a heavy toll.

Despite the perils and difficulties of the climb one band of Gurkhas, the toughest soldiers in the world, had established themselves high up on the mountain just below the monastery on what was known as Hangman's Hill. It was the ruins of the old funicular railway and looked like a gallows. Supplying them by mule proved impossible and one of our grim entertainments was to see our aircraft dropping food and ammunition on them by parachute with less than 50 per cent success.

We handed over to the Argyll and Sutherland Highlanders and for the next three weeks we licked our wounds at San Michele, receiving reinforcements and forming ourselves back into a four-company battalion.

This particular battle for Cassino was over and the monastery was to remain unmolested until the final and successful outflanking attack in May. Meanwhile the front line had to be manned and for a week we had to go back to our old position. All was quiet on the Cassino front and we did not have a single casualty.

Between our two visits to Cassino I went back to Caserta to visit Denis in hospital. He was astonishingly cheerful considering that he had just had his leg amputated, but his description of his journey by stretcher, jeep and ambulance over the bumpy mountain tracks and roads to hospital made one shudder. Literally thousands of our casualties went through the same torture.

15
Positano

If my last chapter on Cassino could be described as 'con brio' I now
quieten down to 'piano' reflecting the sudden reduction in the pace
and noise of my existence.

It is always interesting, at least to oneself, to ruminate on the turning
points of one's life. One of mine certainly came after the Cassino battle
was over when I received an order posting me home to England - a
complete surprise.

I later discovered how this had happened. Every battalion has an
honorary colonel - usually an elderly retired general who has at some
time served with distinction in the regiment. The honorary colonel of
my battalion was General Sir Charles Bonham Carter. He had always
taken a great interest in our affairs so from the time I took command I
used to rather enjoy writing to him at length every month. In my last
letter I happened to say that I personally had been in continuous action
for quite a long time. This was not meant as a complaint and certainly
not as a request for a change. I was unaware that he had any influence
in these matters.

However, he happened to be a close friend of the adjutant general,
General Forbes Adam, and suggested to him that it would be useful to
have somebody with my up to date fighting experience to take
command of some training establishment in England.

My emotions were mixed. Getting back to Betty and England was
too good to be true. But you can imagine the strength of my ties with
the battalion which I had joined as a private soldier in 1939 and had
never left. I hated leaving it in such a depleted state. To have lost the
second in command, Denis Forman, and two company commanders in
one battle was bad enough but for me, the commanding officer, to go
too was devastating.

I need not have worried, of course. No-one is indispensible and for
the rest of the war the battalion was under the command of the
admirable Gordon Defrates, who led it through all the fierce fighting in
Northern Italy until its demobilization in Austria in 1945. By then the
6th Battalion had won more decorations for gallantry than all the other
battalions of the Queen's Own Royal West Kent Regiment put together.

I was not able to brood on these thoughts for long. My immediate replacement, Lieutenant-Colonel Dick Fyffe, MC, of the Rifle Brigade soon arrived - a pleasant man who gave me Wavell's book of poems 'Other Men's Flowers' to mark the handover. I said my farewells at length, finishing up with dinner with my officers. Dick Fyffe kindly let me keep the command car, a driver and my batman and I was soon in Naples reporting at the transit office. The officer on duty regretted there was no convoy for another month. Would I please stay in the officers' hotel until then?

I declined to do that but said I would come back in a month's time and set off down the beautiful scenic coast road past Pompeii, Sorrento, Positano and Amalfi, looking for some desirable place to drop my anchor.

Positano looked perfect. I found the officer in charge - a wounded guardsman - who said he could fix me up with a villa overlooking the beach, the property of an Italian film director then in Rome.

My batman, Lance Corporal Myers, was the son of a Durham miner, but in civilian life he had been a butler and never forgot his profession. It was an unusual luxury for a commanding officer to have a gentleman's gentleman at hand, bringing meals on plates, and sometimes even with a napkin, in the most unlikely places. Here in Positano, setting up a household in the 'Villa of Figs' he was in his element. Within hours he said: 'Sir, we need more staff.' This meant that he had found an Italian cook whom we paid at the rate of one tin of bully beef per day.

Society in Positano was lively and mostly feminine, for though Italy had by then surrendered, the husbands were still in the army. My next month passed in utter contentment. To have a nasty time behind you and assured joy ahead is the recipe for a contented present. In my elation I rather tactlessly wrote to Betty saying 'this is the happiest month in my life.'

After a late reveille, breakfast in the sun on the verandah, bathing beach and book in the morning, I used to join cafe society which flocked to the Miramare Hotel at 12 for lunch, which went on until about 4pm. A long siesta, a late dinner at either the Bucca Di Bacco or the Miramare, a little dancing and bed when weary.

I was popular because I was the only one in the village with a vehicle. I had had to return my command car but Dick Fyffe let me have a 15cwt truck, the perfect conveyance for an eightsome picnic. A

trickle of officers on leave livened the company and some of my
officers came to stay.

When Dick Clarke and Ian Roper were dining with me in the villa, at
half time in came the Italian cook. He bowed, smiled and said:
'Contento, Colonello?' My guests suspected that I had rehearsed him in
this act - that was not so.

After the war Betty and I came on holiday to Positano a number of
times. It became our favourite place. Carlino, the handsome Italian
playboy hotel proprietor who became quite a friend of mine during my
wartime stay, continues to flourish at the Miramare until this day,
together with another and even smarter hotel which he has built. He
always gave us top treatment as long as there was nobody more top in
his hotel. If there were a cabinet minister or a peer present he would
get the invitation for the morning run in his super speedboat.

Positano is doubly defended against exploitation. Its old houses are
so tightly packed that it is hard to develop any sites without knocking
some down. But many of the houses are untouchable because their
owners live in America and their whereabouts are unknown. Added to
this is the fact that the climb to and from the beach is not everybody's
cup of tea.

* * *

My orders were to report to the War Office when I got back to
England. When you report to so massive an organisation you do not
expect anybody to know who you are. To my surprise a staff officer
welcomed me and said: 'The Adjutant General wishes to see you, sir' -
and I was ushered into the presence of General Forbes Adam.

With little preamble he said: 'I would like you to tell me about the
morale and welfare of the infantry battalions in Italy.' I did not stop
talking for an hour. I do not remember his contribution to the
conversation except that it ended with the unforgettable words: 'And I
would like you to take command of 164 Officer Cadet Training Unit' -
the OCTU which later became well-known as Eaton Hall.

This was beyond my wildest dreams. An OCTU was a wartime
Sandhurst, a unit which received cadets and turned them out in due
course as officers. There was no job for which I felt more suited.
Comparatively young myself and straight from the battlefield I was to
prepare these would-be young leaders for the battlefield. I later

discovered that I was the first non-regular soldier to command an OCTU and certainly the only one who himself had never been to Sandhurst or an OCTU.

I was bubbling over with joy as I took the train to Carnforth, Westmorland, where Betty was going to meet me. Not only was I at last going to see her and Elizabeth but I could give her the news that we should be living together in Barmouth until, probably, the end of the war. All this was going around so fast in my head that I did not read a word over that long journey. In the last 10 minutes before Carnforth I could hardly believe it was true so long had I waited for this exact moment.

The next days were pure joy, rather anxious joy for two year old Libby who had never had to share her mother with anybody else before. The joy was tempered too by some terrible news which Betty had to break to me in bed the next morning. My brother, Michael, had just been killed, shot down over France. I wept copiously. I was used to facing death, the death of friends I knew much better than I knew my brother, for we had never seen very much of each other. But the death of your kith and kin seems totally different. I was overcome.

He died as gallantly as he had lived. He went ahead of the squadron he was leading in order to draw the fire and so locate the enemy defences. This he did to his cost.

Among the wonderful letters I got were ones from our friend Denys Gillam, who was also his commanding officer, and Francis Blackadder, then a senior staff officer in the RAF who also knew him. Francis told me what I had not known - that Michael in addition to being a star pilot was one of a small team of fighter pilots who advised the staff on tactics.

One of the tasks I set myself before going to take command of the OCTU was to visit as many wives and mothers of men in my battalion as possible.

I got a special ration of petrol from the War Office and started my visiting in Kent where most of the battalion came from. Meeting these wives was depressing. They looked worn out. The war had been going on too long for them, as every sort of rationing had lowered their standard of living to the dreariest level. They had seen too much of the German bombers which were now replaced by the terrifying doodle-bugs, pilotless, bomb-carrying aircraft, pre-set to fall on their targets with an enormous explosion. As they roared into sight one prayed not to hear the engine cut out which signalled the coming explosion. Kent was on the direct route of these monsters. The wives were such a contrast to their husbands whom I had just left, maybe in greater danger but looking so fit in the Italian mountains. They clearly appreciated having first hand news of their men but I nevertheless felt inadequate to do much for their comfort.

I felt less so when I visited the wife of Stephen Fletcher, whom you may remember as the gunner officer who fell beside me with a volley of bullets through his leg on the mountainside of Rivoglia in Sicily. By now he was back convalescing in his home in Halifax but being by nature a taciturn fellow he had told his wife little of all the things she wanted to know about his life in the war. I was able to fill in the gaps with dramatic effect, for the tale of how he won the DSO on the bridge in Tabarka was copy for an exciting thriller. When I went home she said she had heard more in one evening from me about Stephen than she had heard from him since the war began.

I got a warm welcome at Dumcrieff, Denis Forman's home in Dumfriesshire. There I was greeted by his father, a six foot six parson, teacher and rugger player, who lived to the age of 100, and his talented and charming mother who, among other things, composed music.

Denis was by now back in England in hospital. As far as I remember they had still not seen him and were longing to hear of his exploits in Italy, not least those on the Sangro river, so I chattered away for a long time. Having got to know Denis very well very quickly in far away places I felt I knew him even better now that I had met his father and mother, his sister, Kathleen, and seen whence he came.

16
O.C.T.U.

It was July 1944 and time for me to report for my new job - commandant of 164 Officer Cadet Training Unit which was to be found at Barmouth, an old-fashioned Welsh seaside resort at the mouth of the Mawdach river.

I took the train from Paddington and changed at Dolgellau onto a branch line where both the train and the stations took one back to Edwardian times. We moved at a leisurely pace with plenty of stops. It was spring-like, the sun shone brightly and it seemed a long way from Cassino.

At Barmouth I was met by an old man, a Captain Hollebone of the Buffs, with thick glasses and a withered hand. He was the adjutant of the OCTU. His grey hair and looks belied him. He was in fact only in his fifties, far from stupid and carried authority. Over the next few months he became a boon and a friend. His New Zealand wife, Helen, was beautiful, intelligent and charming. Her two daughters, Bud and Sally, took after her.

As head of the leading fur-broker he had been a considerable figure in the City, and lived in style in a village near Sevenoaks. Kenneth had been adjutant of the OCTU from its foundation, knew everybody, both in the unit and in the town, and once you learned how to adjust his judgements for bias he was an invaluable guide. Most important of all, we liked each other.

An Officer Cadet Training Unit (OCTU) is a wartime military academy to which cadets selected as future officers in the infantry go for training. Those successful are granted commissions in the county regiments or in some other branch of the infantry, such as the Guards, the Rifle Brigade, or the Parachute Regiment. There were similar establishments producing officers for the Royal Artillery, the Royal Engineers, and so on.

Sandhurst could not possibly cope with the wartime demand for officers, hence the creation of a number of OCTUs. Each month 100 cadets would arrive at Barmouth. The course took four months so our average population of cadets was about 400. Each intake formed a company on the lines of a company in an infantry battalion and was commanded in the same way by a company commander and three platoon commanders who were responsible for their instruction. There was a quartermaster and staff and, a new command for me, a company of women, providing cooks and so on. One of the new disciplines I had to learn was keeping a straight face when, taking the salute at the church parade on the Sunday, I watched their buxom sergeant trying to march like a guardsman.

I did not try to make much of an impact for the first week or two but necessary changes soon became obvious.

The organisation was well run, everything happened to time, the place was clean, routine was strictly carried out. The turnout of cadets and their instructors was adequate but the whole outfit seemed miles away in every sense from the battlefield on which these cadets were going to be launched within weeks of leaving Barmouth. Only five of the officer instructors had ever seen action. When I complained about this to the War Office I was told that nothing could be done about it, that at this stage of the war, with British infantry taking part and suffering casualties in three major campaigns, no fighting unit would be willing to release its experienced officers.

I did not believe it. One thing all generals have in common is their keenness on officer training. So I wrote to my general in Italy, General Keightley, explained my dilemma and asked by name for a number of officers whom I knew had seen a lot of fighting and could do with a rest.

This worked marvellously. Quite soon I had recruited Fred Majdalany, whom you have met earlier as my hospital visiting companion in Africa and Malta, Dick Clarke, a company commander in my battalion, and at the end of six months over half of the officer instructors at Barmouth wore the Military Cross and everybody had seen some action.

This had a magical effect on the cadets. They could now talk with instructors who had just come from where they were just going to. They were eager to learn what it was really like.

Equally important when dealing with cadets is the quality of the warrant officers - the company-sergeant-majors who set the standards of discipline. I inherited a brilliant regimental-sergeant-major, Mr Copp of the Coldstream Guards. One of the four company-sergeant-majors was also a guardsman and excellent. The other three were poor. I did not think my general could do much to help in the way of sergeant-majors so I rang up the colonel commanding the Guards depot at Pirbright, introduced myself and asked him if he had any Guards sergeant-majors to spare. I could not think of any reason why he should have, but to my astonished delight he said: 'Yes, I actually have three whom I wish to place.' To this I clumsily replied: 'Would you like to send them then to this OCTU on trial?' As you would expect he replied: 'We do not send our warrant officers on trial.' Anyway, having patched up that little blunder I secured the three and found myself with what must have been one of the finest teams of warrant officers in the Army - just what the cadets needed.

Regimental-Sergeant-Major Copp was the complete Guards sergeant-major. Six foot three, 16 stone, a voice like a foghorn and all the standard Guards panache. The first time I met him he was taking a parade of cadets, his voice echoing down the coast. The parade ground was the sea front so the public could not be excluded and quite large crowds gathered to see these poor cadets being vocally belaboured by Mr Copp.

As he took the parade, just behind him there were two military policemen. I asked him why these were necessary. It then transpired that on a previous parade a lady in the crowd was so incensed by his cruelty to the cadets that she ran across the parade ground and hit him on the head with her umbrella. Hence the necessity for protection.

Inordinately pleased as I was with the improvements I had been able to make in the staff, the best was still to come. The chief instructor, Major Freddie Brunton, an admirable Green Howard, who had won the Military Cross in the desert and owned a chain of butchers' stores in Darlington, wanted to go back to regimental duties. By then Denis Forman was back in England on crutches, convalescing from his leg amputation. I certainly owed him the greatest possible compensation for the loss of that leg. It was I who ordered him to Cassino Castle where the fatal smoke shell struck. I now combined the payment of my debt with doing myself a good turn by writing and asking him if he would like to be my chief instructor. He was elated. He had been lying about convalescing in great depression, cudgelling his brain to think of what worthwhile job he could do in the new inactive, out of character mode of life forced upon him. My letter was an answer to his prayer.

So far you have seen Forman the leader of men. Chief instructor at the OCTU brought out the creative side of his character - the ability to lead a creative team and the imagination to know what would interest and what would please.

One day he came to our house at Barmouth on his crutches. My daughter, Libby, aged two-and-a-quarter, had never seen a man with only one leg before. She ran away and hid. The next time Denis came he brought with him a doll dressed in soldier's uniform with crutches and a leg that would come on and off via a lamp socket. She was intrigued and spent hours walking the doll on his crutches to and from the hospital.

The last and equally welcome new addition to my staff was Fred Majdalany whom we last left, I think, asleep on thė loo in Malta. Maj was described in his obituary as 'the best selling military historian, war hero, urbane wit and for 11 years film critic of the *Daily Mail*.'

The secret of his success as a military historian was that he was that rare bird - a historian who himself has been part of the history. You don't often get a fighting soldier who is also a brilliant writer. In his books *The Monastery* and *Cassino: Portrait of a Battle* he was writing of a battle in which he himself fought. *Patrol* he wrote with the same personal experience, as a company commander in Tunisia. A reviewer wrote of him as 'one of our finest epic writers, a master of dry prose and condensed fact.'

He started his career as a freelance journalist and before the war wrote cabaret songs for Douglas Byng, revue material for Binny Hale and work as a publicity ADC for C.B.Cochran. It was typical of Maj's elegant wit that he should have described Cochran's publicity maxim as 'Don't spoil the ship for three or four hundred poundsworth of specially imported tar.'

The role of the OCTU was training, not selection. We rejected about seven per cent of the cadets but rejection was not our primary role. The selection was done by the recently created War Office Selection Board. In place of the old method of selection by interview the candidates were put through an exhausting three days of interviews, discussions and physical tests. It was bound to be a better system than just interviewing, if only because the examiner saw the examined for a longer period of time and in a wider range of activities. In fact the system was a good deal more scientific than that and over the years became the model widely copied by the more advanced companies in industry. I thought I had better see how my cadets were selected so went to the War Office and spent three days watching the process. The creator of the system was an academic turned brigadier called Buchanan Smith. I had reason to recognise him straight away because he had been the commandant of the company commanders' school in Scotland which I had attended for a fortnight's course before we sailed for Algeria. I thought highly of him because I had passed out top in the grading for which he was responsible.

The cadets could be divided into three categories - the public school boys, the grammar school boys and the promoted sergeants.

The public school boys took to the training like ducks to water. They were used to being away from home and a system in which they were trained both to give and to accept orders. The grammar school boys, to begin with, were less independent, able to give orders but less at home at taking orders from their equals, especially when they considered the wretched cadet in command of the platoon for the day to be a nonentity. The promoted sergeants were sound material. The winner of the Sword of Honour at the end of the course was seldom a sergeant but a sergeant very seldom failed the course.

One day I got a message from the War Office that I was to be visited by a Professor Stevenson, a psychologist from Oxford. He arrived dressed as a brigadier. He was a strange man to find in a military establishment, certainly more of a professor than a brigadier. He told me that he had permission from the War Office to do an experiment at one of the OCTUs in methods of instruction. I pressed him to do it with us. I reasoned that if there were to be any new methods of instruction it would be better to create them yourself than to have them imposed from outside. Furthermore, with Denis Forman and Fred Majdalany I had an unbeatable team for this very purpose. Before they joined me I had already introduced some experiments of my own with which I was well pleased.

For his part Professor Stevenson realised he was more likely to get a welcome for his unorthodoxy from me, the only non-regular OCTU commander in the army, than from the standard regular commanding officer.

The Professor arrived and set up his methods office - or rather Denis Forman did it for him. He also set up his house with a wife and two little children. His wife was clearly also going to create new standards in her field. Playing on the beach with her children she turned on them in desperation and said: 'Darlings, do play a game with some future in it.'

The Professor kept thinking of simple ideas which you wondered why you had not thought of yourself.

Once a month the platoon commander instructor would have an interview with each of his cadets to review progress. The Professor sat in on a number of these interviews. He reported that many of them were confused in form and ended up with the platoon commander saying to the cadet: 'Jones, you really must pull your socks up,' leaving the cadet more muddled than he was to start with. The Professor argued that the cadet only needed the answers to two questions: (1) 'Am I going to pass?' and (2) 'How can I do better?'

As only one in 13 cadets was failed the answer to the first question would almost always be 'yes.' So the summing up of the interview should be more like this: 'Jones, you are going to pass, so don't worry about that. How are we going to help you to do better? Well you are good at A, B, C and D but weak at E and F. This is how I suggest you can improve at E and F.'

I found that this 'You are going to pass' element was an important feature in the cadets' psychology and conduct. A certain strata of cadets would tend to stay in the background for fear of making fools of themselves and courting failure. In my opening address to cadets I therefore made a point of telling them that they were almost bound to pass therefore don't be frightened, have a go.

The final demonstration of new methods of instruction owed more to Forman, Majdalany and Bryan in that order than it did to the professor. His main value was the entree he gave us to extra staff and materials. The demonstration took the form of a three-day conference at Barmouth attended by all OCTU commanders, not only those of the infantry OCTUs but all other arms of the service. There were about 25 of them and not all came with particularly good grace. The regular in command at Sandhurst in particular doubted if three amateurs had much to teach him.

My own contribution was quite a success because it offered an easy way out of one of a commandant's standard difficulty - teaching officer qualities. Not every commandant can give impressive lectures on such daunting subjects as leadership, responsibility, courage - the teaching of which seems the natural responsibility of a commandant.

The War Office produced a film which told the story of a group of young men from the time they were recruited from civilian life until the time they actually went into battle, embracing all the period of their training. It featured Richard Greene (later Robin Hood) as the bad officer, David Niven as the good officer and Peter Ustinov as one of the privates.

I took a company of cadets and said: 'I am now going to show you a film,' which I then briefly described. 'When you have seen it I shall ask you what was the platoon commander's most un-officerly action?' - or some such question. Once the film was over I opened up a discussion asking cadet after cadet his answer to my question. This went on for about half an hour without my giving my view at all. I then showed them the film again, so that they could think about it again in the light of the discussion. I then summed up the film in the most downright terms.

The film was long enough to split up into four different parts, so it provided long and heated discussions on four different occasions, not to mention debates that went on afterwards in the canteen. Oddly enough several commandants wrote to me after the conference and asked me for a script of my summing up of these films. This would have rather lost the point, which was to provide a commandant with an opportunity to put across his own views in an effective way.

* * *

Barmouth was a blissfully happy period for Betty and me. To be together again after so long was happiness enough, but to be in such a perfect place, doing a more than satisfying job with pleasant friends, many of them of my own choice, was a luxury. After our long separation we settled down again together easily and felt our marriage would be happy forever.

Elizabeth was rather shy of me when first I got back. I did not hurry to put this right. By now all awkwardness had gone. She was, of course, in our eyes a gem - a long-awaited gem. For quite a time we had wondered whether we would succeed in having children. She had winsome ways. When asked her age she would answer: 'I am two-and-a-quarter' (the 'a' pronounced as in 'art'). 'My name is Libby Brown, I can't say Libbyliss.'

Libby's favourite game at that age was one for which she was temperamentally unsuited - hide and seek. She was too impatient to wait in her fairly obvious hiding place whilst you prolonged the search behind every sofa and chair and soon, unable to stand the stress any longer, would jump out of hiding crying: 'Here me are.'

To crown our joys, in a few months time Felicity was on the way.

Social life at the OCTU was bright enough. There were plenty of wives and families about; picnics on the beach or in boats up the river, trips in the cranky old train to pubs up the valley for supper - all this against a background of summer weather and the beautiful countryside. We were content with the present at Barmouth and our future had become more reassuring.

Betty's father, Jimmy Hoyle, asked me if I would like to join him after the war in the family clothing firm, J.B.Hoyle and Company of Hebden Bridge. I liked this prospect. Jimmy had built it up in the years between the wars to a workforce of 400. With wartime clothes rationing the numbers were about halved, but I saw no reason why it should not recover and with Jimmy looking towards retirement there should be plenty for me to do. By good fortune my two years with Louis London & Sons, also a clothing firm, just before the war were the perfect training.

Betty's brother, Peter, had just started in the firm at the beginning of the war and might possibly return, but he had been posted missing in the Far East for a long time and our hopes were running out. Were he to come back I felt sure that he and I could work happily together in business.

The long-awaited and long-delayed victory in Europe came and was officially celebrated on May 8th 1945. Every church bell had been rung, beacons were lit on the hilltops as they had been to warn England of the coming of the Spanish Armada.

Each military unit devised its own form of celebration. Our main effort over and above widespread singing, drinking and dancing was the most enormous bonfire on the seafront. This was to be ceremonially lit by Betty with a flame thrower mounted on a tank against the background of the sea. There were to be a number of boats at sea firing tracer into the air in the shape of Vs.

The appointed hour arrived. Betty and I mounted the tank. At her elbow was the sergeant who would tell her when to press the button which would release the great jet of flame at the bonfire.

The tank started moving slowly forward. On each side of our route towards the bonfire at a reasonably safe distance stood and cheered the massed crowd. The sergeant in due course stopped the tank ready to fire but then said: 'No, I think we had better get a little closer, there is a very strong cross wind.'

It was as well that he had second thoughts for when, at rather closer range, Betty pressed the button, the great belch of flame was blown sideways by the wind and only just struck the edge of the bonfire with no damage done except to the bonfire. Had Betty pressed the button from the spot originally selected by the sergeant the flame would undoubtedly have gone into the crowd.

Other victory celebrations, of course, included a parade and a thanksgiving service. These looked worry-free as far as I was concerned until late on the eve of the service when I was told that the chaplain had fallen ill, leaving a nasty gap in the pulpit. Clearly on such an occasion an oration of some sort was required and I spent the night preparing my maiden sermon which in the event and at least to my own ears sounded better than I expected.

I was demobilised in the Autumn of 1945 but Denis Forman, being rather younger than me, had to wait for another year. During that time he was posted to Deira Dunn, the Indian OCTU, to introduce the methods of instruction that we had invented in Barmouth.

As my war came to an end my family remained scattered around the globe.

My dear and wonderful mother died in 1945 after closing years which were less happy than she deserved. These were the war years which were clouded with the death of Michael, and worries of a different sort about Helen's divorce from John Hare which she took very badly. Her other children too were all abroad throughout the war, just at a time when she needed them most. All this comes out in my father's letter in the appendix of this book.

1. The author in 1945

2.   The Bryan family in 1916; the author on his mother's knee

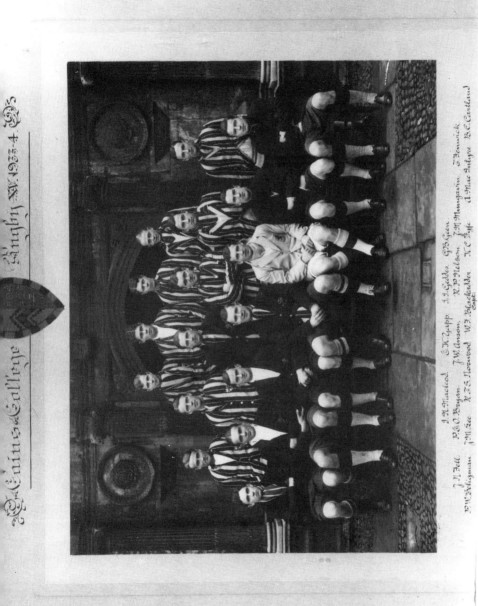

3. Caius College rugger team 1933-34. PB middle row second from the left; Ian MacLeod back row left

4. Mardi and Jimmy

5. My wedding to Betty, 1939

6. The Allied invasion fleet under air attack, Tunisia 1942

7. Tunisia: Longstop, 6 RWK mortars in action

8. Sicily: Centuripe

9. Sicily: looking down from Centuripe

10. Monty

11. Italy: rain, always rain

12. Italy: mud, always mud

13. Italy: Sangro patrolling; enemy front as seen from 6 RWK Observation Post

14. Italy: Sangro patrolling; moving up to an OP

15. Italy: Cassino. View from the town; ruins of the castle with Hangman's Hill above and Monastery Hill directly beyond it

16. Italy: Cassino. The Monastery after the bombing

17. OCTU, Barmouth 1944. PB (left) with Denis Forman and Fred Majdalany

18. White Cottage

COUN. P. BRYAN (CONSERV.)

19. Sowerby by-election, 1949. PB canvassing

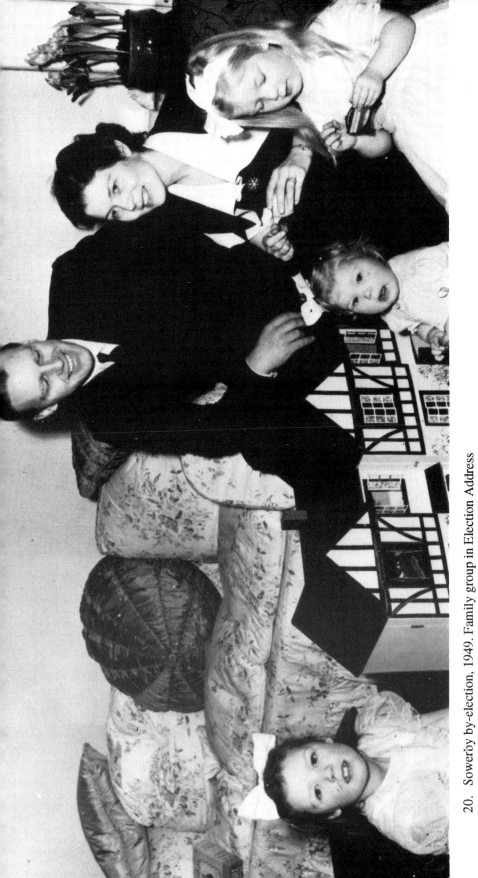

20. Sowerby by-election, 1949. Family group in Election Address

21. Felicity and Bunny off to school

22. The children, 1951

23. Howden, 1955. MP at last

24. The Prime Minister and Government Whips, 1959. Front row: Harwood Harrison; Peter Legh; Ted Heath; Harold MacMillan; Martin Redmayne; Edward Wakefield; Dick Broomam-White. Back row: Graham Finlay; Willie Whitelaw; John Hill; David Gibson-Watt; Michael Hughes-Young; Robin Chichester-Clark; Paul Bryan

25. Felicity electioneering, 1964

26. Libby and Judy Scott-Thompson electioneering, 1964

27. PB with Ted Heath, in the constituency, 1971

28. Park Farm

29. Parliamentary Golf Society, West Hill 1985. Top, left-right: Neil MacFarlane MP; Mr Speaker Weatherill; Viscount Whitelaw. Below, left-right: John Silkin; Sir Paul Bryan (Captain); Hugh Brown MP.

Intermezzo

When Denis Forman was writing his book *To Reason Why* he sent me the manuscript of the parts in which I featured to check up on the facts.

When writing this book I in turn sent him the manuscript of the book up to this point. This was his helpful reply.

Chelmsford

6 September 1991

Dear Paul

Well of course I simply could not lay it down. It reads very well and combines the arts of compression and exclusion coupled with shrewd selection of detail. It is also a good yarn. From wool sorter to war hero in twelve easy chapters.

Some haphazard points:

1. The letters from your father are amongst the most boring examples of English prose I have ever read. From an author's point of view their effect can only be to lose friends and bore people.

2. Suggest you include one letter only to show how your father could make almost anything about English prose as appetising as sawdust and otherwise extract the odd sentence (the odder the better) from each letter. As they stand they will be skipped by anyone who is not actually mentioned in them.

3. You should consider whether Betty's diaries do her justice. She was such a remarkable lady. They are no more than a bald index of events - they might be a catalogue of her colour slides, but they have no colour.

4. You have a habit of making a major change of subject without starting a new paragraph.

5. The things that you have remembered most vividly ('By Mr Paul, thous look a bugger in yon'), Monty's 8 points (which you don't actually remember, only his method), reflect your character in a most interesting way. Can't you remember a few more?

6. Similarly everyone is agog to know what being in battle is really like. It would undoubtedly add to the interest if you could describe in more detail your part in the several actions where you were in the thick of it.

Two specific points: Christmas 1943. Clearly you and Madge had left for North Africa when Christmas was celebrated at Baranello. Yet I have a clear memory of going the rounds with you (and I am pretty sure Lionel) eating at least four dinners, whose start time had been carefully staggered in company after company, finishing with Wakkers who produced all sorts of bizarre but unappetising dishes and finally poured each of us a half pint of brandy. You then made a speech. If this was not Christmas day what the hell was it? A special farewell party organised for a beloved C.O. who was going to miss Christmas?

The sixty-four dollar question is, of course, how would the book strike a complete outsider? I simply could not answer this one. Perhaps Felicity could, but her judgement might be prejudiced too. Perhaps she could send it anonymously to two or three of her readers to get a candid professional view.

I find the restraint, the self-deprecating tone and the sparing use of words very attractive. How very unlike my own flamboyant heart-on-sleeve, extravagant prose. But would the general interest carry to wider public? Who knows.

Finally - throughout the latter half of the book there are references to a saintly figure, name of Forman. Who is this man? I do not recognise him.

Yours ever
Denis

Part Three: Peace

17
Peace - White Cottage

During our last few months at Barmouth we had been planning our home to be. The Hoyle family house, Ashfield, stood on a hilly site of about 10 acres on the outskirts of Sowerby Bridge which adjoins the much larger town of Halifax. The Ashfield garden of perhaps three acres ran down a steep slope to a stream. The other bank was a grass field, also fairly steep, running up to Bairstow Lane, where there was an isolated row of four cottages. Three of these were built in about 1850 and the fourth, more picturesque, looked as if it had been built in the sixteenth century, with a weaving window of that period. In its time this older cottage would have been the farmhouse. About 100 yards away at the bottom of the field, there was a small set of old farm buildings.

Jimmy Hoyle gave us these cottages and we decided to modernise the two end ones, including the oldest of the four, and make this our home. The other two cottages were still occupied.

Betty started organising the modernisation of the cottages whilst at Barmouth but, pregnant and living far away, she could not get down to this with her usual vigour. To make progress more difficult wartime builders were understaffed and materials scarce. White Cottage, as we called it, was nowhere near ready by the time I was demobilized. It looked as if we were going to have to impose ourselves on Ashfield for quite a time. Then Betty's old Aunt Miriam died. She had lived at Byclough, a large, not very beautiful, modern house in a big garden outside the small town of Mytholmroyd, only three miles from Hebden Bridge. We were offered Byclough, until White Cottage was ready, and there we lived happily and conveniently for the next six months.

From our family angle the first months after demobilization were perfect. Felicity was born at Ashfield, safely if rather belatedly. We saw a lot of Jimmy and Mardi and picked up many of our old friendships.

I found my new job difficult simply because there was not enough to do. The changes and chances of war had given me more responsibility at a younger age than I could continue to expect. The difficulty was that even before my arrival the top management was only half-employed. Between the wars, J.B.Hoyle and Company had been built up to a workforce of 400. Competition had been stiff but the firm had more than held its own in the lower end of the clothing market, selling men's working clothes to small and medium sized shops in small and medium sized towns. There were two big customers - Fosters and Bradleys, each of which had a chain of 150 shops. In those days the sky was the limit to your business. If you could beat your competitors there was nothing to stop you taking on more workers and producing more.

The situation I came to in 1946 was very different. Strict and severe clothing rationing was in force so clothing companies were not allowed to produce more than a set amount. You were not able to buy more cloth than your ration. A third limitation to expansion was a shortage of labour. We took in a few school leavers each year to replace wastage but had one wanted to expand on any scale it would not have been possible in Hebden Bridge or any of the nearby towns.

In its heyday the management at J.B.Hoyle's had been headed by Jimmy as Chairman, who took an interest in the sales side, in particular the two big customers and our London warehouse. In the war he became preoccupied with the local Home Guard and was less and less at the firm, which pretty well ran itself anyway, especially on the sales side as with clothes rationing there was no selling to do. The works manager, Jimmy Thornber, a strong character, had risen from office boy and much of the firm's early success was due to his drive. By the time I arrived, with Jimmy Hoyle somewhat in the background, Jimmy Thornber was completely dominant. He never arrived until after 10 in the morning but no decision could be taken until he arrived.

The third member of the management was Harry Earnshaw, a diligent, excellent chartered accountant of a quality far higher than you would expect to find looking after the finances of so modest a company. In ability he was every bit Thornber's equal but never stood up to him in any battle of wills.

I was well received by this trio and could not possibly complain of the welcome I got throughout the works, but this did not solve my problem of how to pass the time.

I was dubbed Sales Manager but answering customers' letters took on average less than an hour a day. I went through the customers' records, finances of the company, spent a good deal of time getting to know the personnel and visited some customers.

Once you have had responsibility you are unhappy without it. For the last few years my responsibility had always been increasing. It was a personal, human responsibility in that I was in direct charge of a growing number of men whose welfare, happiness and sometimes lives depended directly on me. I missed the opportunity to do any good, to help anybody much except within my own family circle. Truth to tell, I did not like feeling unimportant.

I racked my brains to think of some original development that I could introduce in the firm, but the limitations I have already described seemed decisive.

Gradually other activities presented themselves. I was asked to be President of the British Legion at Sowerby Bridge, quite time-taking. We acquired premises and started a British Legion Club in the High Street, which was only partially successful in competition with the long-established Working Men's Club. There were other activities to be organised such as the annual parade on Armistice Day, the sale of poppies and running other functions to raise money for the Legion.

Among my duties was the finding of speakers for their dinners and openers for their functions.

One year, as the date for the Christmas Fayre once more came over the horizon, I was asked to find a suitable opener. A letter from the secretary read: 'Our first choice would be Len Hutton but failing him the Princess Royal.' In the end I managed to get them Councillor Herbert Saltonstall, the Chairman of the Sowerby Bridge Urban District Council. He was also the local undertaker.

When one of the local councillors died and a by-election loomed up, my British Legion friends suggested that I should stand as an Independent, with the assurance of their active support. When I asked one of them if he thought I had any chance of winning he said: 'Oh, aye. They 'ave nowt against thee.' It seemed a negative compliment at the time but less so now that I have been through a good many more elections.

Betty and I decided that standing for the council would be an interesting thing to do. We would get to know the area and a lot of new people. If I won I would be committed for three years but not necessarily for any longer. I was more than likely to lose as North Ward had been a Labour stronghold for many years.

We got hold of the electoral roll which showed that there were 600 houses in the ward. We reckoned that the only way to win would be for one of us to call on every single one of those houses and to come back again if the voter was out on our first visit. We cooked up an election address between us and our helpers delivered them.

Our door-knocking on the 600 doors was more of a toil than I had anticipated but we carried it out and won the election by quite a comfortable majority.

Betty was naturally good at talking with people. As a physiotherapist, she must have spent hundreds of hours talking with patients as she massaged away. Little did she know that North Ward was only the first of many Yorkshire wards that she would canvass with me over the next 20 years.

Meanwhile family life at White Cottage was going fine. It was small and after all our alterations something of a maze but little children like it that way.

Betty made the garden pretty, with lawns at the front and side. The long front lawn looked across the wooded valley to Ashfield and the children used to go into the field and down to the stream at the bottom. There was a sunken garden which led to the kitchen garden where they also had their own individual gardens.

I had a black and white Wendy house made by the local joiner where they played for hours, with a large sandpit adjoining. Out of the field we made an orchard area where we had a swing and there was a tortoise amongst the apple trees. In the early post-war years when food was still short we kept a couple of pigs in the old farm buildings at the bottom of the field, which were tended by a character called Walter who played rugger for Halifax at the weekends. The whole setup was picturesque, peaceful and remarkably rural considering we were on the edge of industrial Halifax.

There was another set of cottages opposite us on the other side of Bairstow Lane in addition to the two adjoining our house, so we had neighbours.

There was Henny who lived next door and did a lot of work in the house; mostly cooking meals and ironing. She was short and substantial, the shape of so many West Riding women who seemed to have no waist at all. She would wear that unbecoming kind of pinafore which is floral and wraps around the body, and her hair was in a little bun with a hairnet. Felicity claimed a particularly intimate relationship with her as she liked her a lot and her bedroom had a door which led through to Henny's. She had on occasion seen Henny in her nightie.

Across the road there was Kathleen Jowett, about Libby's age, fair, fat and daughter of a window cleaner. Being an only child she was dependent on our household for her fun. Time and again, answering a knock at the front door, we would find Kathleen there asking: 'Is Libby playing out?'

Whilst I was starting down my political road with the council election, other family careers were taking off. In 1947 at the age of five Libby started her education at Miss Oakley's School on The Moor.

We had no idea how good or bad a student she would be. Hours of working at 'the Cock, the Mouse and the little Red Hen' in bed with Betty and me in the mornings seemed to show that she was slow to learn reading. Nor could she learn by heart as easily as Felicity, three and a half years her junior. On one occasion when, after much labour, Libby recited 'I have a little shadow' to us, infuriatingly Felicity said 'Me, too?' and repeated it perfectly after one hearing.

On the first day at Miss Oakley's Libby went up to her mistress and said: 'I don't like to be teached. I like to do what way I like.' These early unhopeful indications proved misleading. Head of her prep school, Duncombe Park, scholarship to Benenden, Deputy Head of that school, she emerged the schoolmistress's dream. She became a medical student at St Thomas's Hospital, very hard for a girl in those days and blossomed into a Fellow of the Royal College of Physicians.

Felicity started her education at a younger age. Mardi had started a nursery school for a dozen children at Ashfield under a wonderful teacher, Mrs Dewhurst. On her first day Felicity talked too much. Mrs Dewhurst produced a piece of string and said to Felicity: 'If you talk any more I shall tie up your tongue with this string' and she put it on the desk. Later on the string had disappeared and Mrs Dewhurst asked Felicity where it was. She answered: 'I put it down the lavatory and pulled the plug.' This lack of co-operation with authority was an entirely accurate sign of the way her school career would go. At Duncombe Park she was normally at the bottom of her class - always naughty - but accelerated suddenly in order to get into Benenden where she was unhappy and at first not very successful.

The contrast of the two sisters at the same schools produced tensions. In 1990 the *Sunday Times Magazine* carried an article about my three daughters in the 'Relative Values' series under the heading 'Happy Trinity.'

This is what Libby said:

I was at prep school with Felicity and that was a very difficult time, because I was at the top of the school and she arrived at the bottom. She was very naughty, leading all the others on not to do what I said and I think that was the time of our least good relationship. Again at Benenden I was the top girl when she arrived and the same thing happened.

Felicity said:

My first memories of Elizabeth are of this very responsible older sister. Libby was a classic first child; responsible, thoughtful and earnest. She was good to me, very protective. She was Head Girl at both schools when I arrived, and everybody thought she was simply splendid. We got on very well at home but during school time it was rather difficult because I was not at all like her; I was the naughty one, the irresponsible one. I don't think she understood why I didn't wish to achieve - but I just wasn't that kind of person then. So during school time we weren't close at all.

It was this complete lack of any sense of competition that I remember about the early Felicity. She saw no virtue or joy in excelling. She was perfectly happy playing on her own making daisy chains on the lawn. Luckily all this changed as she grew up for she got into the Courtauld Institute, took a degree in the History of Art, went on to be a journalist for the *Financial Times* in Washington then on the *Economist* in London and has since been a successful literary agent.

Very small for her age and very blonde, inappropriately she was always a champion for the weak against the bullies. I once spanked Libby with a hairbrush. I can still see the minute Felicity rushing at me with flailing fists which I could hardly feel saying: 'You mustn't hurt Libby.'

On the 26 September 1948 Bunny was born. Libby and Felicity were born at Ashfield but in Felicity's case Betty had had a difficult time, so for Bunny she went to Leeds Infirmary. Bunny entered this world 8lbs and well, but poor Betty was very ill indeed and this was clearly to be our last child.

To the children Ashfield was a place of great size and comfort. It was also a source of treats. There were lots of summer events around the pool which was a rather dirty pond with a boat that belonged to Libby called 'The Libbyloo.' There were large summer parties there featuring Fosters, Bairstows and Hoyles.

It was also the place for bonfire night. Betty deceived the girls with a tale that the rockets had glass balls inside which expanded when they flew up in the air. The next morning we would collect coloured Christmas tree balls, supposedly from the rockets.

And again, Ashfield was the place for Christmas afternoon and dinner - having had stockings and family presents at White Cottage. Jimmy could never be there for Christmas tea as he always 'had a meeting,' but was in fact acting Father Christmas. He kept up his disguise to our wishfully believing company until the children were quite old, when one of the presents from his sack turned out to contain a school cardigan forwarded by post from the school.

Jimmy adored being Father Christmas, rather surprisingly for he was a shy man and generally tongue-tied with children. Mardi was a perfectionist; the Christmas tree was exquisitely decorated and the dinner table looked glorious with all kinds of ornaments and bumper crackers sent each year from Mr and Mrs Mackintosh of Mackintosh's Toffee who also owned Caley's Crackers.

Unlike Libby and Bunny who attended Miss Oakley's school, Felicity went to Miss Starkey's, presumably at four or five. Retta Foster was her best friend there. Her mother, Amo, used to pick them both up sometimes and found it so funny that Felicity was always late and often had her shoes on the wrong feet. They wore brown uniforms.

Felicity was a dud at most things in those days, but in particular sports, where she was the last in everything except the 'thread the needle' race which she won. At about the age of seven she went on to Waverley School, Huddersfield, at just about the time when Bunny started at Miss Oakley's. We have a wonderful photograph in the family album of the two of them, both in their new uniforms, both with room for growth, outside White Cottage setting off to school.

That was a period of storytelling. Often in the car, in a traffic jam, one of the children would say to me: 'Who is that?' pointing to the driver of the next car. I would have to invent a story about him - 'That man is called Mr Bottomley. He is a butcher from Barnsley. The reason his wife looks so grumpy is that he has left the door of the fridge in the butcher's shop open and all the meat has gone bad. That means there will be no meat to sell on Monday and they won't be able to go on their usual holiday to Filey' - and so on and so on.

On the same theme, once when driving Felicity to the bus stop in the morning en route for school a man waved at me from a bus stop. She asked who he was - I told her his sad tale. The fairy Stinkerbell had cast a spell on him which forced him to spend every night in a different bed. This led to many adventures in search of ever new beds and a blossoming friendship with a man who had a bed factory. Thus was a soap opera born.

There was also a soap opera 'Jean and Joan' which went on forever. Jean was always good and Joan was always naughty. Their family programme was usually much the same as the Bryans. If we were on a caravan holiday, so were Jean and Joan.

White Cottage had the usual family menagerie. Scamper, the Corgi, was a goody. Sparky, the Persian cat, most definitely a baddy. He would sharpen his claws on the furniture.

I was always composing poems for the children. About Sparky I wrote:

Now that school reports have come
Half a crown for everyone.
All his daughters - oh so good
Father in a topping mood.
But, alas, this morning's post
Turned Dad paler than a ghost
Bad report has come for Sparky
Written by the fierce Miss Starkey

I can't remember the rest of the poem which went on to catalogue Sparky's crimes. Miss Starkey was Felicity's schoolmistress.

Here is another of my poems, written after I had spent a night in the Halifax Infirmary, having some cysts taken out of my scalp. With it went a newspaper photograph of a giant black nurse called Oladile who looked after me there.

Oh here is the maiden who nursed your Papa
No wonder so jealous was poor old Mama
Observe her sleek beauty, her teeth that so shine
Her face black and gorgeous, her figure divine.

She's frisky as whisky and choc full of fun
She can hug like a bear and she weighs just a ton
How lucky was Pa to have bumps on his head
Oladile might never have tucked him in bed.

We were also great hymn singers and actually kept a hymnbook in the car. This was strange for neither Betty nor Libby could sing in tune, not that this deterred Libby in the slightest.

Once my hymn singing caused embarrassment. When Betty and I arrived at Duncombe Park just in time for the evening service we were greeted by a rather unusually worried-looking Libby. After the service Betty said: 'Why were you so worried?' She said: 'Well, you were the only parents there and you know how loud Daddy sings.'

Our various helps, Henny, Mrs Barker and the enormous Mrs Blagborough, all became part of the family in their time and remained our friends forever.

Our nannies, or nannie types, were a more mixed lot.

Iylish, a beautiful redheaded Irish girl, was a star. She said she would come for a year and then decide whether to get married or go into a convent. Betty was confident that a year with the happy Bryans would convince her of all the advantages of a family life. After the year she went straight into the convent. We then got regular letters from Sister Dolorosa.

Her letters were rationed, but when they came they were long and quite high-flown in their language. Once when reminiscing about her time with us she wrote: 'You, Mr and Mrs Bryan, were the perfect example of earthy (sic) love.'

Troudel was very different. A large, unpleasant German girl, I can't think how we got hold of her but she did not stay long.

On a brief visit to Germany I remember sending the children a postcard which read:

Troudel land's the place for me.
Sausages for lunch and tea
Sausages at night as well
What's for breakfast - who can tell?

Gretel, our other German au-pair, the daughter of the baker in Titmoning in Bavaria, was as sweet as Troudel was sour.

The super-nanny was Nurse Elliott. She was what was termed a 'monthly nurse,' i.e. she would go to a family at the birth of a child and see the mother through the first months of its life. Thus did she build up a network of friends, all of whom loved her. She first came to us for the birth of Bunny but continued to come to us from time to time when she happened to have a spare period between engagements.

One year we went on holiday to the Marine Hotel at North Berwick in Scotland, where Betty and I had a spectacular room overlooking the golf course and the sea. A few hundred yards away was the St Annes Children's Hotel so we left the children under the care of a team of trained nurses. This was a luxurious arrangement. As we had breakfast in bed Betty would pick up the telephone and say: 'Please bring the children round for tea' or some such instruction. The children did not seem to miss us at all and were as happy as were we with the arrangement. We got to know the nurses and one of them, Nurse Scarth, came to us at White Cottage to see us through difficult situations, such as elections.

Our children's best friend at the St Anne's children's hotel was Haile Selassie's son, Prince Paul, who had two nannies and was as black as Felicity was blonde. Sandsend near Whitby was another place we went to for family holidays.

The children loved visiting J.B.Hoyle and Company, with all those lovely girls at the mill who were so friendly, but best of all were the works outings to Blackpool in a charabanc with a mammoth lunch then rides on the Big Dipper.

At that time Betty and I were playing quite a lot of golf, although I was still far from good. In 1948, to Jimmy's astonishment - for his opinion of my golf was poor - I won the Ogden Cup, the annual handicap championship, from a field of over a hundred. For those not familiar with golf I should explain that there is a welcome system of handicapping which, with luck, can enable a moderate player to defeat his golfing betters. Though my handicap was never less than 14, I had many happy years of golf at Ganton, a championship course in what later became my constituency, including a time as president of the club when both its centenary celebrations and the Amateur Championship took place. With the Parliamentary Golf Society, of which I was Captain for my last four years in parliament, one had the privilege, year after year, of playing on such world famous courses as St

Andrews, Muirfield, Prestwick, Royal Lytham, Royal St Georges, Sunningdale and Walton Heath.

* * *

By 1950 life at J.B.Hoyle and Company was brightening up somewhat. In addition to our works at Hebden Bridge we had a small unit making overalls in the village of Delph near Oldham. This was about three quarters of an hour in a car from Hebden Bridge - a drive over wuthering moors.

There were only 12 machinists in this building, which had started in the last century as a mill for making the shrouds in which bodies are wrapped in coffins. The next owners converted it into a blanket mill and this it remained until part of it was burnt down between the wars.

I do not know who set up a clothing works in the surviving buildings but we were asked to take it over during the war when a team of about 20 girls were making boiler suits for the Navy. The building would have taken up to 80 girls and in the Oldham area it might have been possible with great effort to recruit them, but the shortage of cloth had prevented our making any effort in that direction.

After a time more drill cloth for overalls became available and I set about trying to get the numbers increased. I buttered up the headmistresses of the two local schools, myself took the top form on a tour around our very unattractive mill, which I had tarted up in every possible way and also used some of the methods of presentation I had learned at the Barmouth OCTU. This was all successful and within three years we were up to 80 eighty girls - a jolly young team in contrast to the old birds at Hebden Bridge. The 'girl' in charge, aged 40 and 16 stone, was my favourite Elsie Buckley who writes to me every Christmas until this day.

18
Conservative Candidate

The general election of 1945 took place between VE Day and the end of the Japanese War. It was the greatest turnover in parliamentary history since the time of the great Reform Bill of 1832. The Conservatives were reduced to a parliamentary strength of 213; only twice before had they been reduced to less, in 1906 and 1932. This came as a surprise to many. As Churchill toured the country Union Jacks came out everywhere. The VE spirit seemed everlasting. But when it came to voting people were thinking of the peace. Their minds were on housing and food, employment and pensions.

In his election address Aneurin Bevan hit the nail on the head. He laid all his emphasis on the need for a national plan, on tackling the housing problem in the same way as the nation went about the task of making Spitfires:

> Low rents, spacious homes, fitted with all the labour saving appliances, can be made available to all only if the task of housebuilding is organised on a national plan. In particular the returning soldier, yearning for a home of his own, should have it provided for him without having to spend the rest of his life half starving himself and his family in trying to pay for it.

The Conservative Party had been in power for virtually the whole period between the two wars so all the evils of that unhappy period could be put at their door.

Amongst one's companions in the army there was a strong feeling that the planning which had produced victory should be converted into a national plan to produce prosperity. Planning became the 'buzz' word, greatly to Labour's advantage. Remembering the soldiers' wives I visited when I came back from Italy and their depressed state after going short of everything for too long, it was hard to see them voting against a party that promised a new National Health Service, a revolution in social service benefits and full employment. I myself only just voted Conservative.

With the advent of the Welfare State, free false teeth for all was the order of the day. The facial appearance of hundreds of people was totally changed, each in a standard sort of way. Clearly 'made to measure' was not practical, but the variety of ready-mades on offer seemed unduly limited for no-one seemed to have new teeth anything like their old ones.

The same problem arose with the demob suits. On return to civilian life every service officer and man was entitled to a new suit and a pair of shoes. Many never got worn because they were unwearable. Those that were worn were as immediately identifiable as 'demob suits' as those false teeth stood out as 'National Health.' Even with my training in the clothing trade I could not imagine who could have made the things. All uniforms had a clear label on the hip pocket showing the name of the maker; no firm was apparently willing to admit to making the demob suits.

Once in Italy when I was actually walking up a hill into battle with shells exploding all over the place I was heartened by the sight of the label on the backside of the soldier climbing just ahead of me bearing the homely words: 'J.B.Hoyle and Company, Hebden Bridge.'

* * *

My Council activities had brought me a little into the limelight. I was nevertheless surprised when in 1948 the local Conservative Association, with whom I had had nothing to do, asked me if I would be willing to be their prospective Parliamentary candidate.

Sowerby was then a Labour seat with a majority of 7000. One might, by the size of their majority, assume that accepting the candidature did not involve much risk of winning the seat. This did not necessarily follow. It had been a Conservative seat from 1931 to the end of the war and had only changed parties with the Labour landslide of 1945. So in making our decision Betty and I had to think of whether we could manage, or indeed whether we wanted a parliamentary life. There was also the question of J.B.Hoyle and Company. I might complain of not enough to do now, but in a few years time with Jimmy Hoyle and Jimmy Thornber heading for retirement age, I would be needed.

There was also the question - was I actually a Conservative? At Cambridge I took no active part in politics as most future politicians do. My subsequent life had made me interested in public affairs but I was certainly not what we would nowadays call right wing. Like many servicemen returning to civilian life I had not good memories of the way the Conservatives had governed the country between the wars. I was impressed with the success of central planning in the winning of the war. I liked the whole concept of the Welfare State. Nevertheless, seeing the Labour Government in action I had no doubt that Conservative was how I would vote in an election.

Jimmy Hoyle actually encouraged me to go ahead. I think he felt embarrassed that I had not enough to do and said that if by chance I won and remained in Parliament for 10 years I would still be young enough to come back and take up the reins with J.B.Hoyles.

Betty, to her eternal credit, finally clinched the decision with the words: 'It will be more fun than not doing it.'

My selection was unorthodox. The standard procedure normally observed is for the constituency to notify Conservative Central Office of their intention to select a candidate and ask for a list of suitable names. A selection committee in the constituency considers this list together with the names of any local candidates who apply. Out of this procedure emerges a short list of three or four candidates who appear before the constituency Executive Committee, numbering perhaps 120 members, who hear a speech from each candidate and put questions to him or her, after which the final selection is made.

The Sowerby Conservative Association did not bother with any of this palaver. I was the only candidate they considered. My adoption meeting was the first political meeting I had attended in my life and my adoption speech certainly the first political speech I had ever delivered. I did not realise it at the time but I was not officially the prospective parliamentary candidate because by the rules of Central Office such a candidate has to be on the list of approved candidates which is held at Central Office.

Hardly had I been selected when the prospect of an actual election drew closer. The Labour Member of Parliament for Sowerby was John Belcher, a railway clerk who had become a junior minister at the Board of Trade. He was in trouble. His name kept appearing in the newspapers in connection with bribes, or at least favours he had accepted from one Sidney Stanley in return for help in dealing with some of the thousands of regulations which still restricted business in Britain. The allegations got so serious that the matter came to a head with the appointment of a tribunal under Judge Lynskey. The proceedings of the Lynskey tribunal filled the popular press for several weeks with the Attorney General, Sir Hartley Shawcross, in the lead role and the artful Sidney Stanley as the unchallenged lead comic.

In the end John Belcher had to resign his seat in Parliament but public sympathy was with him. The scale of the 'bribes' he had accepted was so paltry - a suit of clothes, a crate of sherry, a few meals in luxury restaurants - everybody's heart went out to poor Mrs Belcher who was required to present her National Savings Books in Court showing deposits totalling £17. In the election campaign in Sowerby which followed Belcher's resignation there was no political capital whatever to be made out of the 'disgrace' of the resigning member.

As early as my first Council election in North Ward I discovered that fighting an election is like infantry fighting. It is very simple, it has to be simple to work, but at the end of the day you have actually to fight. Betty and I won North Ward because we knocked on doors and went on knocking on doors until one of us had personally met somebody from every household in the ward. I always wanted to go home one street before Betty but she kept my nose to the grindstone.

With 20,000 houses in the Sowerby Parliamentary constituency compared with 600 in North Ward we could not possibly call on every house, but the general policy of finding ways to meet the maximum number of people and to be seen by even more was still valid. To this end I buzzed about on a horrid little motor scooter in the freezing Yorkshire winter so that people at least knew what I looked like.

It did not matter much what you said when you called at a house. Most of them did not want to talk politics.

In preparation for canvassing Betty had swotted up her Conservative leaflets and was all ready with a little set piece when she called at her first house in the Wakefield Road. A typical Wakefield Road housewife came to the door with a child at her side. Betty said her piece but appeared not to be making a great impression. So she said: 'Perhaps you don't agree with what we Conservatives think?' The lady replied: 'Nay, lass. I'm eether way fer tuppence.' This lesson in canvassing stood her in good stead for life.

At the beginning of the campaign Conservative Central Office suggested that I might like to have an experienced Member of Parliament to hold my hand. They proposed Robin Turton. I looked him up in the directory of members to find that he was the member for the super-safe agricultural seat of Thirsk and Malton which he had inherited from his father. This sounded as big a contrast to marginal

Sowerby with all its smoking chimneys as you could get. I declined the offer. When eventually I became a Member of Parliament I had the agricultural constituency next door to Robin's. He was an extremely good member and had much to teach me - about an agricultural seat.

The main guidance I got from Central Office was a constant curb on my spending. They were terrified that I would spend more than the amount authorised by law and be disqualified. When I asked when a candidate had ever actually been disqualified in Yorkshire for this crime, the answer was: 'Never.'

In the constituency we had a marvellous local newspaper - the *Halifax Courier and Guardian* - which was delivered to almost every house nightly and weekly. One could not spend election money more effectively than through advertisements in this newspaper and this is where I wanted to spend the last available penny. Infuriatingly, when months later the election accounts were finalised, I found that through Central Office caution I had underspent by £2,000.

Once the election was announced the first necessity was to get my position regularised by inclusion on the Central Office list of approved candidates. To London I hurried and on reporting to Central Office was ushered into the presence of the great Lord Woolton, the Chairman of the Party, best known as the famous wartime Minister of Food who gave his name to the revolting Woolton Pie, with its crust of potato and filling mainly of other root crops. He was charming and I much enjoyed our talk.

* * *

Covering the election for the *Hebden Bridge Times* was the 19 year old Bernard Ingham, broad-spoken, a typical product of those valleys. Little can he have imagined that exactly 30 years later he would start a colourful, nay notorious 11 year stint as press secretary to Margaret Thatcher. Nor could I have imagined that 20 years later I would get to know him well as press secretary at the Department of Employment where I was Minister of State.

The Labour Party opened their campaign sensationally by choosing as their candidate one Douglas Houghton. The name meant nothing to Betty and me but struck terror into the hearts of our supporters. It transpired that he starred in the weekly radio programme with the wonderfully endearing title 'Can I help you?' He was well known in every house in Sowerby before he had knocked on a single door. His programme was particularly popular at that time when people were still plagued with so many wartime restrictions and really did need guidance.

In 1949 there was no television and very few motor cars so people came to political meetings by the hundred. At such places as the Co-op Hall at Hebden Bridge or the Town Hall at Todmorden, three or four hundred would pack the hall. I even had open air meetings in the market squares of the cotton towns in March.

West Riding audiences are not demonstrative. Walter Elliott, a wartime cabinet minister, and one of the wittiest speakers I have met, addressed 400 voters in the Co-op Hall at Hebden Bridge. He started with a joke. No reaction. He tried another, and another. Still no reaction. So he joked no more. As we were having beer and a sandwich in the pub afterwards he said to me in his rich Scots accent: 'You know these people here - they suck your blood.'

This was a good verdict. One could not say they were inattentive and their questions were twice as sharp as you would get in the south of England. Ultimate proof of their serious attitude was the turnout on polling day - 82 per cent on a cold March day - surely a record for any by-election.

The attraction at these meetings was not me but my supporting speakers. In this respect Conservative Central Office did me proud. A string of famous wartime cabinet ministers came and spoke for me. Harold Macmillan, Maxwell Fyfe, Walter Elliott and Lennox Boyd come to mind. All wished me luck, accompanied by such phrases as: 'Hope you win.' All except Harold Macmillan. Characteristically, and no doubt with memories of his Stockton past he said: 'You know you won't win? All you can do in a situation like this is to present yourself to the people as the sort of person they could vote for when the tide comes your way.'

Here is the letter I got from him after the campaign:

From the Rt Hon. Harold Macmillan, MP
10-15 St Martin's Street
London WC2

29 March 1949.

Dear Mr Bryan

I had meant to write to you before, but perhaps a little delay is not a bad thing, for it has left you a little time to think things over.

First, I do want to congratulate you most warmly on the wonderful fight you made at Sowerby. I do not think I ever remember going to a by-election where there was such obvious feeling of affection and admiration for our candidate. I do hope you will decide to stay on and fight Sowerby again at the General Election, for if you do, I believe you will win it.

I had a somewhat similar experience in 1923 at Stockton where I did not do quite well enough. I was urged to go elsewhere, but I stuck to Stockton and I have never regretted it.

Yours sincerely
Harold Macmillan

Councillor P.E.O.Bryan, DSO, MC
The White Cottage
Bairstow Lane
Sowerby Bridge

By now I have given thousands of speeches, ranging over the House of Commons, the Conservative Conference, every conceivable lunch and dinner, Commonwealth conferences in Uganda and Canada, sermons, constituency speeches in anything from a Dutch barn to the village hall. From all this I conclude that given the basic skills such as actually making yourself heard, the good speaker is he who can sum up or anticipate the nature of his audience and adjust his performance accordingly.

When on delegations abroad, I have noticed that British members of parliament speak far better on the whole than their foreign counterparts. Wide speaking experience is imposed on our MPs; if you can speak well in the House of Commons you can speak well anywhere.

Having said this, just as Faldo can hit a bad golf shot, the most brilliant speaker can make a bad speech. I have heard Churchill give a bad speech. Bob Rothery, one of the cleverest speakers I have known, gave an awful speech at his daughter's 21st birthday - when he must have been trying his hardest.

The meetings programme was formidable, 55 in all - two, three or even four each night. The prospect of actually giving a political speech did not worry me unduly. I had done quite a lot of talking to troops in the army. My speech at my adoption meeting was well received by an enthusiastic audience. I soon discovered that this was a honeymoon period. If your audience is violently biased in your favour as at the adoption meeting, or if you know your subject inside out as I did in the army, speaking seems easy.

Change the scene to giving a speech on Nationalisation and Economic Policy in a freezing schoolroom to 20 dour trades unionists plus three or four wives and one child and you discover that you have a lot to learn.

Alarmingly too, no two audiences seemed alike. My speech might be well received with lots of good natured questions to follow at Triangle. Motor over the hill to Ripponden and exactly the same speech would be frigidly received with no questions to brighten the occasion.

One learned the value of a good chairman who would jolly up the audience before you arrived and provoke them into questions when you had finished your speech. A good supporting speaker to precede your efforts could do wonders to ease your path.

Fifty-five evening meetings, out of door loudspeaker meetings to bus queues and at factory gates, any spare minute filled by canvassing with Betty or showing myself on the motor scooter - you would have thought with such activity that time would go fast. The election seemed to go on forever. One could not believe after 10 days of it that we had only just got to half time.

At last polling day arrived. The invariable routine is for the candidate and his wife to spend the whole day motoring around the constituency calling at the party committee rooms each situated near a polling station to thank your workers for their efforts. They have been sent your timetable and it is important to keep to it as a number will gather especially to meet you again, receive your thanks and give you a cup of tea. The endless cups of tea are what makes it difficult to keep to the timetable.

I suppose all English county constituencies have plenty of villages with quaint names, but as we did our polling day round it did strike me that Sowerby had its fair share - Lumbutts, Mankinoles, Mytholmroyd, Luddenden Foot, Bottoms, Heptonstall, Triangle, Cragg.

At last the day ended and we got back to White Cottage full of tea, exhausted, elated. I opened a bottle of champagne, not being able to think of anything else to do.

The count took place the next day in the Town Hall at Todmorden, the cotton town at the extreme end of the constituency on the Yorkshire/Lancashire border. Television has made everybody familiar with the long drawn out process of the count. The candidates arrive at the later stages with their wives and talk awkwardly to each other and try not to look anxious. Though Felicity was only three at the time Betty thought we ought to take both children to the count: 'They will probably never go to another,' she said.

Douglas Houghton was there when we arrived wearing the most enormous red rosette. I went forward to shake him by the hand; a loud stage whisper came from Libby, aged six: 'But, Mummy, I thought we did not like the red man.'

It was tense and very exciting. The result looked like being a close run thing as the voting papers were stacked beside each other on the tables. The lead seemed to change every few minutes. But finally a really hostile box of voting papers was opened. I suspected it was the village of Walsden, which we called 'Little Russia,' and Douglas Houghton won by 2000.

I was not unduly depressed. As you motored through Sowerby with all its factories, chimneys and terraced houses, it did not look like a Conservative constituency. To have got 20 votes for every 21 that Douglas Houghton got was not bad. I had no regrets. My active supporters had been excellent, a happy lot to work with and could not have been nicer. My agent, the modest Margaret Palmer, daughter of the Vicar of Sowerby, was perfect. My driver throughout the campaign was Tony Garner, then Young Conservative organiser for Yorkshire, later to become Sir Anthony Garner, chief agent at Conservative Central Office. Margaret too rose to a senior position in the party hierarchy. The star of the campaign was, of course, Betty.

Hardly were we home from our post-count lunch in the pub in Todmorden when there was a knock on the door.

It was Bob Rothery. Bob was the highly intelligent, articulate, forceful managing director of a large Huddersfield company, English Card Clothing Limited. He was the best out-of-doors speaker I have ever heard and took a big part in my elections. He was one of the few who could rouse a grim Yorkshire audience. I have heard him literally provoke a packed audience in the Town Hall at Todmorden into interruption. He would make a mental note of the interrupters then quite quietly and calmly describe some outrageous act on the part of the Labour Government. Then he would turn, pointing straight at an interrupter and shout: 'Now, you interrupter, tell me that you approve of that.' I have seen him play this trick in an open air meeting in a market square so effectively that shortly after you would see the interrupter skulking away out of the crowd.

Bob had called to congratulate me on the result. Only 'one more heave' was required to regain the seat. There was bound to be a general election within a year. He and I should conduct a summer campaign of evening open meetings in the market squares of the two main cotton towns, Todmorden and Elland, one at each end of the constituency.

I was not exactly raring to go at this particular moment but post election deflation had not yet set in so I rashly agreed.

These open air meetings did actually take place, the best lessons in open air speaking that I have ever had. The plan was to start with four meetings at Elland, two on Tuesday and Thursday evenings for two weeks. He would start the speeches and I would not come into bat until he had attracted a crowd of at least 25.

We duly arrived in the Elland Market Square at six o'clock on a sunny Tuesday night. There was nobody there despite our notice in the papers. This did not deter Bob. We set up our soap box. He bellowed out his message. Gradually a few people began to come in from the side roads and after half an hour 20 had assembled - not quite a quorum for my performance. Bob finished by assuring the company that we would be back again on Thursday at the same time.

On the Thursday there were a few people already waiting for us. The 25 mark was soon passed and I was in full song. By the end of the fourth meeting we had a crowd of well over 100 with plenty of interruption and everybody was enjoying themselves. We then went through the same process with the same results in Todmorden. These activities pleased our own people. Whether they changed a vote in the following general election we shall never know.

'One more heave' was our motto up to the next election. The reasoning was that so modest a majority could be reversed with more helpers and even more effort. The unmentioned snags to this theory were firstly that in a year's time Douglas Houghton, who promised to be a good MP, would be well-established. Secondly in a general election the results of the work of the local faithful are as nothing compared with the national swing, one way or another. Thirdly the Liberals had vowed to take part in the general election and a three cornered fight was almost certainly to our disadvantage.

All these factors played their part in the general election of 1950 which the Conservative Party lost by five seats. In Sowerby we lost by 3500 votes.

I fought Sowerby for the third and last time in 1951 and lost this time by 1600. We were getting closer.

Betty said: 'What are you going to do now?' I said: 'I think I have had enough of politics - at any rate for the time being.' She said: 'Then let's do what we have always wanted to do and buy somewhere which the children would enjoy in the country somewhere north of York.'

19
Park Farm

By now we were bursting out of White Cottage. The choice was to get a bigger house in the Halifax area or somewhere in the country to which we could expand at weekends and holidays. Betty was keen to buy a working farm and if she was keen to do something it usually happened. She pushed her reluctant father into agreeing to the idea and before long we were seeking the advice of John Cundall, an auctioneer and estate agent in Sherburn, north of Malton, whose father had been a shooting friend of Jimmy's. I swotted up several books on farming in the vain hopes of not looking too ignorant when being shown around a farm.

The first farm we looked at was Ochre Farm, whose sign you still see by the roadside on the road between Scampston and Yedingham. It was on flat land, not very attractive. We were not tempted but the viewing was good practice for us. The farmer threw me a small blue sample bag of barley and said: 'You've never seen a better sample than that.' This was true - I had never seen a worse one either.

We then looked at Manor Farm in Allerston on the Pickering-Scarborough Road. The attraction there was the farmhouse, a small mediaeval manor house in the centre of the village with an enormous attic which would have brought joy to our children. The land lay on each side of the main road. This was a great disadvantage in any event, but especially so in the case of this farm whose main asset was a Friesian dairy herd. I think we would have been tempted into buying it but in retrospect I say thank goodness Colonel Porter had already made his successful offer.

Exploring the countryside we happened to be motoring up the lane north of the village of Sawdon. Standing half a mile away across a wooded valley and some wide fields stood a lovely looking farm in a beautiful position with a view right across the Vale of Pickering and the Yorkshire Wolds. Betty said: 'That's the one we want.'

There was no reason to think it was for sale and when we knocked on the door the tenant, a Mr Watson, gave us to understand in the gruffest terms that it was not for sale. The more we saw of the farm the keener we were to have it. We also felt that there was something fishy about Mr Watson.

We went to see the owner, who proved to be a Sheffield snuff manufacturer called Harland. He was a delightful old man and the whole story came out. Park Farm consisted of 100 acres of woodland and 120 of grass and plough. It had been in the Harland family for many years. Before the war he had run it on the loosest possible rein with a so-called farm manager in residence. To him it was a place of beauty to which he and his wife would repair when convenient in the summer months. There was no question of controlling vermin because the Harlands liked seeing rabbits running about. In later years I was told by neighbours that sometimes there was no harvest at Park Farm because Mr Harland had forgotten to buy the seed.

When war broke out and maximum food production was the order of the day, exceptionally bad farmers were dispossessed by the government and the land let to chosen tenants for the duration of the war. Not surprisingly Park Farm came under this category and Mr Watson was the government-chosen tenant. He was not well chosen. He had abused his tenancy by cutting down trees without permission and knocking down an old wall, using the stones to fill up the well.

Dispossessed owners did not get their land back straight after the war because food was still in short supply, but in 1950 it was announced that this could happen. The announcement passed unnoticed by Mr Harland but not Mr Watson. Mr Watson counted on this and reckoned that if he just continued paying his rent as usual without comment, with the passage of time he would be established in law as the rightful tenant. By the time we went to see Mr Harland several such cheques had been paid but he was slack in both opening his post and paying his cheques into the bank and none of Mr Watson's cheques had actually reached the bank. To cut a long story short, with the aid of our agent, Eric Thompson, he gave Mr Watson notice and sold the farm to us for £6,750 - a memorable day in the history of the Bryan family.

There was much to be done. The farmhouse, like many in the Sawdon area, was built in about 1850. There was no gas, electricity or telephone and the water came from an uncertain supply in Troutsdale. The farm had four bedrooms. There were chickens in the present dining room, a ram in the kitchen and a bull where we now have the central heating boiler. There was an open cattle yard filled by 150 tons of manure. The only building in addition to the original farm buildings was a Nissen hut full of hens which stood in the front paddock, the only blight on the lovely view.

Our next bit of good luck came in the finding of the farm manager, George Stephenson, who had been manager of Lord Downe's dairy farm at Wykeham for some years. His daughter, Pamela, had asthma and the doctor said she would be better living on higher ground so he moved to Sawdon to be farm manager on a farm owned by the local member of parliament, Alec Spearman. Spearman was just about to sell his farm and George Stephenson fell into our lap. George was obviously a model of rural respectability and agricultural competence. He did not find my interrogation very testing.

Betty then asked Elsie Stephenson about her cooking. She had started her working life as a kitchen maid in the kitchen of the Duke of Westminster at Eaton Hall. During that period she had been on cooking courses on sauces at the Ritz and soups at the Berkeley. She was then cook for many years for Lady Cayley at Brompton Hall until she got married. In addition to all this, time showed her to be a warm homely character; a great favourite with all children, in particular ours. Her fame spread to the school at Duncombe Park with the birthday cakes that she used to cook for them.

During the next two years we got planning permission for two cottages and re-conditioned the house, including an entirely new roof, built a Dutch barn and covered in the open yard. We had already bought a caravan, which we certainly needed whilst all this was going on.

Another caravan housed some of the workmen who swarmed all over the place. I remember a plumber who, for some reason, was terrified of Betty. One day he was installing a sink in the far bedroom and was balancing on the cross beams. Suddenly Betty came up behind him and, taking him unawares, asked how he was getting on. He was so shocked he slipped off the beams and his legs appeared through the ceiling below. A fascinating nomadic family - the Kirks - lived in their own caravan while they built the cottages.

From the start little Pamela Stephenson became such a good friend of Felicity's that when she went away to boarding school in 1954 they promised to write to each other every day.

The most original idea was Betty's of building a very large wooden hut 80 yards away from the house in the orchard at the edge of the wood. We got planning permission for this as a grain store, but it spent more time as a playroom, theatre or dance floor than sheltering the harvest and was very successful over the years. Its permanent fittings were electric light, a sink, a radiogram and a ping-pong table, but with the aid of large rolls of hessian and the wiring in the roof it could be converted into any shape for any purpose. When the children had a party there we used to decorate the orchard with night lights in dozens of jam jars hanging in the trees.

Setting up the farm did not take many difficult decisions from me. The land agent, Eric Thompson, who had helped us buy the farm, was my guide. He judged George Stephenson to be a sound and frugal farmer, unlikely to waste our money. In 1951 the wartime farming subsidies were still in force. Prices were at a level to make the most modest farm profitable so if you were at all above average you were bound to make money. Having covered in the yard and improved our buildings we crammed them with animals. At the height of summer we had 80 head of cattle in the fields. The buildings and yard were full of pigs and some calves. George was a great sheep man. We had 200 ewes which meant that while the lambs were all on the farm our sheep population was about 350. We usually managed to rent one or two fields to extend the grazing.

The corn we harvested with a binder, a primitive machine which shot out sheaves of corn bound with string onto the ground. Then followed the laborious business of standing the sheaves three at a time against each other in which position the wind was meant to dry the corn, which it often did. But if the rains came and persisted, grass would grow through the bottom of the stooks and, even more laboriously, you had to re-stook them. I had lumbago for weeks after doing my bit at this game one harvest time.

The stooks were gathered together into stacks which stood neatly in our farmyard awaiting the arrival of the contractor with his enormous and ungainly threshing machine sometime during the autumn or winter. Threshing days were quite a ceremony; extra men arrived and beer was so much part of the operation that you could safely put it down in the farm accounts. The older hands so enjoyed these traditional days that they were quite sorry when we caught up with our more modern neighbours and bought a second-hand combine harvester.

The children and the dogs were others to deplore the passing of threshing days. They would stand around the stack when it got to around three foot high and wait for all the rats and mice to run out. Some were caught by the dogs. Those chased by the children with sticks usually survived and now and then a baby rat would become a pet.

Mrs Stephenson was a keen butter maker so we had a succession of cows of the Jersey breed, named Betty, Violet and Elizabeth after the family. Jersey milk is rich and tended to make the children sick so in the end we changed to a plainer cow, a Jersey cross, with less sick-making milk. She was called Felicity.

With the children then aged ten, seven and four you can imagine what a novel paradise the farm with its animals presented.

The sheep, with all the excitement of lambing time, the sick lambs which had to be kept in the boiler house, and the inevitable pet lamb. Feeding calves was fascinating and went on all year round. Sows and their continuous stream of piglets were always there to be gazed at and, with the occasional bullock leaping up the haha onto the lawn, there was always something happening. The favourite pets were orphaned baby rabbits from the wood which, despite loving care and feeding, seldom survived long.

These wild treasures were usually produced by the tall Bill Gough, the head forester from the Forestry Commission, who soon became our close friend and our expert on all things rural. His first advice was to clear-fell 14 acres of woodland in front of the house which had passed its best and to replant with an attractive mixture of conifers and hardwood. The trees have thrived and now, 40 years later, form the wood which you see on your left as you look out of the drawing-room window.

In our second year at the farm the children caught whooping cough and were confined to the caravan. It was then that they got to know Dr Allen, who though childless himself was a genius with children and whom I personally got to know well in later years during Betty's long illness.

Life for the grown-ups was not all bliss until the cottages were built. The Stephensons lived cramped in the west end of the farmhouse while at weekends and holidays we were in the east end plus a caravan. We shared the kitchen and the Calor cooker. There was no central heating or electric light. When the water supply failed George would say: 'I'll go and dig it out' and disappeared with a spade into Troutsdale a mile away. What exactly he did I don't know, but water would then trickle back again.

In addition to George his brother Raymond, who lived in Brompton, also worked on the farm. After the cottages were built we had a third man who lived in one of them and his wife helped at the house. Unbelievably, even with three men to pay, the farm made a profit. In today's conditions a farm of this size on land of less than average quality might just support one man half-time.

From the start the garden was a great preoccupation for Betty. It did not then exist. The present garden was just the extension of the rough field beyond it.

We had Mr Roger of Roger's Roses up to give us advice. He said that we should first decide how big a garden we wanted, how much we could actually maintain. Having fenced that in we could plant a much bigger area with shrubs and rhododendrons, which would take minimal maintenance. The present garden and the area towards the tennis court are the result of our following Mr Roger's advice plus all the additions and improvements which Cynthia, my second wife, has added in the last 20 years.

In the early years progress in building the garden from scratch was not spectacular. Betty had little time to spare and Locket, the gardener, though a great favourite with the children, was no professional. When he left, within weeks the garden became a real wilderness. Then out of the blue came the news that Ken Bean who used to be the gardener at Brompton Hall might be available. I had never met Ken, who lived with his wife in Brompton, but everybody spoke superlatively of him. He had been apprenticed in the garden at Brompton Hall and in time became head gardener, but then the Cayleys emigrated temporarily to the Channel Islands leaving him jobless. He had been driving a bus unhappily for 11 years when he came to see me about the gardener's job at Park Farm. I took him on a tour, somewhat self-conscious at the state of things, then I sat him down over a cup of tea and said: 'Well, Ken, what do you think of it?' His reply will remain in my head forever: 'I never realised there would be such an opportunity, Sir.' Of the many strokes of good luck that have descended on us at Park Farm, the arrival of Ken Bean was one of the greatest.

He was as good a chauffeur as he was a gardener. The cars were always spotless. During his later years with the Cayleys Sir Kenelm was an invalid and Ken had had often to look after him, so allied to his natural kindness, which was boundless, he was perfect at dealing with Mardi in her old age and Betty in her illness. After 14 years he left us because of his arthritis. We all still keep in touch with him, living as he does on the edge of Brompton about four miles away.

20
Howden

Before the Conservative Party Conference expanded to its present gigantic size, which limits the places of its meetings to Brighton, Blackpool and Bournemouth, it used to be held every few years at Scarborough. 1952 was such a year. Though I had 'given up politics,' the farm only being eight miles from Scarborough I could not resist looking in.

As I walked along the front who should stop me but Ted Heath, then a government whip. He had got to know me at the time of the Sowerby by-election and we had met once or twice since. He asked me what I was doing politically. When I said I had had enough of elections, anyway for the time being, he swept my words aside and said I must come with him at once to meet John Hare, Vice-Chairman of the Conservative Party Organisation in charge of candidates.

John Hare invited me to come and have a talk with him in London and in due course this is what I did. He got down to brass tacks straight away. He asked me if I was serious in saying that I was no longer interested in elections or did I really mean I was only interested in a safe seat. I replied that even that would not necessarily do. It would have to be a safe seat in Yorkshire. By now I was so fond of our whole family set-up at Park Farm that I was unwilling either to move my home or represent a constituency far away from both London and Yorkshire which could make life one long travelling merry-go-round.

Then the 100 to one fluke happened. The only constituency in England which we could actually see from Park Farm, other than our own, came on the market. Those wolds across the Vale of Pickering were the Northern end of the constituency then called Beverley which stretched 50 miles all the way down to the Humber river at Howden.

The member of parliament, George Odey, had just announced his intention to retire at the next election. I was still slightly embarrassed to put my name in for this, the most agricultural of all constituencies. I was hardly a countryman. Nor did I know a soul in the whole of the East Riding of Yorkshire, except Brigadier Teddy Tryon, a brewery director in Pocklington, with whom I had served abroad in the war.

Whilst Betty and I were endlessly talking this over, Susan Walker came on the line. She was the Central Office agent in Leeds, a splendid Scots lady with whom we had become friendly, not only politically but socially during the Sowerby by-election. She insisted that I put my name in. She would be the Central Office representative during the selection process and without her actually saying: 'I will do my best for you,' one did feel she could do us no harm.

Several hundred people always apply when a Conservative safe seat becomes vacant and Beverley was no exception. My application did not look so bad on paper. In addition to a war record and having fought a Labour seat three times I was actually able to pose as both local and a farmer.

The selection committee reduced the list of applicants to a short list of 12 who were interviewed. I had no idea how I did in my interview before these good people, none of whom I had ever seen before, but having nothing to lose I felt quite relaxed and seemed to get on well enough with the chairman, Sir Ivo Thompson, Bt., who asked most of the questions.

Then came Susan Walker on the phone again to say I was on the short list of three, due to appear before the Executive at Beverley in two weeks time, the Executive numbering about 120 representatives of all the towns and villages in the constituency.

The routine would be for each aspirant in turn to give a 10 minute speech and then answer questions ad lib. You can imagine how Betty and I polished up that speech on the virtues and beauties of the East Riding in the intervening fortnight. It almost became a question of whether I could deliver it without laughing.

The great day came. My opponents turned out to be Michael Willoughby, the present Lord Middleton, and Tony Leavey, the future member of parliament for Heywood and Royton, and in years to come one of my closest friends. They had both arrived without wives. Tony went in to bat first whilst Michael and I made conversation in an ante-room, the sound of voices and controlled clapping coming through the wall.

Then it was our turn. Betty and I sat on either side of Sir Ivo. The platform of the Church Hall seemed a long way above the crowd below. After a few opening remarks from the chairman, he turned to me and said: 'And now, Mr Bryan, I should be glad if you would give us a speech - on coal.' Betty nearly fainted in her chair. I got up as slowly as I could to give myself time to collect my thoughts on coal and took the plunge.

Within a few seconds I realised I was on a good thing. The audience were, of course, in on the game and fascinated to hear what I was going to say. It is rare and confidence-giving to find you have an audience which is in this expectant frame of mind. I spoke slowly. I remembered that at Duncombe Park Speech Day the previous Saturday I had met a member of the Coal Board. I told the audience about him and what he had told me. I then remembered that I had actually opened a new clothing factory for J.B.Hoyles in Wath on Dearne, in the South Yorkshire coalfield. I had got to know the girls, all daughters of miners, very well, not to mention local contractors and councillors. Once I was on that tack, punctuated here and there with quotes like Ernest Bevin's well-known remark: 'Give me a hundred million tons of coal and I will give you a foreign policy,' I could have gone on for a long time but did not try my luck too far, and finished on the dot of 10 minutes. The question period I would judge to have been neutral. It neither promoted nor harmed my cause.

Luck then intervened again on my side. The inspired Sir Ivo turned to Betty and said in a jolly way: 'Since you have come with your husband would you like to answer some questions?' The answer could only be 'yes.' The questions asked were sensible and friendly. She dealt with them beautifully. The whole situation turned out in my favour. With my experience of dealing with questions in the elections at Sowerby I was more likely to be able to make an impromptu speech on a subject picked out of the hat than the other two. To be the only one of the three accompanied by his wife, especially when she came over so well, was also bound to help.

And so a whole variety of changes and chances and flukes put me into a position to qualify to represent the loveliest constituency in Yorkshire for 32 years. I could not have dreamt of this ever happening as I started sorting wool when I first came to live in Yorkshire 15 years before.

George Odey, the sitting member of parliament, was courteous to me. Congratulations from him came straight away together with an invitation to come and dine and spend a night on his yacht, the *Arminelle*, on the Humber.

George was a bulky, middle-aged, successful businessman, the managing director of Barrow Hepburn and Gale, tanners and manufacturers of specialist leather goods like ministers' red boxes and civil servants' brief cases. He was what you would call a 'character,' indeed a well-known character in the East Riding.

I reported at the quay soon after teatime and before long the *Arminelle* was at anchor and we had started our pre-dinner drinking session.

My plan was to let him do all the talking until and over dinner then ask him hundreds of questions deep into the night. You can imagine how much I wanted to know about the constituency and his life in parliament, what he did about secretarial help at Westminster, what about accommodation in London? And so on *ad infinitum*. Part 1 went to plan; he certainly did the talking. We did a lot of good drinking and dining.

Over the port he rather suddenly fell asleep and remained in a deep snoring slumber only broken by the few minutes it took to get into his bunk round about midnight.

I disembarked in the morning, none of my questions answered. He did at one point, however, give me some advice: 'Never ask questions in parliament. It only provokes correspondence.' I told this to Keith Joseph a year or two later. 'That's better than the advice I got from my predecessor - "always wear a double-breasted jacket; then you needn't wear a waistcoat."'

I was adopted as the prospective candidate for Beverley in October 1953. The latest date for the forthcoming general election was October 1956, but the chances were that it would come well before that. Whatever one's prediction, the only sensible programme was to work hard to get to know the constituency with all speed.

Two years passed between my adoption and the general election and during that time I tended to neglect J.B.Hoyle and Company and spent my time getting to know people and the villages in the very large constituency, which stretched from the village of Staxton, almost seven miles short of Scarborough in the north to Howden on the Ouse river, which runs into the Humber. It was nearly 60 miles long and 35 miles wide, from Heslington on the outskirts of York to Beeford within a couple of miles of the North Sea.

The only town of any size was Driffield, with 6000 voters, which in most constituencies would qualify as no more than a large village. As a result of a report by the Boundaries Commission two months before the election, our boundaries were changed, involving the loss of the town of Beverley and the gain of Driffield. The name of the constituency was changed to Howden. With the change of boundaries one had no indication of what the majority should be but considering the agricultural nature of the area anything but a Conservative win would have been a big surprise.

The Conservative organisation was casual but effective in the 134 villages which made up the consituency. The actual membership of the association was not high. The same little group which ran the Parish Council, the British Legion and the Women's Institute probably raised £100 a year for the Conservative Association with an annual coffee morning or bazaar and manned the Committee Rooms on polling day. I remember arriving half way through the evening at a whist drive in the village of Warter ready to present the prizes at the end and hearing a player say to his neighbour when he saw me: 'Oh, is it the Conservatives tonight?'

In addition to what one might call these periodical activists, there always seem to be about half-a-dozen individuals scattered around the constituency - dedicated Conservatives who put in endless hours of toil for the cause. These became my heroes, or more often heroines.

I was lucky in my chairman, a stout fertilizer manufacturer from Kilpin, near Howden, called Dick Pilling. Apart from the worthiness and pleasantness of his character his profession meant that he knew every farmer in the East Riding, which made my regular visits to the agricultural shows doubly rewarding.

Mrs Pilling, a formidable, childless pillar of Howden society, at first made it clear that we were on trial but once Betty had proved herself, which she did at some speed, Mrs Pilling was her champion.

The agent I inherited was a Major Munn, a ranker from the Indian Army who was very keen that I should use my army rank so that he could use his, which was his proudest possession. He was worthy, diligent, good company and made effective by a superlative secretary, Sonya Ainley, later to become, on Major Munn's death, my superlative agent.

It was not just a question of getting to know the constituency and meeting leading citizens, officers of the association and of the village branches. I had to discover a new world.

I was brought up a provincial and latterly a West Riding provincial. I was at home with mill owners and mill workers. As I walked among all those chimney stacks in Sowerby Bridge and Todmorden I had a fair idea of what was happening in the buildings they towered over. I understood the social hierarchy, who led the way and who followed.

The East Riding was a land of big estates and big farms. In my own constituency there was Lord Halifax at Garrowby with 20,000 acres, Lord Middleton of Birdsall with 15,000 acres, Sir Richard Sykes at Sledmere, with 14,000 acres, the Vesteys at Warter Priory with 14,000 acres, the Legards of Scampston, the Forbes Adams of Escrick - all had estates of several thousand acres. Most of these land-owning families had been in possession for two or three hundred years.

Before the war the estates were in general run-down, but their broad acres had earned high profits since the beginning of the war and this prosperity continued right into the eighties. The idea of land-owners struggling for survival certainly had not been applicable to the East Riding.

Before the war most of these large estates were tenanted and had since been progressively been taken in hand. Many of the wold farms are between 500 and 1000 acres, the perfect size for a family business.

On the land below the wolds on the Vale of York there is a different picture. Lord Manton has a fine estate at Houghton, south of Market Weighton, but the farms tend to be smaller and on sandy land. Going further towards the Humber the land gets heavier and the warpland down by the river is some of the richest in the country. The estates stretched out along the river bank - Yokefleet, Saltmarshe and Sandhall - at 3-4000 acres - are rather smaller than those on the wolds, but with their rich warpland probably just as valuable.

Life in the East Riding when first I became a member of parliament was run by the farming community and by the gentry, by whom I mean those who had owned land over several generations, who ran the hunting, the shooting, the racecourses, the county and local agricultural shows, the Anglican churches, the charities, manned the local bench and took their turn as high sheriffs, deputy lieutenants and officials of the constituency conservative association. They sent their children to the better-known public schools and tended to join the army rather than go to Oxford or Cambridge. The villages were inhabited by families of farmworkers who did not go far afield in their search for husbands and wives and so formed a stable population.

The social mix has greatly changed. The mechanisation of farming has decimated the number of farmworkers, and their dolled-up houses, plus many new ones, are now filled with commuters attracted to country life by the motor car and particularly the motorway. Local Authorities have kept planning permission within sensible bounds, nevertheless, Driffield, Howden and villages like Holme-on-Spalding Moor and Escrick, whose populations had been level for generations, have mushroomed.

The East Riding has absorbed these changes remarkably well. Country pursuits, such as the agricultural shows, hunting and shooting continue to thrive. The roads, apart from those leading to the seaside resorts, are blessedly empty and the area remains one of the most pleasant places in the country to live and bring up your family.

When I became the member of parliament for those parts, Arthur Empson at Yokefleet and Colonel Schofield at Sandhall were from families who had been there for generations. Captain Saltmarshe's family had been at Saltmarshe since Domesday. He became one of my most regular correspondents. His letters were always about hanging.

Major Empson, bachelor brother of the poet, William Empson, asked me to lunch 'to meet some of your supporters.' On my right was the above mentioned Captain Saltmarshe, then in his eighties. On my left was Colonel Schofield. Making conversation I said to him: 'Schofield is surely a Lancashire name.' He said: 'You are quite right. We came over here as tenant farmers.' I said: 'Have your family been here long?' He said: 'Oh no, about 300 years.' Over coffee after lunch the conversation wandered on to 'the war.' This was not the Second World War, nor the First World War, but the Crimean War. Arthur Empson said: 'My grandfather knew Florence Nightingale. I believe I've got one of her letters to him.' With this he opened an untidy desk, fumbled about amongst some papers and out came the letter to 'Dear Mr Empson,' written from the Crimea and signed Florence Nightingale.

Yokefleet Hall is an ultra Victorian house, reminiscent of the architecture of the Palace of Westminster. It bore all the signs of 50 years of bachelor occupation. Once when I was spending the night there after a day's shooting, the good Mrs Sellers brought me my early morning tea. She caught me sitting up in bed reading, muffled up in my overcoat. This was reported to Arthur Empson and it finally clinched his decision to install central heating. Even when installed so recently, in action it did not sound quite up to date. The boiler had been put in the basement under the very centre of the entrance hall. When it came on there was a great rumble like the starting of ship's engines.

Most of these ancient and landed families had for generations supported the Conservative Party in the county and at some time provided Conservative members of parliament and ministers.

Lord Halifax, the son of the wartime Foreign Secretary and Ambassador in America, had been the member of parliament for York. His brother, Richard Wood, was my neighbour for many years as a member of parliament for Bridlington. Lady Sykes of Sledmere was the president of my constituency association, her husband the president of Richard's and Lady Halifax was my treasurer. Over the years members of the Middleton, Legard, Manton and Preston families all took active official positions within the Conservative organisation.

Today the county land-owning families supply fewer members of parliament at Westminster and activists in the constituencies. Indeed I cannot think of a single Yorkshire seat which is held by one of their members.

My admiration for Richard Wood, now Lord Holderness, is boundless. As a young subaltern in the Guards he lost both legs well above the knees early in the desert campaign. A dive-bomber swooped down on his platoon, the men threw themselves to the ground and by a thousand to one chance a bomb fell across his legs and by a million to one chance never exploded. His legs were crushed beyond repair and any lesser man would have retired to the comfort of the family estate.

Instead, like Bader, aided by his two false legs and his marvellous wife, Diana, he has led a more than full public life, firstly as a minister and now in the House of Lords. In his early days as the member for Bridlington, he used to ride around the constituency on a horse. He would shoot from a contraption mounted on the bumper of his Land Rover. How he carried out his duties as Minister of Overseas Development I do not know, involving as it did air journeys and tours to the roughest parts of the world.

He gets solace from his religion and was often to be seen reading his Bible in the train to London whilst I was working through my constituency mail. Diana acts as his secretary and, of course, much more. They have made the most of Flat Top House, a fine wolds farmhouse with the old farm buildings and yard beautifully converted into an entertainment area.

The farmers were less politically active in the central organisation of the association, but often came into action in the villages.

Politically, farmers tend to be sour in bulk but reasonable individually, especially on their own farms. However tactful my opening address at a farmers' meeting, the following question time would degenerate into a competition of who could be rudest about the government of the day. Over the years my tactics were, therefore, to have the minimum of actual farmers' meetings; instead I tried to establish myself as somebody interested in farming and on the side of the farmer in the following three ways:

Firstly, once I had become the member of parliament, I instituted what I called my 'Annual Farm Week.' Every August I got the National Farmers' Union to organise a full week of visits to farms of their choice. Before the week I would have a press conference with the local press to discuss my programme and my actual visits took whatever form the farmer in question wanted. Sometimes it would be a tour of the farm followed by a lunch to which he had invited his neighbouring farmers and at others it would be a tour of the farm and no more. During the week I usually included a visit to an agricultural institution such as the government experimental farm at Duggleby. I visited about 15 farms in the week. By the end of my 32 years in Parliament I had at some time or other visited a high proportion of my constituency farms.

Secondly, on the middle day of the annual National Farmers' Union conference in London I used to take Dining Room A in the House of Commons, which seats 58, and have a lunch for the farmers and their wives who were up for the conference. I was always able to get a minister as our guest, usually the Minister of Agriculture but such other well-known politicians as the present Lords Home and Whitelaw have been among our guests. I included a few other Yorkshire MPs at the table and between us we were usually able to supply our farmer guests with a dozen or more tickets for the House of Commons gallery. The whole thing was organised by the National Farmers' Union so was energy efficient as far as I was concerned.

Thirdly, after harvest I had the four district secretaries of the NFU to lunch at Park Farm. This lasted at least till four o'clock in the afternoon and they seemed to enjoy it as much as I did.

By carrying out these three operations with utmost regularity and keeping in constant touch with the regional secretary of the National Farmers' Union, I was at least seen to be trying.

Most thinking farmers knew that in general terms they had little to complain of. Since the outbreak of war and the advent of controlled prices they had had the longest period of prosperity that any of them could remember. Grumbling resulted from the very fact that welcome government support for prices involved endless discussions on what those prices should be. The annual price review was invariably the occasion for a row with the Minister of Agriculture. I hardly remember a single 'good price review.'

Farming in the East Riding is of a high standard and the farming community a bright lot. Time and again a son joins his father on the farm and brings in a new batch of ideas he has acquired at an agricultural college or when apprenticed to a farm elsewhere. The Young Farmers is by far the most successful youth organisation in the county.

* * *

In 1953 my father died. After my mother's death he gave up his living at Milton Earnest, had a sale of all his possessions and prepared to live on his own. With his academic background I thought Cambridge might be a good place for him and got him some rooms there, but this was not a success. He had at last wearied of reading. He said: 'I have read so much in my life that everything I now read is a repetition of what I have read before.' Nor had he any wish to write. Without reference to me or anyone else he then took on a parish in the East End of London for six months. He can't have had much rapport with such a congregation but he got satisfaction out of preaching and seemed more content than I had expected.

Then, to my great relief, he was accepted by a clergy home at Lingfield, an excellent institution. Built round a quadrangle like a university college, the married parsons were accommodated on one side, singletons on the other. It was well run, there was no need to be lonely and they had frequent services in the chapel at which the parsons took it in turns to preach. Sadly, after a time he was asked to preach no more; he was too controversial. He scoffed at this idea: 'If parsons can't stand controversy, who can?' said he to me. He died soon after.

He was a remarkable man. He did not have a great influence on my life by way of advice or example because I did not see much of him in my early boyhood and he was abroad in my university days when he might have wanted to influence my choice of subjects and career.

His successful career of course had a great influence on my life, for how in the normal course of events could the son of a poverty stricken farmer's boy from Prince Edward Island expect to have had the education which he provided for me? As a self-created academic and writer it was a very great achievement indeed to have put all of his sons through first-class universities and given a good education to his three daughters.

His strength of character emerged in the way he broke out of his humble background and surroundings. Most of us, including me, have mainly reacted to surroundings. Throughout my varied life, even when comparatively successful I have only been reacting to opportunities offered by uncles, fathers-in-law, war, politics, Ted Heath or later, Sidney Bernstein, or C.Y.Tung.

My father created his own opportunities. Plenty of bright boys in Prince Edward Island no doubt went to the Prince of Wales College and in due course became teachers. But he became Vicar of St Paul's, Charlottetown, the biggest church on the island, when he was 29, then went off to get more degrees at universities in America. It was pretty adventurous in those days to go to Japan as an academic. Whilst there, in addition to his University work he launched into journalism and was for 10 years Japan correspondent for the *London Morning Post* and for a period also for the *Economist* - two prestigious papers.

As a widower he seemed full of remorse and guilt that he had not been able to give Mother a better life. A sense of guilt often comes with bereavement but I would think he was conscious that over the years he had too often been a bad tempered and even bullying husband. He had few friends and those he had, he had made through his work.

I knew nothing of my father's financial affairs but instinctively supposed that he would not be good at money management. I was therefore surprised when he left £23,000 - a large sum in 1953, all earned by teaching and writing.

21
Waiting for the Election

The years after the war were a disappointment to the British people. Far from coming back from the war to a land fit for heroes, after the short-lived elation that went with victory, the following years were dreary. Rationing of food and clothing went on for seven long years accompanied by building controls, acute shortage of housing and holidays abroad limited to £50 per trip. It was depressing, too, to have to conclude from our recurring economic crises that Britain's place in the world was no longer what we had become used to over the last few hundred years.

In 1952 the coronation of Queen Elizabeth II brought a burst of sunshine through these clouds. For a few weeks all was optimism and goodwill in every corner of the country. Instinctively, and without apparent effort, celebrations broke out everywhere, with street parties in the back streets of even the dismal Lancashire cotton towns.

The coronation itself was a magnificent show, the like of which the young had never seen and the old had forgotten.

The support from the Commonwealth made us feel a great imperial power again. Heads of all the countries, big and small, each in his own horse-drawn carriage, many in their brilliant national dress, made up much of the procession with the 20 stone Queen of the tiny island of Tonga stealing the show, sharing her carriage with a tiny little man from I know not where. Churchill, asked by somebody who that midget was, answered: 'Oh, didn't you know. He's her lunch.'

There was a marvellous display of cavalry. Our own Life Guards take some beating but I am bound to say that the turbanned Indians, with lances, on their magnificent horses ran them close.

It seemed fitting that on the very day of the coronation came the news that Hunt and Hillary had conquered Everest.

All this was good while it lasted but we all came down to earth again in a few weeks.

At the time I was a member of the Conservative Club in St James's Street on the route of the coronation procession. A stand was erected providing about 100 seats for which members drew lots and I was one of the lucky ones with two tickets in the front row. Betty surrendered her ticket to 10 year old Libby on condition she wrote an account of what she saw.

Those were the very early days of television. Only one channel, BBC1, was offered and probably no more than one household in five had a set. The spectacle of the coronation ignited an explosion of demand; Ashfield was part of that explosion, so Felicity and Bunny, then aged six and three, and deeply jealous of their elder sister's trip to London, were able to follow every minute of this spectacular, then they dressed up to enact the whole ceremony themselves with Bunny as the Queen, Felicity as the Archbishop and Pamela Stephenson, who was staying with us, as Lady in Waiting.

In those early post war years, busy as we were in far away Yorkshire with family, trouser-making, politics and learning to farm, we did not see much of such close friends as Forman, Majdalany, Blackadder, or the Davidsons. They in turn were busy setting up their own families, lives and careers.

Denis Forman, working for the British Film Institute, married his brilliant, beautiful boss, Helen de Mouilpied and had a house in Essex. Fred Majdalany, now a well known columnist on the *Daily Mail*, was becoming famous as a leading war historian. He lived in a pleasant old world cottage not far from Denis in Essex, married Sheila Howarth, a fellow journalist, and was now father of my endearing god-child Emma.

Francis Blackadder seemed to be prospering as a director of the Runciman Company in Newcastle, was happily married to Paddy with a child or two and was not surprisingly a leading figure in the rugby football world of the north.

At that stage we saw little of, but kept in touch with, the Davidsons, whose Army life was mainly abroad.

With my political activities in the East Riding, our children going to boarding school at Duncombe Park, near Helmsley in the North Riding, and our increasing presence at Park Farm, our Yorkshire circle of friends was widening all the time.

In Halifax I suppose we saw most of Larry and Amo Foster and their children, Bruce and Reta, until they emigrated to join her American parents at Colorado Springs, where Betty and I visited them in 1962.

At Park Farm our new friends, in time to be our close friends were the Cayleys, the Guthries and the Chafers. The Cayley family, based on the village of Brompton by Sawdon, have been large landowners for several centuries, the most famous of the clan perhaps being Sir George Cayley, the generally acknowledged inventor of the aeroplane. The first historic flight of his machine actually took place in Brompton Dale with his butler in the cockpit, if it could be so called, in 1809. A model of this contraption can be seen in the Space Museum in Washington.

The Cayleys we have known are Sir Kenelm, the tenth Baronet, his wife, Elizabeth, and their seven daughters.

The last years of his life when I knew Kenelm must have been sad ones for him. In the 50 years that he had held the title he had seen his estate dwindle and his style of life much reduced. He died still much loved but sadly an alcoholic in 1967. None of these changing circumstances daunted Elizabeth Cayley. In her efforts to produce a son and heir for Kenelm she instead produced seven daughters who as a 'pen of seven' could hardly be equalled for charm, looks and liveliness.

Elizabeth was the bravest and most memorable character that I met in our early days at Park Farm. The complications of her life with Kenelm and bringing up seven daughters did not prevent her launching herself into new seas. She started writing articles for the newspapers and in no time she was appearing quite regularly in the *Daily Mail*. I asked Fred Majdalany, the professional journalist, why this amateur had become so successful. His reply was: 'Her writing is different.' These two contrasting characters became great friends.

She was quite fearless of being found out. During a general election she wrote a series of articles for the *Daily Mail*, one of which was entitled: 'Canvassing the Council Houses' - of which there are not many in Brompton. The supporting photograph showed Elizabeth canvassing a lady on the doorstep. Those who knew recognised the lady as the well known Cayley nanny, and the doorstep not that of a council house but of 'The Green,' the house where the Cayleys then lived.

She took to broadcasting and covered the Rainier wedding for the BBC radio. I happened to call at The Green for cup of coffee when she was preparing her piece. She was marvellously confident. She stood in front of the fireplace and said: 'Paul, what do you think of this?' Then started off: 'All the world loves a wedding, etc. etc. Then I shall describe whatever I actually see and then say this...' In later years she appeared on television a number of times. Once I saw her on an antiques programme and asked her afterwards when she had seen the tape what she thought of it. Her only comment: 'Isn't my figure awful?'

She became a leading lunchtime speaker, aided by her carefree and almost reckless approach. Once, speaking in the West Riding to a Business Women's Guild, some wag said to her: 'This lot are known as the Fur and Feather Club.' So she started her speech with the words: 'I hear you are called the Fur and Feather Club.' Not a smile.

The youngest four Cayley daughters overlapped my three in age and so when we came to live permanently at Park Farm they all got to know each other well. The Brompton-Sawdon area in the fifties and sixties was a good hunting ground for a would-be bridegroom, for in addition to the seven Cayley daughters and three Bryan daughters there were also three Chafer daughters at Kirkgate Lodge, halfway between the Cayleys and the Bryans. They also quite naturally became great friends.

Charles Chafer was Master of the local Derwent Hunt and his wife, Elsie, was sister of Jo Owen, a big wolds farmer, whom I got to know as a constituent.

Our friendship with the Guthrie family followed Libby's with their daughter, Elizabeth, commonly known as Gussie at Duncombe Park, and has continued to this day. John Guthrie made a fortune buying and selling agricultural estates and was blessed with a son, young John, fully capable of doing the same.

On the often chilly and windswept front at Scarborough were a row of chalets, two of which were rented by the Cayleys and the Guthries. They were hard to get hold of but after much pressure by Betty on me and by me on the council, the Bryans joined the chalet tenants. Much time was spent there by the families but I was not the only father who was seldom on parade. The only amenity offered was a gas stove, and a few days spent sheltering from the rain, crowded in with small children and wet bathing dresses all over the place, taught me to find excuses to be elsewhere.

The chalets overlooked the huge unheated south bay pool and on arrival our first move was to check the temperature which was chalked up on the board. If it was under 54 degrees Felicity would refuse to go in.

When we bought Park Farm we also bought a caravan to increase accommodation. I had never meant to 'go caravanning' but as the children grew older the pressure to do so increased and I submitted to the following programme.

I said we would visit four of my friends at about 100 mile intervals, Betty and I staying with them for the night while the young Bryans entertained our hosts' children in the caravan for supper.

The selected hosts were the Whitelaws at Penrith, the Leaveys at Gargrave, the Blackadders near Hexham and the Gibsons on the Scottish border. It was all an uproarious success though our hosts were not grateful to us for introducing the whole idea of caravanning into their children's minds.

As we were setting off and I was explaining to Bunny the plans for our friends' children to have supper in the caravan, she said: 'But, Daddy, we don't know these children, do we? What will we talk about?' Next day I asked her how conversation had gone. She said: 'OK, Daddy. I find if you ask them questions then they talk.'

This reminds me of remarks she made some years later after her first oral examination. I asked her how she had got on. She replied: 'I think OK, Daddy. To start with I tried to put him at his ease.' Perhaps this was the first sign of her future career, for as a Deacon she spends much of her life trying to put people at their ease.

Another family trip was to Paris. Some friends had offered us their flat near the Madeleine at short notice and in almost no time we were en route via Stratford on Avon by car to Dover and on by ferry and coach to Paris. Betty, who liked the children to squeeze every benefit out of their experiences, got irritated with Libby who was immersed in her paperback, *The Sinking of the Titanic*, and gave insufficient attention to Anne Hathaway's cottage. Once in the coach Betty fell fast asleep all the way to Paris so Libby had her own back.

Our stay in Paris was a huge success. We did the usual sightseeing; the Eiffel Tower, Versailles and so on but things such as buying breakfast, those yard long rolls, were just as much fun.

Libby had done an exchange with a girl called Chantal de Margerie, of that well-known diplomatic family, one of whom became Ambassador in London. We had supper on the Bateau Mouche with the de Margeries.

Walking through Montmartre with its endless pictures of bare bosomed ladies, Felicity said quite seriously: 'Well, I'm shocked. Aren't you shocked, Daddy?'

* * *

Jimmy Hoyle could not imagine any child or grandchild of his not being a golfer and as she approached her teens he gave Libby a set of golf clubs and some free golf lessons with a professional. Sadly this was a failure. For the first few lessons she was not allowed even to hit the ball. Swing was the thing and what is more his method of perfecting the swing was to tie a string round Libby's arms at elbow level. All this nonsense gave her the perfect excuse to reject once and for all this frustrating game.

Betty brought up the children more by example than by lecture. She was so obviously, if not blatantly, a good person in every sense of the word that the children felt uneasy when they were shown up to be otherwise. She was endlessly kind and considerate for other people but brisk and energetic in the extreme. She demanded a lot of the girls and was always giving them jobs to do. If we were going on a picnic Libby would be told to get it ready and probably to read the map. Felicity might be asked to choose the picnic site. All this suited my military training and no doubt made the children more responsible than they would have been, but it did not necessarily suit all three of them. In the *Sunday Times* article to which I have referred Bunny writes:

> All through our upbringing there was a great stress on getting a lot done and being enormously active. I see that in both my sisters. I'm more contemplative and the inner life interests me a great deal. That's why I do what I do.

She is a Deacon in an inner city parish.

In 1955 Libby finished her school days at Duncombe Park in a blaze of glory - her name on countless boards, Head of the school and with a scholarship to Benenden. The school year ended with the July speech day at which one of the great and the good presented prizes to the girls after the headmistress, the formidable Miss Bowen, had delivered her powerful year's report. The custom then was for the Head Girl's father to give a speech of thanks to the prize presenter. This was a little feature of speech day which the girls enjoyed because all children like to see grown-ups humiliated and, as there was no reason why the Head Girl's father should be a good speaker, this often happened. In my case, being an experienced speaker, I more or less got away with it, or at any rate Libby was not ashamed of me which was what really mattered.

There was no question of Felicity's ever being Head Girl of any school, but six years later Bunny was Head Girl of Duncombe Park and I had to go through the ritual again but in very different circumstances.

By then Miss Bowen had retired to New Zealand, but she had come back to the school she had dominated for so many years to present the prizes on Speech Day.

This was to be her finest hour. I, of course, prepared a speech of eulogy praising her past and saying how much we had all looked forward to the speech which she had just delivered.

This is not how things worked out. The great moment came, Miss Bowen got up and stood there speechless - literally struck dumb by the emotion of the occasion. After a bit she managed to mutter: 'I'll be all right in a minute, please just talk among yourselves.' Far from chatting among ourselves we looked down at our feet in embarrassment until, after a few minutes she managed to utter some disjointed sentences. The sooner this awkward business was over the better so I spoke briefly. I doubt if anybody was listening to what I said.

A few months later in London on her way back to New Zealand I gave her lunch in the House of Commons. I tried to comfort her with assurances that everybody so appreciated her visit, but she was not to be consoled.

By now clothing rationing was at an end and it was time to increase production at J.B.Hoyles. This was easier said than done at Hebden Bridge for the West Riding was still enjoying full employment and the town had a falling population. We had already got some increase in production by the expansion of our factory at Delph near Rochdale, which I have already described. Other textile manufacturers had set up in the Yorkshire coalfield, where miners wives and daughters were happy to become factory workers. The difficulty was to find a factory. I scoured the coalfield calling on the Clerks of the Councils of such towns as Barnsley, Mexborough and Pontefract, only to find that there were practically no suitable buildings available and it was almost impossible to get a building licence. A number of firms from the West Riding had opened branch factories in disused Methodist Chapels with some success but there seemed to be no more of these available.

I finally found an extinct restaurant in the mining town of Wath on Dearne which was completely tumbledown and useless in its present state and managed to extract from the Council a planning permission which, with a stretch of the imagination, enabled us to build a cosy little factory to house 60 girls. Advisers from the Singer Sewing Machine Company told us that it would take years before we could teach miners daughters, with their lack of a manufacturing background, to make satisfactory clothing. They were miles wide of the mark, for under the iron guidance of Marion Walton, the tough former union shop steward from Hebden Bridge they picked it all up at amazing speed and before long were making clothing better and more quickly than their elders at Hebden Bridge.

This little factory at Wath on Dearne proved a double success, for in addition to its own valuable production it provided the backup and training ground for a large factory we were able to build a couple of miles away a few years later when building regulations were relaxed. When this was completed we had in all 180 girls in Wath on Dearne producing far more than the Hebden Bridge factory.

Part Four: Westminster

22
New Boy

The general election for which I had been preparing for so long at last took place on May 26 1955 with the Conservative majority increasing from 17 to 60. Thus the political deadlock created by the negligible majorities of the elections of 1950 and 1951 was fully broken. It was the first time for nearly a century that a political party in office had gone to the country and been returned with a substantial increase in their majority. It could be said to be an emphatic vote of confidence in the work of the Conservative government and in the new Prime Minister, Sir Anthony Eden, who had succeeded Sir Winston Churchill only seven weeks before polling day.

My election campaign in rural Howden was very different from the three I had fought in the textile towns of the West Riding. I had just as many meetings, about 50, but as they were nearly all in villages they were smaller meetings and less lively.

The size of a village audience did not depend entirely on the local Conservative organisation. The small village of Langton in the domain of the Howard-Vyse family, with Colonel Howard-Vyse in the chair, produced a healthy audience of 40. As the Colonel drove me on in the car to the next village, Leavening, I asked him: 'What sort of village is Leavening?' He replied: 'I would call it an ownerless village.' The audience there was only 10.

The only big meeting in the Howden campaign was the eve of poll meeting in the Driffield Town Hall. All three parties had their final meeting there at hourly intervals, so the audience would increase as the night wore on as people who had come for one meeting stayed on for the next. To ensure fairness the parties varied their order of batting from election to election and when it was your turn to have the last meeting it really was fun.

In most political meetings dullness is ensured by the composition of the audience, normally 95 per cent your own supporters. By the third meeting on the eve of the poll in the Driffield Town Hall, the audience could build up to several hundred of all parties in an eve of poll mood.

This was the one and only occasion when I could use the experience I gained in the crowded meetings of the Hebden Bridge Co-op Hall and the Todmorden Market Square. For what it was worth this is where I really could defeat the other two candidates, not that it mattered very much in that the Conservative majority in Howden was so big that I would have had to have been an exceptional Conservative candidate to lose. On polling day Betty and I went with our children to the count at Pocklington, where I became a member of parliament with a majority of 11,399 and so I remained for the next 32 years.

On arriving at Westminster our most immediate problem was to find somewhere to live. Among the few faces that I recognised in the House of Commons on my first day there was that of my Sowerby opponent, Douglas Houghton, who gave me a warm welcome and before I had even raised the question, told me that I must live within walking distance of the House, that he was very happy in a flat at Marsham Court and that although the block was always theoretically full up, if I persevered I would get in.

No-one was a better perseverer than Betty and within a month our London address was 14 Marsham Court until number 36, an even nicer flat on the top floor, came free a few years later.

In those days Marsham Court had its own restaurant and such luxuries as spare bedrooms which you could rent at £2 a night for visiting friends. By lucky chance Willie Whitelaw and Celia had gone through the same routine and had a flat in the far end of the building. Thus it was that he became one of my first friends in the House. Within a year we had both got into Ted Heath's Whips' Office, so often walked to and from our work together.

Bunny was by then seven and for a period was being taught at home by Betty. A game she loved was to go down in the lift on her own, across the lobby and up in the lift on the far side to visit the Whitelaws. I can hear her now pestering Betty to be allowed to do this once again. Betty usually tried to dissuade her but in the end gave in and warned Celia Whitelaw that she was coming. Half an hour later a beaming Bunny would burst back into the flat saying: 'But, Mummy, Mrs Whitelaw was terribly pleased to see me.' Years later, when Bunny as a deaconess was preaching in her sparsely attended church in Slough, whom should she see at the back of the congregation but Celia Whitelaw, by then wife of the Home Secretary, who was staying for the weekend not far away at their official residence, Dorneywood. So their friendship has lasted well.

There are various customs in the House of Commons which seem unfriendly when first you get there, but which in time you can see are inevitable. When you pass another MP in the passage, even if you know him quite well, you soon learn to be unoffended if he gives no signs of recognition. It is, of course, bound to be thus otherwise you would never stop smiling and halloing.

The almost complete separation of the political parties seems strange. The Conservatives do their coffee-housing in the smoke-room, the Labour members in the tea-room. They eat at one end of the dining room, we at the other. You soon see that this is the only way to live a reasonably relaxed day-to-day parliamentary life without having to constantly mind your Ps and Qs.

Nevertheless, to begin with you do rather wonder whether you will ever know any members of the other side at all. In due course this problem solves itself. You perhaps find yourself on a committee with Labour members and after 20 sittings you cannot help knowing some of them pretty well. Or perhaps you go on a parliamentary delegation abroad, with the same result.

Despite all the apparent inter-party aggression it is a unique place for making friends. Whereas in normal life one can only manage perhaps half a dozen close friends, you have no difficulty in having many more there because without any effort on your part your friendships are constantly being renewed. For instance Willie Whitelaw and I clearly knew each other very well in those early Marsham Court days, living close to each other and being thrown together in our daily parliamentary work for our first few years.

Our parliamentary ways parted - his rising into the political stratosphere - and there have been times when I have seen very little of him, but we meet sufficiently often, and expect to see each other sufficiently often to continue to know each other well. To this day, despite the intensity of his life, he comes to stay with me at Park Farm to play golf at Ganton.

In the House of Commons you also have many friendships 'in bud,' ready to blossom. To explain what I mean - if an MP whom I did not know very well told me his boy had just gone to York University, I should undoubtedly say to him: 'Come and spend the weekend.' When that MP and his wife walked through the front door at Park Farm, our friendship would not start from scratch, for in the daily life at Westminster I would have already seen him for a long time in a wide variety of circumstances. It only remains to pass some time together over a jolly family weekend and you will feel that you know him well and, as I have said, the friendship continues because from then onwards parliamentary life automatically keeps you in contact.

When I arrived at Westminster in 1955 the Second World War was only 10 years away, the Korean war had taken place and the threat of war was in the air. A high proportion of one's fellow MPs had been in the forces, with the wide variety of experience which that entailed so we were in that sense a military lot and my own military experience stood me in good stead.

In social composition the House I entered in 1955 was very different from the one I left in 1987. Then, probably a quarter of the Tory members came from Eton, Harrow or Winchester and many from the landed classes. This background did not mean they were amateurs. Churchill, Home, Macmillan, Eden, Edward Boyle, would have been stars in any political firmament. It did, however, mean it was easier to rise in the party if you came from those particular strata of society with all its family and territorial connections and friendships. The door was not closed to others for there was a bright band of distinctly non-cavalry men - Heath, MacLeod, Powell, Maudling - who were clearly on their way to the top.

The Labour party in parliament was equally stratified with its enormous block of trades unionists, actually paid to be there by their unions. It was this matter of pay which was one, but only one, of the reasons for the unbalanced social makeup of the house. We were so poorly paid, with no allowance for secretaries, that you could not attempt to be a member without some private or other outside source of income. I would not have been there had I not had an income as a director and shareholder of J.B.Hoyle and Company.

Now that members of parliament are reasonably paid the landowners and Etonians have been replaced by up and coming businessmen, lawyers and merchant bankers; the trades unionists by schoolmasters, university lecturers and journalists. The IQ of parliament has risen, the quality - who knows? Watch the TV and judge for yourself.

I found members of parliament interesting either because they were interesting people in themselves or because their life involved them in doing interesting things. I never quite got used to the privilege of strolling into the dining room, sitting down at the first handy table and finding that on the right you had the Chancellor of the Exchequer, on your left Airey Neave, the hero of Colditz and opposite you somebody who had just come back from India and been talking to Nehru.

You could never rely on an MP to be useless. Somebody who always appeared to you to be dumb would surprisingly rise in the House and give a speech which showed him to be a world famous apiarist. It was quite easy to pick future ministers, but not future prime ministers. As prime ministers one would have picked Eden, Wilson and Heath but not Churchill, Macmillan, Attlee, Callaghan, Home or Thatcher. Nor did I foresee, as in 1956 I walked home to Marsham Court with Willie Whitelaw, that I was walking with a future Deputy Prime Minister.

In 1956 Churchill had just finished the first volume of his 'History of the English Speaking Peoples' and I thought a signed copy would be an excellent birthday present for Jimmy, my father-in-law. I bought two copies and seeing Churchill drinking brandy at tea-time in the smokeroom, with one copy under my arm and one in my outstretched hand, I went over to him. To the other members there it must have seemed like a Bateman cartoon for they knew he was slow to sign things. I said: 'I wonder whether you would be good enough to sign this copy of your new work, Sir?' A long silence, and then he said: 'I'll sign one of 'em.' Which he duly did and the signed and now inherited book is in the bookcase beside my chair at Park Farm.

The knights of the shires produced a number of 'characters,' of whom I would pick Lieutenant-Colonel Sir Walter Bromley-Davenport as one of the most striking. He was a landowner, a guardsman, an army boxing champion and fast bowler for the parliamentary cricket team. He had a voice as loud as that of a typical sergeant-major of his regiment and on the few occasions that he rose to speak in the chamber of the House of Commons he started by slowly booming out the words: 'Mr Speaker,' at which the members in their most prep-school form would chant: 'Can't hear.'

I did not know him well but once he asked Cynthia and me to Capesthorne, his estate in Cheshire, for the weekend to shoot. He said to me: 'You can't miss my house. It is wider than Buckingham Palace' - and so it was. He was blessed with the most wonderful American wife, Lenette, to whom he and Capesthorne owed much.

Over dinner on our first night there I said to her: 'Now that Walter is retired how does he pass his time?' She said: 'He loves having rows. He goes round the estate having rows. We have had a Spanish cook with whom he has had a row almost every day for the last 20 years and tragically she is leaving. I don't know what he will do.' I pointed out to her that a senior Arab wife in her position would certainly recruit a junior wife to replace the row-taking cook. She seemed interested in the idea.

Walter had the distinction - to my knowledge, unique - of having been knifed, and quite badly knifed, at a Conservative garden party held in the grounds of Capesthorne. After dinner over the port I asked him: 'But why did he knife you, Walter?' 'Well, he was one of my constituents,' he replied.

I must not give the impression that Walter Bromley-Davenport was a mere clown. He was a brilliant actor and maintained the acting tradition for which the theatre at Capesthorne had long been famous. Apart from a wonderful wife and an admirable son and daughter he also had many excellent friends and you can to an extent tell the quality of a man by the quality of his friends. His memorial service held in the open in the courtyard at Capesthorne with David Howell giving the address could not have been more fitting.

An MP's weekly programme within the House of Commons is governed by a document known as the Whip issued by his party Whips' Office every Thursday. On the first page is set out day-by-day the parliamentary business for the following week. Each item is underlined one, two or three times.

If underlined once it is followed by the words 'your presence is requested.' Oddly enough this means 'your presence is voluntary.' If underlined twice it is followed by the words 'your presence is essential unless you have obtained a firm pair.' This means that you must be there at the end of the relevant debate to vote for your party unless you have arranged for a member of the Labour party to 'pair' with you, that is - to be absent also.

To have a permanent 'pair' is a treasured asset. For 21 years I paired with Arthur Bottomley, Secretary of State for Foreign Affairs in the Wilson government. Every weekend we would ring each other up and we would decide which vote we would attend and which we would miss. The perfect pair is somebody who attends the house about as much as you do. If he is hardly ever there he is no good because there will be plenty of debates you feel bound to attend. If he almost lives in the House, again he is useless for he will never want to pair. Arthur and I were well matched. I was dismayed when he was sent to the

Lords, but by good fortune my golfing partner, Gordon Bagier, the member for Sunderland south, took his place for the rest of my parliamentary career. There are, of course, plenty of occasions when you cannot oblige your pair. For instance, when I was Minister of State at the Department of Employment in 1971 we were taking through the lengthy Industrial Relations Bill. As a minister I felt bound to attend every vote, which did not suit Arthur at all.

If the item of business on the Whip is underlined three times it is followed by the words 'your attendance is essential.' This means what it says and only in the most exceptional circumstances will the Chief Whip agree to your being away.

The second page of the Whip gives notice of the meetings of the many party and all-party committees. There is a party committee to correspond with all the main offices of state and the chairmanship of the main committee parties is a position of status, usually held by an ex-minister. I was at one time chairman of the Employment Committee after I had been a minister and we were in opposition.

There is an all-party committee to cover almost every conceivable subject and country. After I had finished being a minister I was asked to be chairman of the all-party Hong Kong group. This grew into a major commitment. By the time I left parliament Cynthia and I had been to Hong Kong 22 times, and to China half-a-dozen times, including in 1972 with the first parliamentary delegation to China. Hong Kong, China and the Far East became one of my main political and later business interests.

The third page of the Whip carries a variety of notices such as particulars of any forthcoming delegations abroad, mostly organised by the Commonwealth Parliamentary Association or the Inter-parliamentary Union.

Within a few weeks of arriving in the House of Commons a notice appeared in the Whip of a visit of a five-member delegation to Peru for three weeks. I put in my application which included the words: 'Degree in Spanish, including South American history.' I suppose no-one else was able to say that, for to my delight and to everybody else's surprise I, a new boy, was included in this attractive trip. I was also rather shocked for it dawned upon me that as the only one in the party alleged to speak Spanish, a heavy load would fall on my shoulders. I found a Nicaraguan doctor and practised Spanish with him every day trying to dig out my dormant fluency, which never really existed.

It was as well that I took the trouble to loosen my Spanish tongue even to this extent for on night one of the tour I was required to broadcast on Radio Lima. This was easier than it sounds. Our embassy produced a polished script which I read out in my Cambridge Castillian, which was in fact quite good and more up-market than the local Peruvian Spanish. Things got tougher the next day when we were being shown around the Law Courts and our haughty Labour delegation leader, Lord Winster said: 'Bryan - tell them that the Lord Chancellor is the keeper of the Queen's conscience.' I declined - it sounded rubbish to me in English; I certainly could not manage it in Spanish. Gradually the Spanish became less of a burden and the tour a real pleasure.

I read Prescott's massive *Conquest of Peru* and became interested in the Inca civilization, the old capital of Cuzco, 13,000 feet up in the Andes and the lost city of Machu Pichu. I found it just as interesting when I went back 30 years later with Cynthia, this time on a South American tour as deputy chairman of Furness Withy and Company, the owner of the Pacific Steam Navigation Company, which has been trading along the west coast of South America since 1845, in those early days in sailing ships.

The first step up the promotion ladder of a member of parliament is to become Parliamentary Private Secretary to a minister or a minister of state, naturally the more senior your minister the grander you feel. Your duties depend almost entirely on how much use your minister wishes to make of you. If he is taking part in a debate in the chamber you sit on the bench directly behind him at his beck and call. If points are raised in the debate on which he needs information he will tell you to go and get it from his civil servant who will be sitting in a box to the right of the Speaker's chair.

Ministers tend to get buried in work in their offices and may hardly come into the House at all for weeks at a time. They depend on their PPSs to keep them in touch with what is happening there. If you want some information from a minister or to get a message to him his PPS is a good channel to use. By frequently going to his minister's department in the mornings he will get to know the civil servants and become generally knowledgeable about the work of the department. Kenneth Baker, the former Home Secretary, was my PPS when I was a minister.

Early in my first parliament I became the first of the new boys to become a PPS. Walter Monckton, the Secretary of State for Defence, lived in Kent and had been in my old regiment. With my military and Kentish background I was a suitable PPS for a Kentish Secretary of State for Defence. I was lucky in that apart from any mutual suitability he was a nice man. A well-known QC, he was probably better known as a friend of Edward VIII who featured in the abdication drama. He brought me into his work to a gratifying degree. Before he was due to give the wind-up speech in a defence debate I would sit in his office in the House with his civil servant as he rehearsed his speech.

There is no doubt that making your maiden speech is quite an ordeal. The bold Disraeli called the House 'The most chilling and nerve-destroying audience in the world.'

Lord North's son gave this account of his maiden effort:

> I brought out two or three sentences, when a mist seemed to rise before my eyes. I then lost my recollection and could see nothing but the speaker's wig, which swelled and swelled and swelled until it covered the whole House. I then sank back on my seat and never attempted another speech but quickly accepted the Chiltern Hundreds.

I did not suffer quite to this extent but was nevertheless glad to get the thing over. I decided to give my maiden speech on transport and went as far as going to Germany to study their autobahn system to give myself some original material. I gave quite an articulate but entirely unmemorable speech and the following speaker, in this case Fred Mulley, was complimentary, as is the custom after a maiden speech.

A.P.Herbert, typically, made his maiden speech on his second day in the House. Winston Churchill said to him: 'Call that a maiden speech? It was a brazen hussy of a speech. Never did such a painted lady of speech parade itself before a modest parliament.' No doubt to his lasting regret, Winston Churchill was not in the Chamber when I spoke so we shall never know what his verdict on mine might have been.

It is as well on arriving in the House to choose several subjects upon which you are going to concentrate, but that choice is not necessarily valid for long. By the end of my parliamentary career I had become knowledgeable on broadcasting, China and the Far East, and industrial relations and in debates on these subjects would always be called by the Speaker. This was a far cry from transport.

A.P.Herbert called the chamber of the House of Commons 'the torture chamber' and it must be conceded that those who choose to give speeches there are accepting conditions quite unacceptable to the average speaker.

As a start you get very short notice of debates. A debate on a Monday can have only been announced on the previous Thursday, giving you only a (probably already busy) weekend to prepare your contribution. Say the debate is on farming, an important constituency subject, you decide you must speak and quickly get in touch with the local National Farmers' Union to hear what they would like you to say. Having put the final touches to your speech in the train coming down from York you take your place in your usual seat in the chamber just before half-past three, when debates normally start, only to find that the Foreign Secretary has first to give a statement on his trip to Russia which, together with questions, takes an hour and by then everybody is ready for a cup of tea and the numbers in the House are reduced to the sprinkling of members who actually want to take part in the farming debate.

By the time the minister and his opposite number have finished their opening speeches it is six o'clock, at which point all those wishing to take part in the debate rise in their places. You are appalled to see they number not less than 30, all hoping to have their say before the debate finishes at 10 o'clock. The Speaker calls members alternately from each side of the House, who seldom talk less than 10 minutes and often almost half an hour, and after a couple of hours of this you get worried and timidly go to the Speaker's chair and politely ask him if he is going to be able to 'fit you in.' He may say: 'I am afraid not. You did after all make a speech last week' - in which case all your labours are in vain and what will the NFU say? Or he may say: 'I will try and fit you in a little later but could you confine your remarks to something under 10 minutes.'

You go back to your seat and wrack your brains as to how you are going to halve that carefully prepared speech. Meanwhile the debate goes on. Each time a member finishes his speech, 30 aspirants jump to their feet, the Speaker chooses one of them, 29 rumps return to their moorings. At about eight o'clock, having had no tea you long for some dinner or at any rate a whisky but you feel that if you leave your seat you may miss your chance. You are proved right and at quarter past eight you are called.

Now the time has at last come to speak you are required to do so in circumstances unknown to any normal speaker. Your audience is all around you and above you in the Strangers Gallery and the Press Gallery.

Just as you have got going nicely a voice pipes up from behind you with the words: 'Will the honourable gentleman allow me...' meaning he wants to interrupt you to ask a question. Keen to please the House you say: 'Certainly' and sit down while he asks you some barmy question which serves no purpose but to put you off your stride.

The audience is constantly on the move. Members go in and out of the Chamber, summoned by telephone messages, hunger or thirst. Just as you think the Minister is absorbing your most trenchant point, he turns to have a word with his junior minister, nods to the Speaker, goes out of the door behind the Speaker's chair to his room, never to be seen again, at any rate for the duration of your speech.

By now your speech is a ghost of its original well-prepared self. The Speaker has caused you to halve it. Coming on so late in the debate several of your best points have already been made embarrassingly often by others and you haven't the face to serve them up again.

When at last you sit down, far from satisfied with your own performance, you long more than ever for a drink in the smokeroom, but good manners decree that you must remain in the chamber until the member following you has finished his speech - by which time the front bench speakers are in action with their winding up speeches and you must be in the chamber for these too in case they mention your speech, which they probably will.

If you are called late in a debate there is no chance of your remarks being recorded in the morning papers, apart from a niggardly phrase which reads: 'Mr Smith, Mr Brown and Mr Bryan also spoke,' though if your agent has done his duty you should get more generous treatment in the weekly *Driffield Times*.

The House of Commons is not an efficient organisation. I know no other country of similar size that requires 640 members of parliament working at the most outlandish hours to get through the business of government. On the other hand the British citizen gets a service from his member of parliament unequalled in the world. The reason that the Ombudsman, so successful an innovation in Sweden and other countries, has never made any impression in Britain is that the member of parliament already provides a better and more familiar service of the same sort. As our constituencies are small, averaging only about 70,000 voters, we do know them well and our constituents can get hold of us easily by letter, telephone or at a constituency surgery. We in turn can easily convey their views or questions to ministers owing to the form of our daily routine at Westminster.

If, say, at the Driffield Show, a constituent asked me a question about the budget I could safely say: 'I will ask the Chancellor of the Exchequer and let you know.' I would know that I would be meeting the Chancellor in the lobby when we were both voting and would have no difficulty in having a word with him. Ministers welcome routine contacts of this sort for it saves them formal interviews or correspondence. I always think that this easy connection between constituent and parliament is one of the most valuable features of our democratic system. Familiarity is said to breed contempt but lack of personal contact breeds disillusion and distrust.

One is often asked what an MP can do for a constituent anyway? Sometimes a lot. Once on a Sunday afternoon a Yorkshire voice came through to me over the telephone at Park Farm saying that his sister's husband in the forces was very sick in Aden. After a few words of sympathy I asked him what he wanted me to do about it, to which he answered that he did not know. I rang up the duty officer at the Ministry of Defence, and told him the story. A couple of hours later he rang me back and confirmed that the man was on the danger list and said that if I could get the lady to London the Ministry would fly her out to Aden. A little later another telephone call came through from the RAF Station at Driffield, who had been informed, saying that they had a special local benevolent fund which could be used to pay the train fare to London. In the event the wife went to Aden and was with her husband when sadly he died.

Not many constituency cases are as dramatic as that. Much of one's mail is about housing and should more properly be addressed to the local council. Other letters are about schooling, where one may not often be able to do much but where, due to one's close contact with the Chief Education Officer, one can give advice.

In my early years one of my most persistent and tiresome correspondents was Sir William Prince-Smith, who owned an estate at Southburn on the Wolds, specialising in pedigree Suffolk sheep and

Aberdeen Angus cattle. He never stopped complaining, was rude and ungrateful even when I was able to do something for him. In the end I wrote saying that I had had enough and I would deal with him no more. The about-turn was immediate and complete. I was asked to dinner, asked to shoot and his letters became positively courteous, his manner more than friendly.

All in all I got satisfaction out of this pastoral side of my life as a member of parliament. I did not often have special surgeries of the sort where, for instance you announce that you are available to constituents at six o'clock in the Town Hall at Goole. More often I put an advertisement in the paper which said: 'Paul Bryan will be in Market Weighton on Saturday, May 4th. Those wishing to see him should make an appointment with the agent, telephone Pocklington 3169.' I would seldom get more than half a dozen replies and I would go and see these people in their houses. This suited everybody. The constituent probably didn't actually live in Market Weighton itself but in a village nearby so it saved his or her coming into the town. As a member of parliament you can get a far better idea of a constituent's problem in his home and probably meeting the family. Often the problem put before you was quite insoluble and the constituent just wanted to get it off his chest - but even that is of some value.

Quite early on in one's parliamentary career one has to answer the question - what sort of MP do I want to be?

Like 75 per cent of my fellow members of parliament I had a safe seat and therefore my level of activity was entirely my own decision. If I overworked myself in the constituency this was my fault and no-one else's. It was also a very easy thing to do. The more invitations to meetings, whist drives, coffee mornings and prize-givings you accept, the more you are asked, and the whole programme gets out of hand. In a constituency measuring 60 miles by 50 with 130 villages, you can find yourself spinning round like a hamster in a wheel.

Sometimes, rather than react to invitations it was more effort-economical to initiate them. For instance, if I had to go 35 miles to Bugthorpe my agent would arrange for me to call in at several other villages en route.

It was important to squeeze every scrap of available goodwill out of the functions I attended. Cynthia, my second wife, was especially good at this. If we were going to a coffee morning at Foggathorpe in the home of Mrs Smith, she would ring her up the day before, ask her at what time she would like us to come, whom we would meet, what if anything she would especially like me to mention in my talk and so on. Thus was I able to make the best of my time when I did arrive. The next day Cynthia would ring up Mrs Smith to ask how much money had been made and to congratulate her on the event. I would write her a note and we would make sure the affair was reported in the local paper.

In all this constituency work, as you can imagine, a wife can be invaluable. Betty was excellent with constituents and she often went to events on her own, though of course she was not always available when the children were at home in the holidays.

Wives can be of importance to an MP, not only helping him in the constituency but keeping him up to the mark. In an election campaign or even over a long weekend when one is delivering speech after speech, it is so easy to get slack and let your standards fall. Not even your agent will point this out but both of my wives certainly did. After the 1979 General Election the 'House Magazine' carried a poem written by the aunt of a former member of parliament, Tom Benyon - it was called 'The Winner.' It should be read, learnt and inwardly digested by all members of parliament.

> When in a hall she must never look tired
> But listen intently and hear him admired
> Perhaps as she listens to speech forty-four
> Not an inkling she gives that she's heard it before
>
> And oh, the post mortems that go on each night
> With 'What did you think?' or 'Was I all right?'
> Then when it's all over, victorious or spurned
> Remember the person who really has earned
>
> That glass of champagne, the speeches, the toast
> Then comes the speech that is truer than most
> 'I couldn't have done it without my dear wife.'
> You couldn't, my friend, you bet your sweet life.

Some MPs set up a regular PR machine in their constituencies, scanning the local papers to see who in the constituency should get letters of congratulation or condolences for this and that and sending letters to children who had passed examinations. This seemed to me a thoroughly unnatural operation. I confined myself to letters to 18 year olds, welcoming them onto the electoral register. This was after all something in which we had a mutual interest.

In constituency life, as in marriage, it is as well to start as you mean to go on. I have heard MPs boast that their local newspaper has asked them to write a weekly article. This is a fearful trap; producing the article week after week becomes more and more of a bind. The article gets worse. In the end you have to give it up and suffer the accompanying discredit.

In my early days in parliament, speeches in the constituencies were quite a toil. You were expected to speak for half an hour and each constituent wanted his special interest to be mentioned. Nor did questions abound to brighten up the show. With the development of broadcasting with its chat shows and phone-ins, people got used to asking questions which made speaking easier and the evening more interesting. In the end I got accustomed to speaking for no more than five minutes during which I told them about the doings in the House of Commons in the past week and then took questions for half an hour or more. This tactic earned you more credit, was sure to cover every subject in which your audience was interested and, best of all, took no preparation.

Speeches did not always go exactly as anticipated. I was once asked to speak at the inaugural lunch of a Conservative Ladies' Luncheon Club. Chatting over sherry before lunch with the lady entitled Speaker Finder, I said: 'Miss Byass, could I be of help in finding you future speakers for your luncheon club?' Eagerly and intensely she replied: 'No, I think we will be all right, Mr. Bryan. To start with we are having people like you who do not charge. Like that we hope to build up a fund so that we can afford some really good speakers.' Her plan must have worked like a charm. I was never invited again.

In my very agricultural constituency there are half a dozen agricultural shows which Betty and I never missed. This was a pleasant part of constituency work. We took the children, and probably some of their friends and as the years went by got to know the farmers and their families in each place really well. Driffield was by far the biggest of these shows. The attendance could be up to 14,000 with probably three-quarters of them my constituents. Inconveniently it took place on a Wednesday but I gave it such high priority that I never missed coming up from London for the day to be there. I used also to put a notice in the Driffield Times which said : 'Paul Bryan will be at the Driffield Show. Those wishing to see him are asked to approach him on the showground.' People seldom did but at least it announced to the populace that I was there in case they didn't see me.

You often read of political lobbying of MPs and indeed plenty of organised groups from time to time want to see you about hanging, abortion, Sunday trading, the Market Weighton by-pass or the closing of the Pocklington railway. In facing these lobbies MPs show surprising courage or lack of it. For instance, on the subject of hanging I think MPs are brave. Nothing is more certain than that there is a large though diminishing majority in favour of capital punishment and yet time and again, at least once per parliament, the majority of MPs vote against the known wishes of their constituents.

On the other hand, on Sunday trading they are weak as water. Shopping on Sunday is already well tried and completely successful in Scotland. More people go to Church there than in England and then they go shopping with their families which gives welcome part-time work to many and everyone is happy. But in one's constituency the anti-shopping lobby is highly organised and vocal while the would-be shoppers are silent. Great meetings are organised, one's political opponents are asked to attend, but I never did. Those sort of meetings just become one-sided shouting matches. Instead I invited the leaders of the anti-shoppers to come and meet me for a discussion and then had it reported in the local paper. On the last occasion this came up I then spoke in favour of Sunday trading in the debate in the House.

The work of an active MP can disrupt family life and all my sympathy goes to a provincial member who has started his parliamentary career with a family of say, three under the age of 10. Inevitably he will see little of them. When he is home at the weekends he is preoccupied with his constituency and his wife can be under intolerable stress.

I was lucky in that my children were at boarding school in my early days in parliament and my constituency being near Park Farm tended to add to their social life. Later when the children got to the university stage I could certainly identify with their lives with greater ease than if I had remained a trouser manufacturer for life.

I have argued so far that it is up to the MP himself to keep his working life in reasonable bounds, but it must be admitted that, especially if a minister, 'impossible' weeks are sometimes unavoidable.

I remember one such week when I was the Minister of State for the Department of Employment. After a busy Monday in the Department, we had an all night sitting. Tuesday was another busy day receiving several delegations, who really would have preferred to see the Secretary of State, following by a fairly late night in the House. Early on Wednesday morning I departed by train with Bernard Ingham, the Press Officer, for Newport, Wales, to open a training school. On Newport station unexpectedly the BBC wanted an interview after which the representative of the local Conservative Association asked me to drop in on a Young Conservative lunch to say a few words after I had finished with the training school. I arrived back that night to find that my Secretary of State, Robert Carr, had 'flu and that I would have to take all his questions at Question Time in the House next day. So all Thursday morning was spent closeted with civil servants swotting up answers to both Robert's and my questions and to the supplementary questions which were likely to follow. All this activity meant that I was far behind with my letters and the documents I was meant to study. I went back to Yorkshire with a red box full of documents to look at in the train and the promise of two more such boxes which would be delivered to Park Farm. On the Friday evening there were three events in the constituency involving about a 120 miles, on Saturday there was a prize-giving at a speech day and in the evening more constituency activity. On Sunday there was certainly no question of golf as I dealt with the contents of the red boxes and by the end of the weekend I was just in danger of being sorry for myself, which would have been absurd, for the golden rule must be - if you don't actually feel lucky to be a member of parliament, give it up.

On such occasions I reminded myself of a conversation I had once had in Hong Kong in the early hours of the morning. My host was a man in his fifties who had achieved every material success he could possibly have imagined when he set out on his career. He was immensely rich with superb houses in Hong Kong, Sydney and the south of France, where he also had a yacht. He was still director of a bank, but otherwise, being childless, had not enough to fill his agile mind. After an exquisite dinner, our tongues loosened by wines and brandy to match, we talked deep into the night. He said: 'Yours is the life I covet. You are successful and active but more importantly, parliament, your constituency and Park Farm give you continuity and friends.'

This was a shrewd judgement for an outsider. I have already explained that in parliament one is able to have an abnormal number of close friends because the mechanics of life there enables you constantly to renew your friendships. But in addition there are all your friendly acquaintances, the clerks of the house, the badge servants, the policemen, the waitresses, the staff in the Post Office, those clever, helpful girls in the library, the man in the ticket office, clerks in the vote office, the Speaker's secretary, my own marvellous secretary - not to mention the lady in the tea-room who, when I reached the head of the queue, used to say: 'Flora with your crumpets, Sir Paul?' - they are all there without any effort on your part, session after session and one blesses the continuity of it all.

The same applies in the constituency. When first I became a member of parliament, I wondered how I would ever get to know the people in the 134 villages stretched across the East Riding of Yorkshire. But there are so many things that you do regularly like attending agricultural shows, the Remembrance Day parade, point-to-point meetings, constituency annual general meetings, which, added to all the constituency cases, builds up a band of friends which due to the stability of the population in the East Riding, is constant and always growing. There are of course those whom you meet regularly and often, such as your agent and chairman. In 32 years I had only five agents and not many more chairmen. Anthony Preston was my chairman for 10 years. How can one be luckier than have a chairman and his wife who are such friends that you become godfather of their child? William Legard, another of my chairmen, married my agent, Helen Lepine, and I am godfather to their Arabella.

Despite its size Howden was an easier constituency to know than, say, a small suburban one because the population if not static was certainly stable. A certain amount of building was always going on around such towns and villages as Driffield, Market Weighton and Holme-on-Spalding Moor, but not to such an extent or at such a speed as to alter the profile of the population. In some Home County seats you are addressing a different electorate from election to election.

23
Government Whip

Ted Heath was a remarkable Chief Whip. His appointment only five years after he had got into the house was in itself exceptional. Historically, Chief Whips were cavalry types who had been in the House for a long time. Ted was the son of a builder and had been in the House for a very short time.

When one day in the lobby he asked me if I would like to join his Whips' Office, I replied naively: 'I take it I ought to accept.' To which he said 'Yes, you should.' I should have been elated, for this meant that Michael Hughes-Young, who came into the Whips' Office at the same time, and I were to be the first of the new boys to join the government.

Joining the Whips' Office was one of the best things that happened to me in my political career. When I arrived at Westminster I knew few members of parliament. Most of my fellow new arrivals had had a longer and wider, if not more intense, experience of politics. They had been prominent in the Union at Oxford or Cambridge, active in the Conservative Party in the country or maybe in local government. My knowledge of MPs was limited to the few I had met in Yorkshire.

Membership of the Whips' Office at once made me friends, and soon close friends, with a dozen specially picked MPs. There it was that I first got to know Willie Whitelaw and Tony Barber who have been friends ever since. The choice of whips was in the hands of the Chief Whip but he never made an appointment without first discussing it with the other members of the office, for it was all important that we should be a harmonious team.

When I entered the Whip's office in 1956 my fellow whips were:

Ted Heath: Chief Whip.

Martin Redmayne DSO: Deputy Chief Whip. Shy and dour he was a successful territorial brigadier in the war. He became Chief Whip in the next Conservative government, not too happy an appointment, and after a spell as a minister went to the Lords where he did little politically but became managing director of Harrods.

Sir Hendry Oakshott. A rather aristocratic timber merchant.

Sir Gerald Wills. A member of the tobacco family.

Richard Thompson. A naval officer who was soon promoted to ministerial rank in the Ministry of Health.

Peter Legh. He succeeded his father as Lord Newton.

Tony Barber. A barrister, wartime pilot and escaper, became Parliamentary Private Secretary to the Prime Minister, Harold Macmillan, and finished up as Chancellor of the Exchequer. He later became chairman of the Standard and Chartered Bank; his personal assistant there was John Major, the future Prime Minister.

Harwood Harrison: The most dogged character I have ever met. Having been through all the trials of a prisoner of war of the Japanese he rejoined his regiment as a territorial officer after the war so that he could finish up commanding his battalion, which he duly did. The Whips' Office was the limit of his ministerial career. Though a highly effective local member of parliament who converted his seat from 'marginal' to 'safe' he was, rightly, so doubtful of his own speaking ability that he got one of us, his fellow whips, to come and address his own constituency annual general meeting, usually, of course, the preserve of the sitting member. Given a few more prisoners like Harwood, the Japanese might well have surrendered without our resort to the atom bomb.

Jo Godber. A horticulturalist, joined the cabinet as Minister of Agriculture.

Michael Hughes-Young MC. The most charming member of the Whips' Office, was a regular army lieutenant-colonel in the Black Watch badly wounded in the war. He and I got into the Whips' Office together and almost at once his wife died leaving him with five children under 16 and a big house. With the aid of a classic family nanny he coped wonderfully well. He lost his seat of Wandsworth in 1964, and went to the House of Lords as Lord St Helens. Tragedy struck him again, for his son and heir, the apple of his eye, was killed in a hunting accident. His daughter, Henrietta, is married to Denis Forman's nephew.

Edward Wakefield. Brother of the famous rugger player, had already had one brilliant career in the Indian Civil Service. He left us to become High Commissioner of Malta, leaving a great gap in the office for he was as entertaining as talented.

Graeme Finlay. A barrister, stayed in the Whips' Office for a long time but never reached ministerial rank.

Dick Broomam-White. An Etonian and well-known horseman with the build of a jockey, was a clever Scotsman who had been a lieutenant-colonel in the Intelligence Corps.

That was the Whips' Office which I entered in 1956. Others to join us during my time were:

Willie Whitelaw MC. Finished up as Deputy Prime Minister to Margaret Thatcher.

David Gibson-Watt MC. One of the very few officers to win three MCs in the war. Became Minister of State in the Welsh Office and is now in the House of Lords.

Robin Chichester-Clarke. From the well-known Northern Ireland family, he succeeded me as Minister of State at the Department of Employment in the Heath government of 1972.

Richard Sharples MC. One of Monty's personal aides in the European campaign. He was assassinated when Governor of Bermuda.

We were a warlike squad - a brigadier, six lieutenant-colonels, three majors, a naval commander and a fighter pilot - and gallant withal for we could flaunt two DSOs and seven MCs between us.

The Chief Whip's task is to get government business through the House of Commons and to do this he must have a system by which he knows how much support or opposition a bill will receive. For example, early in my parliamentary career there was a controversial bill, the Rent Bill, the result of which would have put up the rents of nearly all council house tenants. Ted Heath had a Whips meeting and asked each of us in turn what our various MPs thought of the Rent Bill. From this meeting he concluded that we did not know enough about their attitudes and we were told to go and find out more.

Each Whip had about 35 members to look after, mine being northern members, and during the next day or two I sought them out to get the information Ted wanted. From the information we gave him he was able to gauge how many would vote for the bill, how many would be unhappy about it and how many would actually vote against it. Thus it might be decided that the Minister in charge ought to go and address the party housing committee to explain the bill or the Minister might see personally those who were unhappy about it. The information garnered by the Whips' Office might result in the bill's being amended before ever it was published.

I found all this questioning of my members to be a great help in getting to know them. I would never have found much small talk to offer the crusty old Lieutenant-Colonel Leonard Ropner, the member for Barkston Ash (Selby), but telling him the Chief Whip wished to know his opinions on various subjects pleased him and he became quite voluble. Nevertheless he found it difficult to master my name and for the first two years of our acquaintance he called me 'Kershaw.' When at last he mastered Bryan he still forgot it again under stress. Once he came storming into the Whips' Office to complain of some alleged outrage but, finished his tirade to the Deputy Chief Whip with the words: 'Mind you, Kershaw was perfectly charming about it.'

Early in my life as a whip I received a sharp lesson in tact. One night a vote was due in about three quarters of an hour and I could see no sign of a less reliable sheep of my flock. I therefore decided to ring him up at home and remind him of the vote. The 'phone was answered by his wife who said 'I am afraid John is not here. He is at the House of Commons.' I only just stopped myself saying: 'But he's not.' This was a situation which I was to meet a number of times.

You might wonder how in that maze of a building I knew that John was not at the Palace of Westminster.

An almost infallible method of finding somebody there is via the Badge Servant on duty. Members of Parliament are looked after by an admirable corps of Badge Servants, all ex-warrant officers from the forces, each attired in white tie and tails with a large and splendid badge around his neck. As one of their duties is to deliver messages to members wherever they may be they acquire a miraculous knowledge of MPs' habits and movements. In my search for John I had only to go to the Badge Servant and say: 'Have you seen Mr Blenkinsop?' and the reply might well have been: 'Well, he is certainly not in the chamber. If he is not in his room he is usually in the smoking room or working in the library. But I think he is probably not here. I have not seen him pass through the members' lobby.'

An unenviable job in the Whips' Office and which for that reason only lasts a year is pairing Whip. I took over pairing Whip in 1958 from Tony Barber and handed it on to Willie Whitelaw. Your main duty is to be in a position to tell the Chief Whip at any moment the state of the party in the House in terms of votes. Consequently you must know in detail who is ill, who is on delegations abroad, who is absent or likely to be absent for any reason whatsoever. This can be nerve-wracking. Within two days of taking over my duties as pairing Whip we lost a vote, a very unusual happening, against my prediction. Ted Heath was not pleased. Your second duty, less nerve-wracking but more embarrassing, is to be on the receiving end when members want to be away for a vote and cannot find a pair. As one who had only been in the House for four years I found it embarrassing to have to tell some senior member that he could not attend his granddaughter's christening or his son's first appearance in the school first XI.

When the House is sitting there is always a Whip on duty sitting on the front bench in a position near the Speaker's chair. He is the stage manager. He has to make sure that all the players are present and ready to take their part. Well before the end of a debate he will check up to see that the minister responsible for the next debate is in sight. He will observe all that is happening and report anything noteworthy at the next Whips meeting. This daily duty on the bench taught one a lot about parliamentary procedure and about one's fellow members.

There is a Whips meeting in the House every afternoon at 2.15 and a weekly meeting on Wednesdays at midday at number 12 Downing Street, the Chief Whip's Office, a pleasant Georgian house where the walls of the fine room in which they meet are covered with team photographs of Whips over the ages.

In addition to being allotted a number of members to look after you are given subjects to cover. If for instance you are the Whip responsible for finance you will have to be in constant attendance when the Finance Bill goes upstairs into committee. For a period in the spring the committee will sit every Tuesday and Thursday morning and maybe in the afternoon and evening too. All this time the Whip has to be there, making sure his members are present in sufficient numbers to carry the bill through.

One Whip, entitled Vice Chamberlain of Her Majesty's Household, has the duty of sending a daily report of the proceedings of the House to the Queen. During question time you will see him on the second row opposite the Speaker's chair, taking his notes. You are not allowed to give any speeches in the House when you are a Whip.

You might ask why, with such an arduous life to offer, anybody wants to go into the Whips' Office. The main answer is that it is a well trodden route to promotion. The present Prime Minister was Whip. In my case it was a marvellous way to get to know the House, its proceedings and its members early in my career.

The senior Whips have some high sounding titles. Patronage Secretary, Treasurer or Comptroller or Vice-Chamberlain of Her Majesty's Household describe the four top Whips. The next five are entitled Lord Commissioners of the Treasury. Those below that rank are Assistant Whips and unpaid.

I served under Ted Heath for four long years in the Whips' Office and got to know him well. It was a very satisfying period for me. Just as in the war I felt privileged to serve under an officer of the calibre of Swifty Howlett, so did I feel lucky, in my first parliament, to serve under Ted Heath. Considering he had only been in the House of Commons for five years he had a remarkable grip of the day-to-day parliamentary situation. He had complete confidence in ordering about the senior ministers. He was serious but with a sense of humour which anyone will know who has heard him give an after dinner speech.

He used his whips relentlessly. He seldom gave his own view until he had squeezed us dry. We worked hard for him but great were the rewards in the Whips' Office. Most of us became ministers in due course. In his time many of the best perks went to whips. For instance in 1962 I was picked to go on a wonderful two month tour of the United States as a guest of the State Department and I am sure I would not have been invited to lunch with the Queen had I not been a whip.

At no time did I get an inkling of the disgruntled and sometimes sour character into which - to the public - Ted appears to have developed. In parliament he seemed to forget his friends - a mistake some politicians like Rab Butler or Willie Whitelaw would never make.

As a result, when he was challenged for the leadership by Margaret Thatcher in 1976, he was sorely short of friends.

His bitterness after his defeat by Margaret Thatcher for a time killed his political influence. It was so deep that you suspect it of influencing any judgement he makes. When in the Gulf War, against the wishes of the government, he went on his mission to see Saddam Hussein it was widely suspected, probably quite wrongly, that he did this to annoy Mrs Thatcher. After he came back he was endlessly on television full of scorn for the Allied leaders in their incredibly difficult positions or belittling George Bush as inadequate in such a world crisis, and forecasting a long war, in most of which he was proved wrong.

Perhaps a wife would have prevented the hardening of his nature. To win her he would have had to make his bid early in his life.

Life in the Whip's Office is always eventful and frequently unpredictable. Who would have predicted the Suez Crisis, the fall of Anthony Eden and the rise of Harold Macmillan, all of which followed each other in quick succession in 1956?

The Suez event is now looked back upon as a traumatic blunder which finally marked the end of Britain as an imperial power. For most of the last 300 years Britain, a small power in terms of population, maintained the most powerful Navy in the world to keep open our trade routes and communications with our empire. The Navy had fulfilled precisely this role in a war that had ended only 11 years before. So when Nasser took over the Suez canal, the most fragile joint in the whole body of the Empire, the instinct of the British throughout the land was to resist. I doubt if the cabinet, a very experienced cabinet, was as determined as the average British citizen, but at its head was a determined Prime Minister in Anthony Eden, an Arab expert. From a conversation I had with Walter Monckton a few months later I concluded that it was Eden's absolute conviction that carried the Government into war as, 30 years later, it was Margaret Thatcher's conviction that carried her cabinet into the Falklands War, with happier results.

But he was not alone. Harold Macmillan's diary of August 18 1956 reads:

> If Nasser gets away with it, we are done for. It may well be the end of British influence and strength for ever. So in the last resort we must use force and defy opinion here and overseas.

My only objections to the operation were military. With the prolonged build-up of the assault force, surprise was out of the question; and what was to happen after the army had captured a 100 mile long canal? Were we ready to occupy the area forever?

Weary months followed: by the time the British and French launched an attack on military targets on October 31st, controversy engulfed parliament and the nation and it did not end with the ceasefire on November 6th in compliance with a United Nations resolution. We had been defeated not by the Egyptians but by the Americans, who had made it clear that if we did not respect the United Nations resolution no further economic support could be expected for our creaking economy.

With the passage of more than 30 years Suez still appears as the historic watershed of the post 1945 era, certainly for Britain and only to a lesser extent France. Suez made it clear that henceforth Britain would find it hard, if not impossible, to pursue a foreign policy independent of the United States.

Soon after Suez Anthony Eden resigned, exhausted. His health made his departure inevitable but I do not believe that politically he would have survived. He was a surprisingly bad Prime Minister. From my point of vantage in the Whips' Office he always looked ill-at-ease, irritable and in a hurry. I say 'surprisingly' because he had been Churchill's unchallenged heir apparent for so many years and his record was so immaculate that much was expected of him.

The installation of a new Prime Minister was a cosy affair compared with the traumatic elections suffered by Heath and Thatcher. After seeking advice from Sir Winston Churchill and the Marquis of Salisbury, the Queen sent for Harold Macmillan. His years of progress towards No.10 Downing Street had been as erratic as Eden's had been serene. In his early days in parliament he had been considered very much the odd man out and it was 17 years before he got a government job of any sort. It was his work in the war, as a minister mainly in North Africa and Italy that brought him into the front line of politicians and by now he was Chancellor of the Exchequer.

Relatively unknown and a period piece in appearance, manner and conversation, Macmillan looked an unlikely starter. But he gradually and unmistakably asserted himself in the chamber of the House of Commons and on the foreign scene, starting with talks in Bermuda with President Eisenhower which began to repair the damage inflicted by the Suez operations on our relations with the Americans.

The Prime Minister is traditionally the guest of the Government Whips for dinner every year. At our dinner with Macmillan just before the Christmas recess in 1957 he said: 'Over the last year I think we have got the confidence of the party back in the House of Commons. Over the next year we must get back the confidence of the country.' And this was precisely what happened.

There were plenty of dramas. Shortly after that very dinner the Chancellor of the Exchequer and his two Treasury Ministers resigned on the eve of his departure for a tour of the Commonwealth. We kept losing by-elections, hard-to-defend troubles in Nyasaland and particularly Hola Camp embarrassed us in the House of Commons, but through all these trials Macmillan, with the aid of the newly arrived television, was gaining in stature while his party gained in confidence and on October 8th 1959 the Conservatives won the election, increasing their majority to 100. My majority in Howden went up by 1500 to nearly 13,000. On the same day Margaret Thatcher entered the House of Commons for the first time as the member of parliament for Finchley with a majority of 16,260.

In 1957 Guy Mollet, the French Prime Minister, was worried about the bad press which the revolution in Algeria was getting in Britain. He therefore invited a delegation of Lords and MPs to see the scene for themselves and I was lucky enough to be included in the party, presumably because of my experience in North Africa during the war.

Led by Walter Elliott, the very Scottish wartime Cabinet Minister, we were a varied group. The House of Lords was represented by the eccentric Lord Hinchingbrooke and the socialist Earl of Listowel, brother of the Conservative Member of Parliament John Hare, with whom I was to work closely in my next job. The Conservative members of parliament were Julian Amery, son of Leo Amery, and myself. George Thompson, a Scottish journalist, later to become Chairman of the Independent Broadcasting Authority; Wilfred Fienburgh of the Daily Mirror and Sir Lyn Ungoed Thomas, QC, Solicitor General in the previous government, were the Labour members.

Walter Elliott was a model delegation leader; politically wise, considerate, amusing and, though no linguist, he managed to impress the French. He would start each of the many small speeches he had to make as we toured around with a few well chosen words which you imagined would sound impressive even to those who could not understand them. He would then say: 'I will ask Mr Amery to express the thanks of our delegation in your own tongue,' on which Julian would scintillate slightly overlong in the most perfect French.

Walter Elliott treated us not as a delegation but as 10 individuals, a lesson I remembered when in later years I led delegations to Mexico and Hong Kong. When he was sitting next to me on a flight from Algiers to Constantine he said: 'Paul, are you getting all you expected out of this trip?' I was quite taken aback by his concern. In fact I was fascinated by every minute of our tour.

On parliamentary delegations one often makes unlikely friendships. Wilfred Fienburgh was a character with whom I had nothing superficially in common, but by the end of our tour I had had a number of long conversations with him and felt I knew him well. Denis Healey writes of him in his autobiography:

> Wilfred's good looks and big brown eyes often led him astray. After entering parliament in 1951 he recorded his adventures in a novel *No Love for Johnnie*. It gives a good picture of the post-war Labour party and was made into a powerful film.

He spoke with a nondescript accent which at first might place him as an officer in an English county regiment. Nevertheless I said to him: 'When did you leave Yorkshire?' 'How did you know I come from Yorkshire?' he replied. 'Because you say CONtrol instead of conTROL.' He then went on to tell me with great frankness that in the war he had observed that the only way to become an officer was to speak like an officer, so he completely changed his mode of speech, duly became a subaltern in the Rifle Brigade and was badly wounded in Normandy.

Before the war he had been a fiery young trades union leader in the textile industry. So militant did he become that no mill in Bradford would employ him. This was a world I knew well from my years in Halifax and I said: 'I am surprised you are not more bitter.' He said: 'Ah, but I am.' Denis Healey says:

> In my opinion Fienburgh might have been a candidate for the Labour leadership if he had lived but some demon made him accident prone; in 1958 he was killed in a car crash, when only 37 years old.'

I was expecting to meet a dejected French army depressed by the hopelessness of their situation in Algeria and still smarting from the humiliation of Dien Bien Phu and their ejection from French Indo-China. But as I noticed in the war in North Africa, the French never seem humiliated by what is by now a long tradition of defeat. The army we came to visit in the hills of Algeria was positively perky. The troops were young and their senior officers correspondingly so. They were smart, well equipped, morale was high as it tends to be when you are dominating the enemy and appear to have the upper hand. If enemy movement was detected or suspected an officer and half a dozen troops would jump into a helicopter and fly off to sort out the trouble. This sort of fighting with plenty happening but not too many casualties is what all troops like.

The enemy, if not in evidence, was certainly there in the villages, valleys and crevices of the Algerian hills. The FLN gradually wore the French down, ending in their exit from Algeria, a national trauma from which they have never recovered.

The rebellion was not all that we saw. We flew south over P.C.Wren forts to Ghardhaia in the Sahara desert, an all-white town glistening in the sunshine as we saw it from our plane. One sight we were taken to see was an Arab brothel which seemed to thrive. As we walked away Walter Elliott told me of the trouble we had had in London during the war when due to the mass of foreign troops in the city prostitutes proliferated on the streets to such an alarming degree that the problem finally reached Cabinet level. When explained to Winston Churchill he quickly dismissed the matter with the words: 'I don't see there is much to worry about. If business was brisk the ladies would all be upstairs.'

I had been lucky in that in my first two years in parliament I had been on two delegations, to Peru and to Algeria, both very interesting. In addition to these, during my long parliamentary career I went on delegations to America, Canada, Uganda, Kenya, Berlin, Cyprus, India, Japan, Indonesia, Hong Kong and the first parliamentary delegation to China.

Parliamentary delegations are by no means joyrides. People are so proud of their own countries that they want to show you everything and in addition there is always the local British community who expect your attention. I have been on delegations where with some awkwardness one has had to ask to be excused from some of the carefully prepared outings to keep the programme within bounds.

Nevertheless these visits are a luxury and a privilege in that you have access to sights and experiences which are simply not available to the ordinary traveller and you meet personalities in the flesh whom you have long read about in print.

24
Jimmy Dies

In 1956, quite suddenly and unexpectedly, Jimmy Hoyle died. He had gone into hospital for a simple hernia operation, complications had set in involving a clot of blood and in a very few days he was dead.

I use the word 'unexpectedly,' but in truth he had been in decline for a number of years. The Jimmy Hoyle of 1956 was a different man from the Jimmy I knew before the war. I put this down to the cruel loss of his son, Peter. Peter was reported missing after the fall of Singapore. It was assumed that like most of his regiment he was a prisoner, which indeed he was. But whereas after the Japanese war his fellow prisoners kept returning in groups, he never came back and it was only after many months that Jimmy and Vi knew for certain that Peter had been killed in a motor accident on a working party in the prison camp. To lose his only son was bad enough in any event but for the anguish to be so prolonged was a strain from which he never recovered.

He had a successful life. He inherited J.B.Hoyle and Company from his father straight after the First World War when in his early twenties and was left to get on with it. As I said in an earlier chapter he was ahead of his fellow West Riding mill owners in that he was willing to bring in non-family managers and pay them well. The key figure was the rough but bright diamond Jimmy Thornber who rose from office boy to manager at speed, and the qualified young chartered accountant, Harry Earnshaw, who was such a good administrator.

Jimmy Hoyle gave these two their heads and it worked. His own role was to keep people happy which he did quite naturally. Everybody loved him. This was as well for I cannot think of anybody who more longed to be loved. He could not bear friction. Whenever I was talking with Thornber and disagreement was in the air Jimmy would quietly slip out of the room. This diffident charm served him well as a salesman. Without any of the standard and unattractive attributes of that ilk he was immensely successful in dealing with our two biggest customers, Bradleys and Fosters.

His great love was golf at which he reached county standard and one of the great delights of his life was the day his son, Peter, was chosen to play for Yorkshire.

Surprisingly for so shy a man, Jimmy enjoyed giving speeches of the sort usually required at weddings and 21st birthday parties. He was a bad sleeper so read a lot in the small hours and prided himself on the breadth of his vocabulary.

On a mill outing at Blackpool he gave such a speech feigning great surprise at receiving some presentation. On the following Monday one of the clerks eulogising the speech said to me: 'And there was Mrs James looking up at him with dog-like devotion.'

Mardi had another and less expected experience on that outing. She was always an elegant and shapely lady so it was a surprise when one of the travellers came up to her and said: 'By, Mrs James, it is nice to see thee. But thou hast thickened.' Thickened is such an apt word. As we get older some of us get fat, some of us do not, but we all thicken.

Jimmy, though not particularly at home with children, was a great favourite. In retrospect we were wrong not to let Felicity, aged 11, and Bunny, aged 8, come to the funeral. Instead we sent Bunny to Duncombe Park to be with her sister for a fortnight and both had a feeling of not understanding what was happening.

I could not have wished for a better father-in-law. The welcome he gave me in the very early days when I really was a very unpromising prospective son-in-law could not have been warmer. His whole attitude towards my venture into politics was wonderfully generous for however it turned out it could only increase his burdens.

Jimmy Hoyle's death added an extra, though not an intolerable, load to my weekly routine. In terms of hours spent at the mill he was not active but at the end of the day he was in charge. I soon discovered that my mind was less at ease in the knowledge that Jimmy Thornber was in command. The firm owed much to him but by now he was deep in a very straight rut and while he was controlling the company it was unlikely ever to change direction to meet the much changed and changing conditions of the market. He was such a strong character and so used to treating the whole concern as his own that no new blood that I chose to introduce would have had a chance. I concluded that he must go, not an easy conclusion considering his service to the company and his age, just short of 60. It would have been uncouth to sack him straight after Jimmy's death, but it was then that I made the decision that after a respectable pause he would have to go and I started thinking about how to find a successor.

Harry Roff, the chairman of Management Selection Ltd., the leading company of its kind at the time, was a great friend of mine. This friendship came in particularly useful in solving my problem of replacing Jimmy Thornber at J.B.Hoyle and Company. Harry Roff took a personal interest, came up to Hebden Bridge to see the works and spent the weekend with us at Park Farm.

The happy issue out of all this activity was the appointment of Roy Garside as managing director, a lively rugger playing Yorkshireman from Leeds, steeped in the clothing trade, as good at selling as he was at manufacturing and longing to get his teeth into just this sort of responsibility. It was impossible even for Jimmy Thornber not to like Roy Garside.

I do not believe in long handovers and it was not long before Roy was in charge. The exit of Jimmy Thornber was sad and it worried me. He was not badly off for he never spent any money and must have saved a good deal, apart from the pension which we of course gave him, but his whole life was the company plus his only son and I dreaded to think how unhappy he would be. He had a good wife but almost no friends outside the firm. He was shy and in my time never went out to see a customer, which he should have done, and customers and suppliers did not come to see him unless they had to for he was stern company.

Roy Garside's first task was to increase production at the factory I had opened at West Melton near Wath on Dearne in the Yorkshire coalfield. Roy created a new factory twice as large and just as successful outside the town of Wath and Dearne itself. On the sales side too he thrived, for with his outgoing personality he had many friends and connections in the trade and gave to our nine travellers inspiration of the sort they had never met before.

He also took a great load off my mind, for nothing is more worrying than responsibility for something you can only distantly control through someone with whom you are not in tune.

With Roy there I was positively cheered up by my visits to Hebden Bridge. My usual routine was the night sleeper from Euston to Leeds on Thursday, breakfast with Roy in the hotel, then drive over to Hebden Bridge for the morning and over to the constituency, 60 miles, during Friday afternoon for meetings and other functions on Friday night and over the weekend. Sometimes when I had too much to do in the constituency I would just have breakfast with Roy in Leeds then come straight over to Howden.

Jimmy's estate was complicated but the accountant, Mr Ross, was excellent and the solicitor, Uncle Bertie, was part of the family and in time it was all cleared up.

The next problem was to decide where Mardi would be happiest. She clearly could not live alone at Ashfield, especially now that we were away so much. We decided that we would add a wing to Park Farm, make it our family home, and find a cottage close at hand, perhaps in Sawdon, for her.

Over the next year we rebuilt Park Farm as it is now and where the children happily spent most of their childhood. This was a hectic year with architects and builders all over the place and Betty the inspiration and driving force. We found stone to match that of the farm at Keldy Castle, a shooting lodge on the moors belonging to the Reckitt family, which was being demolished. The stone windows in the present drawingroom I bought for £10 and were the drawingroom windows at Keldy. Our white front door was one of the bedroom doors from Wigganthorpe Hall which John Guthrie had bought and was demolishing. The panels in the bookcases in the drawingroom and in the doors between the dining and drawingrooms were originally window shutters at Wigganthorpe. With the house doubled in size, the two cottages built, also the Dutch barn and the covered yard, Park Farm had come a long way since Betty and I first called on Mr Watson in 1951, when there were chickens in the dining room.

The one part of our plan which did not work was the idea of a cottage in the village for Mardi. The most suitable cottage, with a pleasant garden, perfectly situated on our edge of the village was duly bought. Mardi spent days having it filled with her own furniture and her carpets, but in the end she never spent a single night there. It was no good. She couldn't bear to be alone so she came to live with us at the farm.

Park Farm continued to be a perfect place for the children. Every year we were snowed-up for a few days - the longer the better as far as they were concerned. Sledging, ski-ing behind the Landrover and skating on the duckpond were all new and fun. Though isolated - we were three miles from the nearest shop, in Brompton - there were always plenty of children about. Cayleys, Chafers, Pamela Stephenson the foreman's daughter and the Skilbecks from the other cottage. There were parties in the big hut and endless games in the farmyard.

The pony became a feature of life at Park Farm during the children's teens.

I was not brought up a countryman, but when we came to live at Park Farm I became interested in shooting, farming, woods, dogs, walking - but horses, No. In modern parlance I found them not to be 'rider-friendly,' in the few efforts I made at friendship.

Betty, in contrast, had always enjoyed riding and was determined that her children should do so too. She was not sufficiently at home with horses to make Pony Club and all its works worry free. Catching the ponies, getting them into the horse box, towing it up some impossibly narrow lane to a boggy site, all this and again in reverse to get the ponies and children back again and to bed - were far too much of a struggle for enjoyment. Luckily we had as our next door neighbours a couple of miles away the Chafer family who soon became close friends. Charles was Master of the hunt, his wife Elsie took a leading part in its affairs and their three girls were as keen on hunting and the Pony Club as their parents.

Given all the good advice in the world it seemed difficult to get hold of satisfactory ponies. Felicity had a perfect little animal called Gypsy on which she won prizes at Pony Club events. Though hopeless at ball games she turned out to be bold and the best of our three at riding. Libby had a dull pony called Beauty which belied its name. During the winter months we would take on a beach donkey from Scarborough, which nibbled the bark off the young apple trees. There was a Shetland pony called Juniper which had hoof trouble when he got too fat and had to be kept in the stable half the day to curb his grazing.

In addition to the ponies we owned we usually had one or two of widely differing temperaments on loan. I can't forget a brick I dropped in trying to be a help with Bunny's riding. Lady Ferens had a daughter called Bobby whose pony was called Brandy. Bobby had a new pony and therefore no need of Brandy for the summer, so we were asked if we would like to borrow him. Coming in at the fringe of these arrangements I wrote to Lady Ferens and thanked her for lending us Bobby.

We went as a family to the local point-to-point races and rather further afield in my constituency when later I was a member of parliament. These were good social fun when the sun came out, but at the Derwent point-to-point at Wykeham the sharp winds or drizzle of March left a lot to be desired.

Though I have never become a good shot, shooting came much more naturally to me. There were wild pheasants, pigeons, a few woodcock and plenty of rabbits in the woods around Park Farm so one could go out with the dog at any time and probably come in with something. Gradually, joining up with our neighbours at East Moor Farm and putting down 300 birds it became quite a good little shoot and in our best years we averaged 80 head a day over five shooting days.

Marvellous characters emerged in the countryside and none more so than Joe Hodgson, a retired Forestry Commission rabbit catcher who has made the shoot and our woods his life's interest. If I had paid him by the hour I should by now be broke. One of his shrewder ploys is the way he puts down young pheasants withour buying any. At the end of the shooting season he gathers up 20 hens, takes 500 eggs off them which he gives to a bigger shoot to incubate and in due course takes 300 birds back in return.

Apart from our home shooting at Park Farm I have always had a half gun involving about 6 days shooting on some other shoot, firstly with the MacDonalds at Thorpe, then with Marcus Worsley at Hovingham and then with Graham Mackrill at Elmswell. With these and invitations from friends I usually get about 15 days shooting a year which is all I can manage or want.

I have had a series of shooting dogs - Whisky, Mandy, Cindy - labradors which have given as much pleasure to the children as the ponies. My latest, Gemma, has been well trained by Gordon Dearing whom I got to know as the keeper at Hovingham and I take her picking up at other shoots, which is almost as much sport as shooting and much less worrying.

I am not by nature interested in horse racing but having most of the Malton training stables in my constituency I was bound to get to know something about it and to follow racing politics at Westminster. Every year I would visit two or three of the stables and go to York races which is an agreeable social event whether of not you follow the form. I am a poor gambler and have got used at York to losing £5 if there are five races and £6 if there are six. Once, and only once, my luck turned. Cynthia and I were invited out to Hong Kong to the opening of the Sha Tin racecourse and as it was a very special occasion I put £10 on the first race. After two days I had made £550. On the third day I said 'I will lose £50 but no more' and this I did. Cynthia still wears a costly leather jacket which she calls her 'Quinella' - the name of the sort of bet, first two in either order, that brought me most of my money.

One of Cynthia's conditions for our marriage was that Emma should be allowed to bring Jerry, a small skewbald pony, to Park Farm. He has turned out the most trouble-free and happiness-spreading animal in Park Farm history. He has given excitement to almost every one of hundreds of small children who have visited the farm over the last 20 years. To underline the welcome I wanted to give Jerry when he first came, at the cost of £30 I put up his 'winter palace,' a little corrugated shelter in the corner of the field. He has never been in it except to fetch the hay which we sometimes put there in winter.

* * *

I never fancied myself as a natural skier but always regretted that I had never had a go and was determined that the children should not make the same mistake. So in 1960, when they were 17, 14 and 11, we went off together to St Moritz for a fortnight with the Army Ski Club.

Thus I started my ski-ing career at 47, but I do not think this is the only reason I did not get far beyond the nursery slopes. Betty was quite a good skier, having learnt at her Swiss finishing school and the children proved good enough to want to come back in future years. We were at St Moritz in the Christmas holidays and it was perishingly cold.

There were lots of jolly families on the army scheme whom we later kept up with, notably the Guinesses, and Bunny fell head over heels in love with Timmy Guiness, a jolly boy and brilliant skier. When we got home, Bunny wrote to us in a letter from Duncombe Park:

Today I wrote to Timmy. Not a romantic letter but three pages in my best handwriting.

As no prep school boy can manage more than 'just over the page' in his worst handwriting, try to imagine Timmy's alarm at getting such a letter.

The area around Park Farm was ideal for driving lessons. In a National Park adjoining 10,000 acres of woods belonging to the Forestry Commission there were endless, almost traffic-free roads and lanes on which Libby with Tubby Cayley and Elizabeth Guthrie used to practice from about the age of 13, so when the dreaded test arrived they were more than ready and all passed on the first attempt. Teaching them in these surroundings was less alarming than later teaching Felicity in the streets of London.

25
America

I have said earlier on that Ted Heath favoured his Whips in the matter of promotion and parliamentary perks. One of the more desirable perks was the American 'leader scheme' by which you were invited by the State Department to come to America for two months, seeing what you wanted to see and meeting almost anybody you wanted to meet.

Those selected for the Leader Scheme were world-wide in their citizenship, equally wide in their professions and supposed to be future leaders in their field. One politician went from each of the selected countries and already Ted Heath, Tony Barber and Joe Godber had gone from the UK. I was invited to go in 1960. To show how wide the net was thrown, in the course of my visit I found myself in a lift in Chicago with an eye-catching young thing, and meaning to establish communication before we reached the sixth floor I asked her what brought her to America. She replied: 'I am here on the Leader Scheme. I am a dancer from Bali.'

The more I heard about my impending trip from my preceding Leaders, the more did it seem the chance of a lifetime which if possible Betty should share, and with nothing but encouragement from my American hosts I arranged for her and Libby, who had just then passed into St Thomas's Hospital as a medical student, to join me in the far west in Colorado Springs half way through the journey and spend the last month of the tour together at my expense.

My first week was spent in Washington meeting senators and congressmen, seeing the sights and planning my journey, insisting that I spent most of the time in the west of the country for the opening up of the American West has been a slice of history which has always fascinated me.

I had feared that as it was a tour paid for by the public purse my journey would be too official and I would spend too much time with mayors in town halls. I need not have worried. America seemed to abound in people, mainly volunteer women, only too keen to show foreigners the wonders of their home town and succeeded in giving the impression that you were the foreigner of all foreigners whom they most wanted to please. The American welcome puts us to shame and gets warmer the further you go west and the smaller the town. When Betty joined me a month later she was so moved by these welcomes that she thought in the course of a dozen brief stays that she had established a dozen pen friends for life, only to discover in time that letter writing came more easily to her than to them. This does not apply to Richard B.Peterson, Attorney, of the smallest town of all, Council Bluffs, Iowa, the start of the Oregon trail, who to this day writes me his family news plus his musings on the state of the world, usually glum, every Christmas.

It was in Council Bluffs that somebody telephoned me from San Francisco asking me to give a speech at a three day conference in Monterey, dangling before me as a bait the names of the other speakers who were indeed famous - Walter Rowtow and Dean Rusk, a future Foreign Secretary. The telephone dialogue continued:

Bryan: 'What is the subject of the conference?'

Answer: 'Competitive co-existence.'

Bryan: 'What do you want me to talk about?'

Answer: 'A British view.'

Bryan: 'On which day would I speak?'

Answer: 'The third day.'

Bryan: 'O.K. That gives me two days in which to discover what competitive co-existence means.'

Americans are very generous in their judgements on their fellow citizens. Describing the neighbours who were due to come to supper they sounded such a wonderful bunch that you wondered whether you would be able to keep up with them. Such phrases were used as 'He is a fine man.' 'Fine' in that sense suggests to me something between gallant and saintly. In the event the group that arrived were nice and ordinary but extraordinary in their commendable search for self-improvement. A woman in her sixties would just be taking up the piano. A couple in their fifties were off to a tennis camp - 'the only way to improve your game.' A group had been set up to study the history and future of India aided by nothing more than reading matter from the local library.

I have always thought of my golf as rather a worrying sort of fun, but it is light-hearted compared with golf in Council Bluffs where every single putt has to be holed regardless of the state of the game and duly documented on a card so that you can't even forget the horrors of your performance. This reminded me of a remark of a Scottish caddy after an interminable round with a Japanese at St Andrews when he said to his pal: 'I think we did right to drop the atom bomb on these buggers. Otherwise we would never have finished the war.'

In Portland, Oregon, I was looked after by members of the ESU (English Speaking Union) who seemed to come from a slightly lower social strata than their British counterparts but were much more active. I had to give a speech and was given my first taste of an American audience - a delicious taste. In my experience American audiences are more numerous, appreciative and charitable than those in England, especially those in Yorkshire.

Standing on the hill and looking down on the town of Portland one puzzle of American life seemed to me to be explained, namely how so many apparently simple people have become so rich. I was looking down on a town of a million people. Standing on the same spot only 100 years earlier one would have been looking down on 3000 people. Expansion has been so fast that a small businessman would become a big businessman almost automatically if he stuck to his trade.

San Francisco was as wonderful as the postcards and equalled only by Sydney and Hong Kong in its situation looking down over the harbour and the Golden Gate bridge. Once again I was cossetted by a splendid lady who showed me all I should see including the amazing giant Redwood trees in the forests north of the city.

The conference to which I had committed myself in that telephone conversation at Council Bluffs, Iowa, duly took place in a huge conference centre at Monterey over a sunny weekend. Despite the attractions of a glorious beach and a famous golf course, 2000 San Franciscans unrelentingly filled the hall with a diligence not to be seen in my native country.

Any nervousness which I may have had at addressing such a crowd disappeared after the first session for, as in Portland, the audience was benevolent beyond belief. One after another famous speakers got up, said something homely or funny and then read a paper for 40 minutes. I would have less authority but could not be less entertaining than that.

On the second night there was a large cocktail party. To a forthcoming sort of lady I said: 'I am speaking tomorrow. What do you think I ought to say?' She was first incredulous, indeed horror struck that my speech was not already in print. Then she said: 'For the Lord's sake say something cheerful.' This was brilliant guidance.

By now I had discovered that competitive co-existence meant the problem of the West, which in their eyes meant America, living at peace with Communism, which they saw as a united force embracing not only Russia but the world's most populous nation, China, and several others.

Because of this assumption that Communism was so huge and united and that America was alone holding the torch of Western civilisation this had been a very depressing conference.

So I started my speech with a verbatim account of my conversation with my cocktail party lady. I said: 'She said to me, for the Lord's sake say something cheerful - so here it comes.' I then told them of the renaissance of Europe. It was then 1960, 15 years after the war. The recovery of Germany, France and Italy was well on its way but almost unnoticed in America. So I really could say something cheerful and speaking just from a few notes in an English accent I was at least different.

America was then at its most confident. Pre-Kennedy, pre-Vietnam, pre any disillusion, the unquestioned belief was that everything in America was best. What a contrast when Felicity went there in 1967 expecting the America that we had painted only to find a country in a turmoil of self-doubt and confusion, with young people in revolt.

A month had flown by and by now Betty and Libby had flown in to Colorado Springs, the home of Larry, Amo, Bruce and Reta Foster, the family of whom we had seen most in Halifax in the years after the war.

Larry Foster was a member of the famous Yorkshire textile family, the Fosters of Queensbury, whose enormous Black Dyke mills, in their time world famous, can be seen to this day on the hills outside Bradford. Larry was the last of the numerous Foster family to work full-time in the business, specialising in the engineering side. At Cambridge he was nick-named Sax Foster because he played the saxophone in the Quinquginta Ramblers, the university dance band. Fosters of Queensbury was the home and owner of the Black Dyke

Mills Band, the most famous brass band in England, so running this was a natural interest for Larry.

Amo, an energetic American, even more energetic than Betty 'wore the trousers' in that marriage, but it worked well and there was no happier family. In about 1950 Amo persuaded Larry to emigrate and join her parents in Colorado Springs.

If the purpose of the Leader Scheme was to teach the leader how the Americans lived, our fortnight with the Fosters was appropriate in showing us 'the Americans on holiday.' We piled into their enormous estate car, meandered through Colorado and Arizona, staying nights in motels. The sun was blazing hot, the scenery was either beautiful, sensational or both. It was certainly memorable for it included Bryce Canyon, and most sensational of all, the Grand Canyon, which I believe is nominated rightly as one of the official Wonders of the World.

The Grand Canyon was my ultimate humiliation for it proved with absolute certainty that the world is millions of years old and that therefore the importance of a single human being is infinitesimal. Over the centuries the Colorado river has carved its way through the rock to form the Grand Canyon. A telescope is provided through which from one side of the canyon you can look at the rock face of the other and see the definitive history of the world. Each inch equals so many years or hundreds of years and as you look down the rock face various fossils appear and you cannot doubt that they are the remains of creatures which lived a measurable number of million years ago.

Our time with the Fosters was a mixture of wonder and fun and we were sorry to say goodbye.

Apart from the Fosters at Colorado Springs the only personal introductions we had were to the Klebergs, the owners of the King Ranch in Texas and to the Blaffer Owens at Houston. My MP friend, Richard Sharples, later assassinated as a Governor of Bermuda, introduced me to the Klebergs.

The original King of King Ranch, from whom the Klebergs were descended, was the son of an Irish immigrant who escaped from his jeweller's apprenticeship in New York in 1824. Over the years he became a pilot on the Rio Grande and in the chaos and boom which followed the Mexican War established himself as a considerable river boat operator. It was in 1853 that Richard King bought his first parcel of land - 15,500 acres on the Sante Gertrudis Creek, for two cents an acre.

By the time Betty, Libby and I had reached the ranch, 110 years later, the acreage had increased to 900,000 acres and about 90,000 head of cattle with another 9000 acres in Pennsylvania and joint enterprises in Cuba and Brazil. The Sante Gertrudis breed of beef cattle was developed on the King Ranch and is now world famous in tropical climes.

The breeding of animals is a King Ranch speciality, for in addition to cattle both Quarter horses on the prairies and race horses, which have won many an American classic, made the ranch a place of pilgrimage for those who wished to learn.

The ranch's pastures produce livestock and game - they also produce oil. Since 1933 it has been developed in partnership with the Humbol Oil Company and at the time of our visit was contributing a third of the profits of the ranch. The oil 'christmas trees' are surprisingly inconspicuous and silent. What are conspicuous but not unsightly are the prickly pear cactus trees which form the boundaries of many of the pastures and provide a rich reserve of livestock feed, handily protected and stored up for dry times. Vicious thorns protect their big, thick plate-like leaves, but when needed the store may be unlocked simply by burning off the thorns.

Three weeks later we were back in England at a Hunt Ball at Duncombe Park. I heard the American voice of a lady standing not far away so went to talk to her and astonishingly found that she was Mrs Kleberg, the mother of Dick whom we had met so recently. She and her husband, Bob, were staying with the Syke's at Sledmere for York Races and no doubt to see the Sledmere stud. I took the opportunity to arrange for Bob to sign my history of the King Ranch at the races next day.

We had three fascinating days at the King Ranch before moving on to the Blaffer Owens at Houston. Jane Blaffer Owen had been at finishing school with Betty in Switzerland and had been described by a fellow student as 'crazy as a bed bug.' She was, I thought, rather quaint but could have been better described.

The Blaffer Owens were a very rich oil family who lived in the style you would expect. We stayed in the separate guest house in the grounds of their house and as we got dressed for dinner a black lady brought us a list of the guests.

We dined about 16 strong at a table beside the swimming pool, but before we started a tanker vehicle had preceded us, spraying away any flying insects. We judged that the Bryans were the only non-millionaires at the table. Making conversation with the bejewelled lady on my right I murmured remarks about what a lovely welcome we had had and what nice people they all seemed to be, etc. She took my remarks seriously, took a considered look around at the company and then said: 'Well, if you don't like us here tonight, we're the top.'

New Orleans lived up to our highest hopes. Betty was unwell that night so Libby and I went on the tiles and, stopping the first taxi I said to the driver: 'Where do we go to hear the real New Orleans jazz' He replied: 'You want to go to Pete Fountain in the Bateau Lounge,' and there we went for an evening never to be forgotten. About 200 people sat around at tables of four or six in a large plain hall. On the platform Pete Fountain played the clarinet; a drummer, double bass and piano made up the quartet. They played continuously in sessions of about half an hour, in such a way that it was possible at moments for each of the players to excel at his own instrument at which point the crowd would burst out into spontaneous applause.

The next day happened to be Father's Day in America, something I had not met in our country. Teasing Libby I said 'What have you planned for me?' She said: 'You will be surprised.' went to her suitcase and got out an LP record of Pete Fountain in the Bateau Lounge. This record has since been worn out and replaced.

We finished our American journey in an 'Olde English' inn in famous Williamsberg, perfectly restored to its seventeenth century state. It was perhaps a good preparation for our return for it could not have been more English. When we were signing in at the hotel the girl at the desk said to Libby: 'Gee, what a complexion. Are you Irish?' An old lady had stopped her in the street in New Orleans and said the same.

26
Vice-Chairman

A new parliament always leads to a general post amongst the members of the government. Some ministers go. Some are promoted. Others are moved sideways. Some back-benchers get promotion to ministerial rank.

In 1959 Ted Heath, the Chief Whip, went into the cabinet as Secretary of State for Employment. He was succeeded as Chief Whip by Martin Redmayne, the Deputy Chief Whip. The new Deputy Chief Whip was likely to be Michael Hughes-Young or me. He got the job and I was disappointed - but not for long. Of the two of us I think I would have been the better Deputy Chief Whip under Ted Heath but Michael would have been better under Martin Redmayne. Redmayne was a successful soldier, a brigadier in the war and, though not a regular soldier, a very military character indeed. Michael Hughes-Young had been a regular soldier and suited him perfectly.

So I continued in the Whips' Office for another six months with the fancy title of Lord Commissioner of the Treasury. Then I moved over to Conservative Central Office to become vice-chairman of the Conservative Party Organisation. The chairman at the time was R.A.Butler and the deputy chairman Oliver Poole, the member of parliament for Oswestry and a considerable figure in the City of London. He supervised the administration at Central Office.

I, as vice-chairman, was responsible for parliamentary candidates. I was the person you wrote to if you wanted to be a Conservative candidate. I would interview the applicants and then make my recommendations to a committee who would decide whether he or she should be accepted on the approved list of candidates. No constituency could choose a candidate who was not on the approved list.

This job suited me down to the ground and I did it for four years. In the army I had become very interested in the assessment of people, both as a battalion commander and as commandant of the OCTU, where I also had to do a lot of interviewing. The applicants I interviewed came from every walk of life and many of them had served in the forces. I found the interviewing easy because I had such a broad background that I could find something in common to talk about with almost anybody. I could talk from direct personal experience about manufacturing industry, war, the services, the church, universities, children's education, travel, agriculture, the countryside, sport, a fair selection of foreign countries, fighting local government and parliamentary elections and so on.

My first morning's interviewing showed me the variety I was to meet.

The first person to come into my office for interview was the Deputy Governor of Cyprus, Sir George Sinclair, a man in his early fifties. He had never done any work for the Conservative party and had no knowledge of our party organisation. But he was obviously a man of distinction and talent and I had no hesitation in putting him on the approved list. The only reason the interview took any time was that he was an interesting man to talk to.

The next arrival was a double first at Cambridge (from my old college), a senior economist with Lever Brothers, former president of the Cambridge athletic team, an Olympic runner - Terry Higgins. He also had done nothing for the Conservative party but was obviously a man of quality, so he went on to the list. He later became an extremely good MP and was Financial Secretary to the Treasury in the Heath Government.

The next interviewee was a young man of 29 who had joined the Young Conservatives at the age of 15 and had worked hard for the party ever since so had gradually worked his way up the organisational ladder until he was now vice-chairman of the Area Young Conservatives. I could not see him as an impressive member of parliament, but nevertheless I recommended him for the list because from the point of view of the party workers you simply cannot reject somebody who had done so much for the party. I would have been less likely to pass him had I thought there was any chance of his ever being actually selected for a winnable seat.

I should point out that getting onto the approved list is only the first of many stages before you actually arrive in the House of Commons. For any safe Conservative seat there could be up to 300 applicants. I have already described the tortuous process through which they have to go in my own experience en route to becoming MP for Howden.

The amount of influence Central Office has on the final selection of the candidate by a constituency depends very much on the nature of the constituency chairman. He is entitled to come to Central Office and discuss potential candidates with the vice-chairman in charge of candidates and take the relevant information back to his selection committee. On the other hand he has no obligation to do this. A lot depends too on how much influence the constituency chairman himself has over his selection committee.

After the Independent Broadcasting Authority had once again made a mess of the granting of ITV franchises the chairman, Lord Thompson, made the well-known comment: 'There must be some better way.' After four years of watching from close quarters constituencies choosing their candidates I felt inclined to say much the same thing.

In a safe seat where several hundred aspirants apply the successful candidate should surely be a star. This is not always so. Personnel selection is an elusive skill. The army and progressive business have permanent, well-trained and experienced selection committees which have plenty of practice. In contrast the selection committee in a constituency is only asked to choose a candidate once every 10 or even 20 years so has no permanence or experience whatever. The result is as one would expect. I could give dozens of cases of first-class members of parliament, even cabinet ministers who were rejected a number of times before they succeeded in being selected while others who have proved moderate or even bad MPs were chosen at the first attempt. Why then do we persist with this inefficient system? Answer - because in a democracy constituencies insist on choosing their own candidate. They will not have one foisted on them by the Central Office or the Prime Minister. Indeed an effective way of torpedoing a would-be candidate's chances is any suggestion that he is the special recommendation of Central Office.

Only twice in my four years as vice-chairman could I say that I was directly responsible for a would-be candidate becoming a member of parliament. On the first occasion the constituency chairman, obviously a powerful woman, discussed at length with me various applicants. We got on well together and finally she said: 'All right, which would you choose?' I gave her a name. She said: 'He will be our MP.' And he was. This was an unusual situation. You do not often get a chairman so confident of his or her influence over the committee. It gave me the chance to place an admirable candidate whom I knew would not necessarily appeal to the average selection committee. He became a cabinet minister.

The other occasion arose when Roland Robinson breezed into my office and said: 'Paul, I have just been made Governor of Bermuda so there will be a by-election at Blackpool. The constituency will accept anyone I recommend.' I gave him the name of Peter Blaker and they had a drink together. He became the member for Blackpool and a successful minister. This again was a unique case - a member of parliament who can name his successor is a rarity.

The average constituency chairman had too fixed an idea of the sort of candidate he was looking for. His opening statement would be: 'I'm looking for somebody who will live in the constituency, he must be under 40, married, a countryman, preferably a farmer, not a Roman Catholic, etc. etc.' I had to explain that every time you make a proviso you halve the list so as a result of half a dozen 'musts' your choice has evaporated. The sensible way was to choose the best person then of course if he insists on living at Land's End you might have to move on to your second choice.

Constituencies quite often finish up with candidates quite unlike the image they had in mind. I doubt if Chelmsford had in mind a Roman Catholic bachelor. But who could resist Norman St John Stevas?

In an increasingly mobile and television-informed society, selection committees expect above all an articulate candidate, and a local man has less advantage than in the old days. Nowadays members of the landed gentry seem to have no advantage at all. In the East Riding both the late Lord Halifax, as Charles Wood, and his brother, Richard Wood, were local members of parliament. The present Lord Halifax, then Peter Irwin, did not even get on the short list when his uncle's seat at Bridlington became vacant.

Despite the increase of women in all the main professions the number in parliament remains obstinately low. There are many reasons for this but the main reason in my opinion is that selection committees are largely composed of women and women choose men. I used every stratagem to get my star women onto constituency short-lists and was not unsuccessful, but one of the men on the list almost always won.

Harry Roff, the creator of Management Selection Limited, who had been so helpful to me in finding a chief executive for J.B.Hoyle & Company was by definition an expert in selection and interviewing. I asked him to come and sit in on some of my interviews and see whether he had any suggestions for improvement.

After watching me at work for a morning he said : 'I can't help you. My job is completely different from your's. When I am interviewing somebody for the managing directorship of, say, Cadburys, I have a job description of the person I am looking for. There is no job description for a member of parliament. A number of people with completely different qualifications and qualities can all be successful members of parliament. You are really looking at these people and saying to yourself "From my own experience in the House can I imagine this person being a useful member?"'

During my years at Central Office, among those whom I recommended for the list were Geoffrey Howe, Michael Heseltine, St. John Stevas, John Nott, John Biffen, Ian Gilmour, Leon Brittan and also Colin Mitchell, 'Mad Mitch' of the Argyll & Sutherland Highlanders who won the Sword of Honour at the OCTU when I was commandant there.

One of the less usual applicants was Eric Morley of 'Miss World' fame. He ended up by interviewing me. The conversation went as follows:

Bryan: 'Mr Morley, what are your responsibilities at Mecca?'

Morley: 'I am in charge of the dance halls and the bingo.'

Bryan: 'Why do people play bingo?'

Morley: 'You can't be humiliated at bingo. Have you ever been to a bingo club?'

Bryan: 'No.'

Morley: 'Do you realise that almost certainly several thousand of your constituents play bingo regularly? Would you like to come to one of my bingo clubs and learn how several million people pass their time every week?'

I could hardly refuse his offer. A few weeks later found me dining with Eric Morley followed by an educational half hour watching 1500 people play bingo at the Locarno at Streatham. Betty was ill at the time so Jean Barber, whose husband was busy in the House as a Treasury Minister, came along with me.

In addition to introducing me to bingo, Eric Morley several times asked me to the 'Miss World' ceremony and each time I took one of my daughters. The evening is divided into two parts; the actual choosing of Miss World at the Lyceum and the celebration dance at the Cafe Royal, attended by all the would-be Miss Worlds.

The first part is really better seen at home on the television. The second is truly memorable for seeing all these girls at such short range, nearly every one looks beautiful. On the television there are times when you are bound to say: 'Surely that can't be the prettiest girl in Sri Lanka.' The black girls are of course the outstanding dancers.

One year an Indian girl, a medical student called Miss Fariah, won the crown. At the dinner dance at the Cafe Royale she sat next to me and dazzling she was. I was hesitant to ask her to dance but, pressed on by Felicity, who assured me she was longing to dance with me, I did so and we danced. Later in the evening the wicked Felicity said: 'Go on, Daddy, ask her to dance again. I am sure she would love to.'

So weakly I said: 'Miss Fariah, would you like to dance or would you rather talk?' She said: 'I would rather talk.'

At this dance a young man came and asked Felicity to dance and while doing so said to her: 'I know you. I have seen you at Park Farm when I have come up there on my motorbike from Scarborough Post Office delivering telegrams.' She asked him how he had been invited to this affair and he answered that he had replied to an advertisement in the 'Dancing Times' for a young man with a dinner jacket. On arrival he had been allotted Miss Nicaragua but as they had no common tongue between them they wearied of each other. I suggested to Eric Morley that he would do better to advertise for language students.

* * *

Vice-Chairman of the Conservative Party Organisation is a position in which you can get publicity. You have behind you the whole party machine, you have to give many speeches in the constituencies and, provided you keep the press office well fed with handouts of your speeches, you get into the press most weeks. You also tend to be invited to take part in television programmes. On polling night of the local government elections one year in the early sixties I found myself as the party representative commenting on the results as they came in during the evening. Harold Wilson was the Labour commentator. This is quite an agreeable role if your party is winning but when you are expecting to lose and the incoming results confirm your worst fears you really do run out of excuses. You have to scrape the bottom of your mental barrel to explain why such and such a councillor has lost a seat which has been Conservative for 20 years. It is a relief when at last the evening comes to an end and you can drink a glass of whisky with your opponent who has, of course, had a very happy time. Harold Wilson was good company and we could talk about other things beside the evening's horrors as he comes from Huddersfield, which I know well.

My friends Roy and Margo Smith were out to dinner in Yorkshire that night. On coming home their housekeeper said: 'Mr Bryan's been on telly.' 'What was he talking about?' asked Roy. Reply: 'I don't rightly know but - by - 'e were good-natured.'

Harold Wilson had a nice sense of humour. When my brother Austin was vicar of Preston Candover, at his church fete he invented a competition: 'Guess the weight of the vicar.' How this worked I do not know but it was apparently a success and he wanted to use it again the following year, but as by then everybody knew his weight he needed a new subject and had opted for the Prime Minister. I wrote to Harold Wilson and here is the reply I received:

> Prime Minister
> 10 Downing Street
> Whitehall
>
> March 18 1969
>
> Dear Mr Bryan
> Thank you for your letter of March 11 asking whether we could tell you the Prime Minister's weight for a competition at a Church fete in your constituency. The Prime Minister has asked me to tell you that, having considered the question from all angles, bearing in mind the Official Secrets Act, the Weights and Measures regulations, and the need to make seasonal and other appropriate statistical corrections, he would set his weight officially at 12 stone 12lb.
>
> Yours sincerely
>
> Peter Gregson

* * *

On one occasion when Ian Macleod was my chairman at Central Office he was due to go on a TV programme on the Common Market with Richard Crossman, but at the last minute he fell ill and I was asked to take his place. ITV sent a car to the members' entrance for us and there I met Crossman. He was far from pleased to find that he was going on the box with me instead of a cabinet minister and did not hesitate to say so. He actually explained to me in the car that he felt more at home when pitted against somebody like Lord Hailsham. By the time we got to the studio I had a hunch that he was going to find some way of getting out of the interview.

The producer was David Hennessy (now Lord Windlesham) and he explained how he was going to present the programme. It was the early days of the Common Market and speakers from varying walks of life were to give their views on how the Common Market would affect them and the programme was to finish with the two politicians. Crossman objected saying that the politicians should come at the beginning rather than the end of the programme. After some argument he declared that he would not go on the programme unless it opened with him. David Hennessy was unmoved and said that if this was so would he kindly brief the interviewer with his views so that he could bring these out in the course of his interview with me, which he duly did. You do not often find 'big' men being so small.

I once went on the Frost programme with Anthony Wedgwood Benn. I was impressed with Frost's meticulous preparation. He knew every detail about me, even the fact that we were both at the same college at Cambridge at rather different times.

In my four years as vice-chairman I served under no less than four Chairmen - R.A.Butler, Ian Macleod, John Hare and, very briefly, Edward DuCann whom I was to get to know well in my later years in parliament when he and I were chairman and vice-chairman of the 1922 Committee for 10 long years.

Rab Butler was a man of culture and kindness and, having been married to a Courtauld, was also rich. His second wife, Molly, suited him splendidly. In the 1980s when after Rab's death she wrote her autobiography, Felicity was her literary agent.

Rab was a key figure in the recovery of the Conservative Party fortunes between devastating defeat in 1945 and its near victory only five years later. The Conservative Party has a great instinct for survival and when it was obvious that our lingering image as the party of privilege and country squires had to be expunged this was rapidly done, with Rab the inspiration behind it. It was strange that he had such a feeling for what the people wanted, as shown in the 1944 Education Act for which he was largely responsible, for he could not be described as a man of the people.

Walking back from the House of Commons to Central Office with him one summer's day he said: 'I think we shall beat the Australians in this Test Match, don't you?' I said: 'Why do you think that?' He replied: 'Because our men bowl so fast.'

In the early days of TV party political broadcasts it was decided that the chairman of the party should be recorded in the natural surroundings of his country home in Stansted, Essex. The camera focussed on the front door of the stately Stansted Hall and out walked Rab in tweed cap, jacket and breeches with his gun under his arm and dog at his side. After taking five rather Charlie Chaplin-like steps he discharged his gun into the air as if shooting at a pheasant. The dog was recorded retrieving a rabbit.

In 1963 Rab very nearly became Prime Minister and one can speculate forever the effect that might have had on our history. He finished his career happily and appropriately as Master of Trinity College, Cambridge, where I last met him at his 70th birthday party.

Ian Macleod was a very different sort of chairman, though one of Rab's most loyal disciples. He really was a man of the people and a schoolboy at heart until his dying day. Once Robin Marlar the captain of the Sussex cricket team came to see me for interview and afterwards I said: 'I am sure Ian would like to see you. Let's see if he's in.' The two of them gossiped about cricket for half an hour in the greatest detail, just as I could have done at the age of 18 but not at 45. Ian could have talked in exactly the same way about racing or rugger. At the internationals at Murrayfield he was to be found not in a box but in the crowd or in the bar. At Cambridge - where I played with him in the Caius College rugger team - though immensely clever, he did not get much of a degree for he was too busy playing bridge, at which he was one of the best players in the country. All this seems a strange background for he was the best speaker in the House of Commons and a huge loss to our party and the country when he died as Chancellor of the Exchequer in 1970.

Ian Macleod was one of the people in my life with whom I have been entirely in tune. We did not have to have long talks to understand what the other was thinking - we thought in parallel. This was partly because of the similarity of our backgrounds - the same age, same middle-class professional provincial background, educated at similar minor public schools, same college at Cambridge, same lack of interest in academics or politics whilst there. I played games, he played bridge. Neither of us spent much time having port with our tutors.

Absurdly we actually got married from the same house in Halifax. I spent the night before my wedding with Sam and Winnie Smith. Ian did the same when stationed in Halifax as a soldier three years later.

I had a more spectacular war which showed no indication of my future route through life. His showed the first signs of brilliance which was to make him one of the leading politicians of his time. It was when he went to the staff college and for the first time in his life worked really hard that he discovered that he could master a subject in detail at an astonishing speed and certainly much faster than any other student there. In parliament this enabled him to deliver a masterly speech without a note of any sort.

His parliamentary career got off to a flying start. Having worked in the Conservative research department with Enoch Powell and Reggie Maudling since the end of the war, by the time he got into the House in 1950 he was well informed and this came out in a startling speech in which he bettered the Minister of Health, the famous Aneurin Bevan, into humiliation. Not many months later, when the Conservatives had won the 1951 election, Ian himself became Minister of Health.

With no experience of a department he approached his job with caution, made no great changes, but emerged after two years as a respected minister.

His promotion to Secretary of State for the Colonies was just what he wanted, for he needed experience of foreign affairs. It was, of course, controversial. His predecessor, Alan Lennox-Boyd, was respected but having made his 'wind of change' speech Macmillan wanted a faster pace of de-colonisation in which fortunately Ian believed, but it did not go down well with the right wing of the party. This was a thoroughly satisfying part of his career.

When he was given the joint appointments of Leader of the House and chairman of the party organisation his cup of success seemed full. He was delighted. Nobody performed more brilliantly in the House nor gave more inspiring speeches at conferences and in the country. What is more his background, the son of a doctor rather than a country squire, and an officer in a county regiment rather than a guardsman, put him at ease in the constituencies. He did not have to undergo any great change of attitude which the traditional ranks of our party found so difficult after 1945.

The brimming cup proved to be a poisoned chalice. Ian's period as party chairman coincided with a prolonged trough in the fortunes of the party and history shows that no party chairman, however brilliant, can ride high when party fortunes are low. The country was getting tired of our party, the prosperity of which we had boasted was waning. This was confirmed by a steady stream of disastrous results at by-elections. We were plagued with scandals such as Profumo and Vassal. Even Macmillan was losing his confidence and this came out with his panicky sacking of seven cabinet ministers at a stroke. The final humiliation came when having made entry into the Common Market the main and new plank in our platform, de Gaulle vetoed our entry.

Macmillan did not survive to suffer election defeat for his health broke down. From the ensuing turmoil, with the aid of the ailing Macmillan and much to the astonishment of the world, the fourteenth Earl of Home resigned his title and became, to his own surprise and almost against his own will, Prime Minister of Great Britain.

Ian Macleod was so disappointed that the favourite and his hero, Rab Butler, had not become Prime Minister that he declined to serve under Alec Home. This he realised later was a great mistake and kept him out of the political scene for some time, but not for ever. By the time he died, as I have already said, he was Chancellor of the Exchequer in the Heath government.

As chairman of the party Ian was succeeded by John Hare, later to be Lord Blakenham, as big a contrast to his two predecessors as you could have for he was the worst speaker in the House of Commons. It seemed to me brave of a man so inarticulate on the platform to take up a profession of which public speaking is such an important part, yet despite this handicap he was successful as the Secretary of State for Employment, but he will not go down in history as one of the great chairmen of the party.

He had a good sense of humour. Once at a staff party at the Department of Employment, after he had made a more than inadequate speech in the House, one of the girls trying to think of something comforting and kind to say blurted out: 'I am so sorry.' John said: 'Don't worry, dear. I haven't got to do this. I am terribly rich.' He, like Rab, had married money - in his case to be found in the Pearson family.

Oliver Poole was succeeded as deputy chairman at Conservative Central Office by Sir Toby Low, now Lord Aldington. I had met Toby before as an effective staff officer in the war in Italy. This appointment was destined to have a dramatic and happy effect on my life. Owing to the friendship which followed, 10 years later as a widower I took my daughter, Bunny, to Janie Low's 21st birthday party. There I met Cynthia who took her son, Alex, to the same party. Cynthia and I were the only non-family oldies at the party so we got married. Alex was to become my son-in-law for he married Felicity.

This chapter, starting with the struggles of would-be politicians to get into the House of Commons followed by the ups and downs of some of them once they get there, leads naturally to the question of what are the attributes of a successful member of parliament?

The first essential is a safe seat. Once I had won Howden with a majority of 11,000 I knew I was there for life. Any success I had in parliament could not be negated by the electorate suddenly cutting off my political career. For one's wife and family that was a measure of stability in an inherently unstable career.

When I lost the election at Sowerby in 1951 by the small margin of 1650 votes, I was disappointed. Looking back I can see that it was a stroke of good luck. Had I won with an inevitably small majority I would only have held the seat for nine years until 1964, then when the Conservatives lost the general election found myself with the task of finding a new seat at the age of 51. I would undoubtedly have abandoned my parliamentary career.

The next asset required is luck. You can be a most promising MP but if your party is out of power for a long time your career will not make much headway. Roy Jenkins must have been one of the brightest of the young Labour members when he got into the House in 1948. Within two years the Labour party were out of power and Jenkins spent the next 13 years marking time in political terms but occupying himself writing some good books. In this respect I had both good and bad luck. The appointment of vice-chairman of the party in charge of candidates had the status of a junior minister and I was quite satisfied to have got that far after five years. On the other hand when I had completed that job and would probably have been a minister of state in another Conservative government, my party was defeated and I had no more than a shadow ministerial job for the next six years. As against that, when not a minister, you can accept business appointments, so I was able to accept a directorship at Granada Television, from which I got much satisfaction over the years to come. I finally became a Minister of State at the age of 57 when the Conservatives got back into power in 1970. I have no complaints on the luck front, for in no circumstances would I have ever risen any higher on the ministerial ladder.

Whilst in the period 1950 to 1964 bright young Labour MPs were frustrated and marking time, their equivalent in the Tory ranks, Macleod, Maudling and Powell, enjoyed 13 years of continuous success, rising to the highest ministerial ranks.

A number of members of parliament are outstandingly clever, articulate and ambitious and you can safely forecast from the day they arrive at the Palace of Westminster that more will be heard of them. In that category I would place Churchill, Eden, Butler, Heath, Macleod, Joseph, Boyle, Enoch Powell and Thatcher on the Conservative benches. Wilson, Healey, Crossman, Crosland, Jenkins, Castle, Bevan come under the same heading in the Labour ranks.

More interesting perhaps is to try to decide why less promising starters got to the top. Michael Foot, always acknowledged as brilliantly clever and an orator, was regarded as a permanent rebel. No-one would have guessed that he would end by leading his party.

Willie Whitelaw, not academically distinguished nor a fluent speaker in the technical sense, was certainly not picked out by me as a future Deputy Prime Minister. Yet as the years went by whenever a really difficult job had to be filled, for instance the first Secretary of State for Northern Ireland, people in our party instinctively said: 'Willie should do that.'

When John Major became an MP in 1979, Lord Barber, who had been his chairman at the Standard and Chartered Bank, rang me up and said: 'One of our best people, John Major, has just got into the House. Would you make yourself known to him?' So I did get to know him slightly better than you would expect considering our disparity of ages. I recognised a competent and charming person but certainly not a Prime Minister to be.

* * *

When you finish your parliamentary career you are offered a free medical check-up. Making conversation while the consultant from St Thomas's gave me the once-over, I said: 'Are MPs more or less healthy than the average individual?' To which to my surprise he replied: 'Much more healthy. For a start they are stronger. An individual who is happy to stand up in the House of Commons and face that mob is temperamentally strong. Anyone who has arrived in the House of Commons is by definition physically stronger than the average.' It is noticeable that despite the rigours of parliamentary life the sick list is not abnormal.

If I had to name a quality common to all top politicians it would be resilience. It is remarkable how Prime Ministers and Foreign Secretaries after a gruelling foreign schedule then return and within hours deal with a statement followed by an hour or more of questions from a critical House.

The public is apt to judge parliamentary success in terms of ministerial appointments, but there are plenty of other roles which in the House of Commons community carry a status as high as any minister outside the cabinet. The chairman of the Public Accounts Committee (for a long time Harold Wilson and now Terence Higgins); chairman of the 1922 Committee; chairman of the Labour Party; chairman of the Interparliamentary Union; chairman of the Commonwealth Parliamentary Association are all highly regarded positions. After I ceased to be a minister I found great interest in being vice-chairman of the 1922 Committee and chairman of the All-Party Hong Kong Group.

The Speaker of the House of Commons is the most prestigious parliamentary position. Having been through the hands of half a dozen speakers during my long career I still find it hard to define the qualities required in the perfect Speaker. Selwyn Lloyd QC, ex-Foreign Minister, ex-Chancellor of the Exchequer, with immense experience of every sort was qualified to be the perfect Speaker. Yet in my view he was not as good as Speaker Weatherill, who had far less experience and never rose above the rank of Deputy Chief Whip. What is required is that elusive quality which commands the respect and even affection of the House in really difficult situations.

The Speaker is elected by the Members of Parliament. They are very sensitive at any attempt to interfere with this prerogative. When the rumour spread that Mrs Thatcher had tried to persuade Jack Weatherill not to stand for Speaker, his election was assured.

At about the same time that I was manufacturing corduroy working trousers in Hebden Bridge in the limited colour range of tan, drab and mouse, Mr Speaker was starting his career in the family tailoring firm of Bernard Weatherill making nether garments of a more regal class. When, after taking the chair in the House of Commons, he was received by the Queen at Buckingham Palace he was able to remind her that his first visit there was when she was a girl, to measure her for jodhpurs.

It is nice to have friends in parliament, but history does not show that they are essential for success. I would not have thought that Churchill, Attlee and Heath were rich in friends but they all became Prime Ministers. Nobody has more friends than Willie Whitelaw; Rab Butler had a crowd of disciples, yet neither of them quite reached the top.

27

Courts and Queens

In 1960 a friend of mine got into trouble. When I was commanding the battalion at Cassino and thereabouts, my intelligence officer was John Wheater, then aged 19. I got to know him well.

When the time came for my second assault on the Sowerby constituency I got a letter from him, by then a solicitor, offering to come and be my chauffeur for the three weeks of the election campaign. Nothing could have been more welcome. He was offering to do the peacetime electoral equivalent of what he did for me in the mountains of Italy. He was a great success and lightened the drearier moments of the campaign. He was a social success too, particularly with my mother-in-law who, as I noted earlier, gave him the accolade of 'dear boy.'

Ten years later came one of the trials of the century - the Great Train Robbery trial. A gang of hardened criminals hijacked the Glasgow-London night mail in Hertfordshire by tampering with the signals and got away with several million pounds. The boldness and the meticulous planning of the operation captivated the public, and had the criminals not made the mistake of hitting the guard on the head with a truncheon they might have emerged as heroes rather than villains. Imagine our surprise when on television we saw the face of John Wheater among this infamous band. The media was full of the trial for weeks and we never missed an episode. Suddenly the trial got even nearer home when John Wheater's solicitor asked me if I would give evidence of character in the court at Aylesbury.

On the appointed morning I reported to the solicitor at the court for instructions. He said that our case was that John was a fool rather than a knave - could I say that he was incompetent? I did not particularly savour this. I had come there to say favourable rather than derogatory things about John. However, if this was going to help him avoid prison I could say something of that nature without perjuring myself. In truth he was not particularly reliable.

I passed an unforgettable day. I had never been in a court of law before and this was a spectacular maiden voyage. I saw the accused, Biggs, Wilson, et al, the 10 toughest men in England, jump out of the black maria cheerful and laughing. The last to get out was John Wheater, looking hopelessly out of his element.

All day long I sat in the court until I was summoned to the witness box at about 4.30pm. Our counsel then started cross-examining me. His first questions were aimed at establishing my standing as a witness. How long did I command the battalion? Did I win the DSO and the MC? How long had I been the member of parliament for Howden? Was I now the vice-chairman of the Conservative Party Organisation? This I found all very comforting.

Then he turned to John Wheater's assets. Was he brave? Was he respected by the troops? All easy questions for me to answer. Then he asked: 'Was he meticulous in his duties?' I thought to myself: 'Oh dear, here comes the rough water.' I answered: 'Not particularly.' He then said: 'Thank you very much, Mr Bryan, that will be all,' and I left the witness box.

I thought that in cutting me off like that he had made a mess of it. In fact he was being sensible. All he wanted to do was to insert a scintilla of doubt into the minds of the jury. Had he carried on with further questions about the incompetence of Wheater, prosecuting counsel would have started asking me questions as to why I had ever employed him as my intelligence officer.

In the end justice was done. John Wheater was convicted of aiding and abetting the criminals with a sentence of three years' imprisonment. The main criminals got 10 years.

After the war John Wheater had qualified as a solicitor and gone into practice with an intelligent, hard-working partner called Lomer. Lomer sailed ahead because of those very qualities. John, less clever and certainly less hard working, trailed. He then made the blunder of setting up on his own as a criminal lawyer. He got too friendly with his clients and on some occasion, in what respect I do not know, he sailed too close to the wind and put the train robbers in a position to say: 'You buy Leatherslade Farm for us or else.' This farm, strategically placed near the railway, was the headquarters on which they based the whole exercise. The verdict was right. He did aid and abet, but he was not privy to the main plot.

In an effort to get him fixed up with a job when he came out of prison I made enquiries about the opportunities for English solicitors in Australia. This was naive. Australia had already had enough of our convicts over the ages. There was luckily a family laundry in Harrogate in which he was able to work. He came regularly to our regimental reunions.

In 1985 when going round the new prison at Full Sutton in my constituency, in conversation I said to the governor that the only jailbird I had ever known was John Wheater. To which he replied: 'Oh, he was one of my inmates at Wormwood Scrubs,' and went on to say what an admirable influence John had upon the place. One morning a black warder reported to the governor some trouble that had occurred in the prison the night before and what action he had taken. In self-defence the warder said: 'Wheater said that that was the right thing to do.'

* * *

Every year the Queen gives a number of small private lunches at Buckingham Palace for an unusually assorted group of guests. In 1962 my name happened to come out of the hat and at the appropriate moment I was heading for the palace gates in my hired car. As I came to the gates it was clear that there were to be more important people than me among the guests as a great crowd had gathered. As I went through they all peered into my window and looked away in disappointment. The person they were looking for was Uri Gargarin, the first human being to enter space. The rest of the guests were not quite so sensational but by no means nonentities. There was Prince Philip; Lord Mountbatten; Sir John Hunt, the conqueror of Everest; Joanna Kelly, the governor of Holloway Prison; Sir William Holford, the architect; Herman David, the president of Wimbledon; Bud Flanagan, the funny man; Colonel Sir James Hutchison, MP. Under what heading James Hutchison had been invited I do not know, but I had always known of him for an act of bravery the like of which I had never heard before. Working in the underground in France he became recognised by the Gestapo and so lost his usefulness. He therefore came back to England and underwent a facial operation to completely transform his looks.

Before and after the lunch there was a long period for sherry and coffee, no doubt arranged like that so the Queen would get the chance personally to talk to everyone, which she did with pleasant ease. The guest most at home with her was Bud Flanagan. He told me when we were sitting next to each other at lunch that he had gone down to

Windsor every Christmas to entertain the royal family. He was the court jester. Gargarin sat next to the Queen, an interpreter sat behind and between them and got no lunch. After a respectable time the interpreter switched to the other side of Gargarin so he could talk to Mountbatten. Up to then the remaining mystery about the space flight was how Gargarin had returned to Earth. Mountbatten told me over coffee that he had asked him that very question. The reply: 'Particulars of my landing will be published shortly.' He was surprised to learn that Mountbatten knew a lot about the Kremlin, his various relations having lived there in pre-revolution times. On my other side sat Sir John Hunt. He was not very chatty.

As I went out I asked advice from one of the courtiers on how we would deal with the press, for with Gargarin there we were bound to be questioned. I was told that as this was a private occasion nothing should be said. I need not have worried. The only one of us they talked to was Bud Flanagan who had no hesitation in answering their questions with such comments as: 'The pudding was a sort of toffee apple.'

Some months after my Buckingham Palace lunch my constituent Charlie Elsey, a famous trainer of racehorses from Malton, was coming to the palace to receive the CBE. I therefore asked him to lunch in the House of Commons beforehand. When I told him about my lunch with the Queen he replied: 'I did that too a few years ago - during lunch I sold the Queen Mother a horse.'

At one question time in the House of Commons some ill-natured member of parliament grumbled to the Prime Minister about the over-effusive welcome that Gargarin had received at Heathrow. Macmillan replied: 'That's nothing to the welcome they would have given to that dog.'

Members of Parliament get plenty of opportunities to go to the royal garden parties, and sometimes they can arrange for their daughters to be received. Just after Felicity had left Benenden she came with me and was introduced to the Queen. On that very day it had been announced that Princess Anne was to go to Benenden so this seemed a natural subject of conversation. Talking about the stern headmistress, Miss Clark, I facetiously said: 'She is rather frightening for fathers.' The Queen replied: 'Fathers only?'

Normally the atmosphere at Buckingham Palace does not stimulate such liberties. My first ever visit to the palace was to receive my war decorations at the hands of George VI. I suppose that, covered with medals, we were a self-satisfied lot, but the admiral on duty soon brought down the mighty from their seats with such orders as: 'Hurry up, you VCs.'

Personally my most memorable meeting with the Queen was 20 minutes in conversation with her *à deux*. Not long after I had ceased being a Minister of State at the Department of Employment in 1972 I was summoned to the palace for her to thank me for my services as a minister. She clearly hasn't time to thank all retiring ministers, but I suppose in my case, being re-shuffled at the age of 58, I was unlikely to be a minister again. One is told that when talking with the Queen she should be left to lead the conversation. I can't remember who led our conversation. She made it all so natural. She had just been on one of her tours to foreign parts which I knew so that gave us a simple start. After my various brief contacts with the lady over the years I am a confirmed fan and bridle at any criticism of her.

* * *

On the 30 June 1963 I got my name into the world press in an uncharacteristic way. That Sunday morning I played golf at Ganton with Roy Smith, Derek Roberts, and the professional. There are two short holes on the Ganton golf course, the fifth and the 10th. We came to the fifth and I holed out in one to laughter and derisory cheers. When we came to the 10th hole I holed out in one again. I can still hear Derek's shout: 'He's bloody well done it again,' ringing across the course.

We went on to the 12th hole where by the tee there is a refreshment hut manned in those days by a Mrs Henderson. Roy said to her: 'Mrs Henderson, Mr Bryan has holed out in one twice in this one round.' This was clearly not the most important news she had heard that morning. After a pause she said: 'Which were they?' Roy replied: 'The fifth and the 10th, Mrs Henderson.' A longer pause and then she said: 'Oh, he would pick the short ones.'

My brother in Montreal heard this item on the radio news. My nephew in Buenos Aires sent me the cutting from the local paper. Friends I had made in Council Bluffs, Iowa, did the same. My sister in Sydney heard it on the radio. The Guinness Book of Records rang me up to know if it was true.

For some years I appeared in the *Golfers' Yearbook* under the heading 'Freaks;' then others repeated my feat and I was displaced.

As one who views telepathy with scepticism I do not expect you to believe the following but it is true. On that day Betty rang up the golf club during the morning with the message: 'Please ask Mr Bryan to bring Derek Roberts and Roy Smith home after golf as I have got out a bottle of champagne. I am sure there will be something to celebrate.' There was no way in which she could have known what happened at the fifth and the 10th holes.

I see an entry in our Park Farm visitors book 'Henry and Barbara Brooke, August 1963.' Henry Brooke was the Home Secretary at the time and Barbara, Dame Barbara Brooke, was my fellow vice-chairman at Conservative Central Office. Working in the next office to mine and attending most of the same meetings and conferences it followed that I knew her very well, and to know her was to like her. She was the acme of intelligent respectability and the perfect example to our Conservative ladies, whom she dominated.

The Brookes were proud of their bright children, the eldest of whom, Peter, is currently (October 1992) Heritage Secretary. After dinner Barbara Brooke rather suddenly announced: 'We feed our dog on Pal.' She went on to tell us that on the Pal packet there had been a competition with the prize of £100 and that prize would go to the person with the best answer to the question - 'How would you spend the £100 if you won it?' Henry, an Oxford scholar, put his whole intellectual weight into answering this question and came out with this offering: 'I would put my wife in kennels and take my Pal for a holiday.' He, of course, won the £100.

Barbara Brooke said: 'So we bought a motor mower.'

28
Betty's Illness

In 1962 when Bunny was 12 Betty fell ill with manic depression. Her illness was to dominate our family life until she died in 1968.

The symptoms first appeared when she went to St Thomas's Hospital for treatment to her back. The consultant, a Mr Cyriax, summoned Libby, then a new medical student, and asked her to tell me that Betty's main problem was a mental illness. She was soon in the mental hospital at Dollis Hill in North London. For the next three weeks I motored daily up and down the crowded Edgware Road, 18 sets of lights, for she was in that stage of the cycle of her illness, which later I got to know so well, in which she had to see me at least daily and any of her other close friends who would come. Betty Barber, Muggs and Bridget responded wonderfully. She sacked her doctor, came home and was soon absolutely normal.

Then a real crisis broke. I will never forget it. As I got out of the train at York station on my journey back from London the loudspeaker barked out: 'Will Mr Bryan go to the Stationmaster's office.' There I was told that Betty was in The Retreat, the mental hospital in York. She had tried and nearly succeeded in committing suicide at Park Farm, but our marvellous Dr Allen had got there just in time.

The principal at the hospital was reassuring, saying that there had been great advances in mental treatment, that Betty's case was not uncommon. A few months' treatment and she would be well again.

This was not to be. It was a cyclical illness. She would go into a depression which would last about six weeks during which she had to go into a hospital for fear of suicide. She would then get better and for a period of perhaps three weeks she would be perfectly normal, her bright intelligent loving self. Then for a slightly shorter time she would go into an elation, during which time she had to communicate. On holiday in Spain she wrote 84 postcards in three days. On another occasion she spent £100 on about 100 articles from the shop 'Ideas' in Helmsley. She telephoned everybody she could think of.

Once when Felicity had passed some minor examination Betty wanted Libby to ring up all our friends with the news, which Libby declined to do. Betty then accused her of being jealous of her sister and absurd though the idea was it was nevertheless upsetting to see someone you love behaving so out of character.

Another distressing part of this stage of her illness was that she embarrassed the children by telling all the family secrets to anybody and everybody. Finally she would be overcome by remorse when she realised what she had done and this seemed to be a factor in her relapse into a depression. It was then that I, not the doctor, had to decide when she should go into hospital again because, from experience, I got to know when there was danger of suicide.

Putting her back into hospital was the most painful thing I have ever had to do.

The regularity of her cycle of illness made me as a layman think that her weakness was mechanical rather than mental. Some activities would bring her temporary relief. For instance, if, when in a depression, I took her for a long walk in the woods at Park Farm, she was perfectly all right as long as we were walking. The moment we got indoors she trembled and was back in depression again.

I was surprised how easily the doctors were deceived by what I understand is a well-known illness. We, of course, tried all the so-called best doctors, each of whom had his pet cure. At St Thomas's Hospital they filled her with huge amounts of assorted tablets, up to 30 in a day. At one time the consultant there was so pleased with her 'cure' that he asked her to address an audience of nurses to explain how this had come about. Highly articulate and an experienced physiotherapist, she had no difficulty in doing this. I raised no objection, indeed there was no point in stopping it but I knew that she was not cured. We had merely arrived at the stage of the cycle in which depression gave way to normality.

At another hospital psychoanalysis was the vogue, but this was useless for Betty was so much cleverer and quicker than the analyst. The analyst's case seemed to depend on an allegedly unrealised but deep down unhappiness in Betty's childhood and her marriage. Betty hit all this sort of rubbish for six for she was proud of our happiness. Before her first appointment with the analyst we agreed that I should go in first and explain to her the background of the illness. She thought this quite improper and could not believe that Betty had agreed to my doing this. Betty carried on her appointments with this lady for a time but they came to a stop in a horrible way, for which I blame myself. As we came up to Christmas I asked the analyst whether it would be all right for Betty to have no appointment for the next month. She agreed, saying that Betty was stable and there was no risk of attempted suicide. This proved to be exactly the opposite of the case, though luckily again she did not succeed.

At the Retreat in York they went in for electrical treatment, which was alarming in that one could not believe that such a violent disturbance of the nervous system could do anything but lasting damage.

For a time Betty's illness knocked the family off balance. We all adored her, she was a powerful character and quite irreplaceable. Bunny, aged 12, especially missed her - but so did we all. What with nursing, hospital visiting, visiting the children at school and so on, I calculated that Betty was taking 25 per cent of my working time and a much higher proportion of my thinking time, which was difficult in that parliament, the constituency, J.B.Hoyle and Company and Park Farm gave me more than enough to do anyway.

For some months Libby gave up her training at St Thomas's Hospital to look after her mother and I wondered whether I would have to give up being a member of parliament. Knowing how much any break in our careers would have distressed Betty, Libby and I decided to go on doing what we were doing and to see how we got on.

Ironically, what made life possible was the seriousness of her illness. The fact that she had to go into hospital for lengthy periods made our task lighter. I got to know my daughters better than ever as I had to visit them at school and do a lot with them in the holidays. Libby became almost a mother to Bunny. She writes:

> We were very much together over her illness. There was never any antagonism or difficulty as to who should help or how we would manage it. It was much easier for me because I had a more obvious role by this stage. I had left school, my father was an MP and often needed somebody to help him with things, so in a sense I took on a wifely role as well as having to help Bunny in a motherly role. My tasks were quite clear. I think for Fliss and Bunny it was much harder.'

Betty died when we were on holiday together at the Marbella Club in Spain. She had had one of her good periods and in my judgement was just heading for the elation stage. We had just played golf the day before for the first time for five years. We danced that night, also for the first time for years.

At about 7 o'clock the next morning she said she was going down to the swimming pool. I said I would follow when I had had a cup of tea and this I did about half an hour later.

When I arrived she had drowned. The attendant had laid her body beside the pool. She looked infinitely peaceful. I was overwhelmed, not with grief, but with relief. At last she had been released from the living torture which had been her life for seven years.

Why she died, to this day I do not know. I do know it was not suicide because she was not in that stage of her illness.

The Spanish officials and the Hotel Manager were correct, courteous and kind and the funeral on the next day was beautifully done. Betty's grave is in the Roman Catholic cemetery surrounded with cypress trees on the hill overlooking the sea outside Marbella.

29
Shadow Postmaster General

A lec Home had been in office less than a year when he was faced with the general election of 1964. During that time our standing in the country had not improved and I was personally surprised that Labour won with a majority of only 13 over the Conservatives and four over all other parties combined. There were some who blamed Home, unfairly I thought, for our defeat, but the main reason for the Labour victory was that the Conservative government had been in power for 13 long years and the electorate wanted a change.

The vice-chairman of the Conservative Party Organisation in charge of candidates usually does the job for one parliament and is then promoted to Minister of State in some department. No doubt this would have been my lot had we won the election of 1964, but as we lost I did not become a minister for another six years, in the Heath government of 1970.

In the event the election had been won by so small a margin that it was obvious there would be another election quite soon and Alec Home therefore asked me to stay on at Central Office until all the constituencies were fixed up again with candidates. This took about six months. I was succeeded by Jim Prior.

Alec did not enjoy being leader of the opposition, and his least fine hour was Prime Minister's question time, which took place every Tuesday and Thursday afternoon. This in contrast to the nimble footed Harold Wilson, whose favourite game this used to be when in opposition. The leader of the opposition does not have to take part in Prime Minister's question time, the questions are not, after all, aimed at him, but his supporters expect him to rise from time to time and score points off the government. This did not come easily to Alec and he asked me to help him.

For six months I used to meet him each Tuesday and Thursday in his office at midday to go through the questions on the order paper with him and advise on when and how he should intervene. Often I would advise him not to intervene at all.

This little job took time. In the morning I would go to the library or the research department and study the questions; at 12 o'clock I would meet Alec and in the afternoon I had to be in the House to listen to the result of our discussions. All this gave me the chance to get to know him well, in itself time well spent.

One day I got a message from him asking me to report a little earlier for our meeting as he had something he wished to discuss. This turned out to be his resignation which he announced that afternoon. Typically he wanted me to know before the general public. He need not have resigned. He was judged by most Conservative MPs to have done well in the election, in which the party fared better than had been expected, but there were the usual 'time for a change' murmurings which follow lost elections. He had sacrificed a lot, giving up his peerage, to become Prime Minister because he thought he was wanted, but he was not interested in out-staying his welcome.

This was not the end of his political career for in 1970 Ted Heath was lucky enough to have him as Foreign Secretary. In the years between he did a certain amount of public speaking and drew the most enormous crowds, especially at the universities. Though caricatured as an 'old world' figure, wedded to making speeches from scribbled notes on Basildon Bond notepaper, he had a great attraction for the young. I am not surprised. He is in every way a good and delightful man.

In 1965 Winston Churchill died. His funeral matched his life. He had laid down in detail how it should be conducted, naming the regiments to be involved; the bands and the tunes they should play. This had already proved an inconvenience to the Ministry of Defence, forcing them to postpone the disbandment of several regimental bands.

His body lay in state in the lofty historic Westminster Hall like kings and queens before him. For three days four guardsmen stood at the coffin whilst the crowd in thousand slowly and silently moved by. The queue stretched from Westminster Hall down the embankment, over Lambeth Bridge and past St Thomas's Hospital. As an MP I was able to get my daughters into the Hall without queueing, but having done this they felt so unworthy that they then joined the end of the queue for three hours to pass the coffin again.

The British genius for pomp and ceremony was at its best with the bands and the magnificent marching of the troops and as the gun carriage went by you could not but think of how approving the old boy must be. One could not help being moved. My war medals had been in a brown paper packet at the back of a drawer in my wardrobe. I felt that Winston would have wanted me to wear them so I took them off to the jeweller to be mounted.

As an MP I had a place in St Paul's Cathedral where I sat for a very long time, but the hours did not drag for there were television screens mounted on the pillars so one could follow the coffin and the music from the moment it left Westminster Hall on the gun carriage then up the Thames on a naval barge and finally into the cathedral on the shoulders of guardsmen. Typically the service was brightened with rousing hymns like 'John Brown's Body' and I am sure influenced future funerals for I have noticed that nowadays funeral services tend to be more cheerful.

The second world war was the first in which radio had covered the world. This made Churchill's voice the most potent, not only in Britain but in the universe. On one occasion when somebody was recalling his leadership he said: 'The people were the lion. I was only the roar.'

* * *

Whilst my career in politics had somewhat run out of steam, Denis Forman's in broadcasting was at full steam ahead. He was a director of Granada, already acknowledged as the leading independent television company.

The Independent Broadcasting Authority laid down that each television company should have one or two non-executive directors. I doubt if this was a proviso which appealed to Sidney Bernstein who had created Granada in his own image with his own team and needed no outside help. Nevertheless the rule had to be obeyed and to give him a hand Denis Forman said he knew a harmless Yorkshire MP called Bryan who actually lived in the Granada franchise area and would not interfere too much. The outcome was that I joined Granada; it was a happy association for me which lasted 25 years, with a break during the time that I was a minister.

In the first parliamentary recess after my appointment I spent a week at the studios in Manchester, where I watched the cast of Coronation Street rehearsing and sat in on the build-up of the daily regional programme, from its start of no more than an idea being discussed around the table by a dozen lively young researchers, to its going on the air only nine hours later. The staff I met were young, intelligent, talkative and welcoming. The fact that in those days everybody wanted to work for a glamorous television company meant that the calibre of the staff was likely to be high but this was ensured at Granada by the enormous trouble that was taken in recruiting. Huge numbers of people were interviewed in the search for the best.

Granada was not a gentle company, certainly not genteel, but warm, lively and welcoming. I always looked forward to my visits.

Sidney Bernstein set high standards. He meant Granada to be the best and instilled in the staff the belief that it was the best so successfully that they were always talking about 'Granada standards.' Nor was this empty talk for the television company has certainly led the field from the day it was launched, 35 years ago.

Coronation Street was the first of the soap operas. It has maintained its audience in this country ever since and despite the Lancashire accent and often incomprehensible dialect, has a big foreign following.

In drama it established an early reputation with the aid of Laurence Olivier, David Plowright's brother-in-law, and rose to a crescendo with Brideshead Revisited and Jewel in the Crown, arguably the best dramatic series ever produced on television.

World in Action is not the most loved investigative programme but is certainly the most investigative. The freeing of the innocent Irishmen - the Birmingham Six - after 15 years in prison was acknowledged to be the result of the persistence of this programme.

As recently as 1992 Roger Graef wrote:

> Of all the ITV companies Granada most symbolises quality television. Its commitment to innovative current affairs, long documentaries and extension dramas and to nurturing talent, has produced much of television's finest work and recently that of the British Film Industry as well.

Granada Television was always a successful commercial business, but a business run by showmen or programme makers. For the first two decades it was run by showmen, Sidney and Cecil Bernstein. Then the programme makers took over, first Denis Forman who produced Jewel in the Crown and was responsible for Brideshead Revisited then David Plowright, an early editor of World in Action and the driving force behind many of Granada's successful programmes.

The successful showmen and programme makers were clearly backed by a team of quality. The questions then arise: not only how has

Granada assembled such a team but more pertinently how have they kept them in an industry in which there is much tempting away of stars? As a start Sidney Bernstein is not everybody's cup of tea. I know several intelligent and sensible people, in particular my old friend Majdalany, who have found him impossible to work for. He is interfering but he is also considerate.

In later years, when I was a director of the Granada Television Rental company, I remember him asking at a board meeting: 'Has each of our shops got a full-length mirror and a shelf by it for the girls' cosmetics?' Nobody knew. The managing director said he would report at the next meeting. At this it was announced that all the shops except eight had got the mirror and the shelf. Sidney said: 'Have those eight shops got no doors to the girls' lavatories?'

Nobody could feel unnoticed. A feature of the monthly board meetings at all the companies was the individual reports that managers had to present, explain and defend, with Sidney Bernstein himself frequently at the table. Though frightening, Sidney did not seem to inhibit discussion.

Like the *Financial Times* in journalism Granada has been a training ground. Jeremy Isaacs, Anna Ford, John Birt, Michael Parkinson, Michael Apted, Gus MacDonald, Roland Joffe, Jonathan Powell, Graham MacDonald, Mike Newall and Mark Shivas - all started their careers in the Manchester studios.

There were moments of deep satisfaction. On the eve of poll of the 1974 election I happened to be in Manchester performing on the BBC. I naturally called in for a drink with my Granada friends to find them engulfed in Barry Head's notorious sweep. I, the only Conservative there, joined the gamble and was alone in forecasting a Conservative defeat. This was not a popular win.

Granada's most remarkable achievement has been to produce a high proportion of leading actors in the broadcasting world, while at the same time retaining a nucleus and more than a nucleus of the best talent in the home team so consistently that at no time has anyone disputed its claim to be the best television company.

This has also been the reason why it is such a pleasant company to be associated with. For it makes friendships easy to retain.

* * *

When I rejoined the Granada board after being a minister in the Heath government Sidney Bernstein said he would like me to find a new director for the board who, for want of a better description, one might call a director for public affairs. He gave me a long description of the sort of person he had in mind then said: 'I would have a word with Bernard Levin or Harold Evans' (editor of the *Sunday Times*) and a number of such people. 'I am sure they could suggest somebody.'

I came out from my meeting with Sidney and told Alex and Denis Forman what Sidney had in mind. They both burst out laughing. Denis said: 'We have been through all this before. Such a man does not exist.'

In this cause I gave a number of lunches to a number of people, some of whom said: 'What about me?' With not much confidence I produced a few candidates whom Sidney duly turned down. Then I gave serious thought to the way Granada recruited its board as a possible guide to how I might land my elusive fish.

The television board consisted of Bernsteins (Sidney, Cecil and Alex), those who had come up through the business (Wharton, Forman, Peers, Amyes, Plowright, Heads, and later Mike Scott and Quinn) and others previously known to the board for one reason or another (Carr, Bryan). In those days I do not recall anyone being recruited for the television board through a headhunter. This led me to the conclusion that my best hope was to find somebody already known to Granada and by a lucky stroke such a man immediately came in sight.

Conservative Central Office normally employed a prominent newspaper man as chief publicity officer and as a rule he would stay for the duration of one parliament. At that time Don Harker had the job and as we were coming up to the 1974 election he was likely soon to be free. He fulfilled the qualification of being already known to Granada for he had worked for the company successfully in his early days before he moved on to Rank. He agreed to join us and over the next 17 years became renowned in his role with Granada where he quietly established an entente with the political world unlike that of any other company.

When it came to the independent television industry having to react to such things as the report by the Annan Committee or a parliamentary select committee, Granada invariably took the lead and with everybody's agreement and indeed enthusiasm Don did the writing. He became my most constant contact with Granada whom I could enjoy ringing up at any time with or without good reason and often meet for lunch.

In 1977 I was at a cocktail party and met Sir Brian Young, the director of the Independent Broadcasting Authority, then chaired by Lady Plowden. At that time television franchises were up for re-consideration and I was shortly to be one of the Granada team to be interviewed by the authority about our franchise application.

Young said to me: 'What we shall want to know from you as a non-executive director is your reaction to some of the disgraceful programmes put out over the last few months by World in Action.' When I reported this conversation to Denis Forman he very sensibly wrote to Brian Young and asked him to enlarge on his remarks. He wrote a brilliant reply castigating three of the World in Action programmes in, to me, unanswerable terms.

The great day came. Each of the members of the authority asked his questions, most of which Denis Forman firmly blocked, or glided politely to the boundary. At last the question forecast by Sir Brian Young was put to me, fortunately by a member of the authority and not by him.

I answered to the effect that as the only director of a television company in the House of Commons I was vulnerable to all sorts of complaint and criticism but all in all I remained proud to be a director of Granada Television. We might make a few of the sort of mistakes that the member had mentioned, but we should be given credit not only for the quality of the general run of our programmes, but in particular for the fact that, incomparably more than any other company, we produced programmes like State of the Nation, Disappearing World, Nuts and Bolts of the Economy and several others that I had memorized which used up a tremendous amount of our management time and creative talent despite the low ratings which of course we knew such programmes would attract. I was asked no supplementary question.

I don't expect my answer mattered very much. We duly got the franchise again. The IBA would find it difficult to demote the producers of Coronation Street.

One day in 1973 Sidney Bernstein asked me to dine with him in his flat overlooking St James's Park. Over coffee he said: 'Paul, I would like you to join the board of Granada Theatres.' At the time the theatre company was composed of a dozen cinemas, the remains of the

original theatre company on which Granada was built and about 40
bingo clubs, many of these housed in the grand former Granada
cinemas. To my obvious question: 'What do you think I could do for
the theatre company?' Sidney replied: 'Paul, I think you could tighten
up the bingo,' When I told my secretary of my new appointment she
said: 'Wool sorter, soldier, trouser maker, politician, television direction
- now bingo - what next?' I had seven interesting years as a director of
Granada Theatres but in the forthcoming history of the Granada group
I do not foresee a chapter entitled: 'How Paul Bryan tightened up the
bingo.'

I have hardly mentioned an all important character in the Granada
set-up - the charming and clever Cecil Bernstein, the peacemaker who
picked up the pieces behind his brother, Sidney. Apart from his general
duties, he was brilliant at nursing the cast of Coronation Street and in
the early days of Granada Cinemas was regarded in the industry as the
great expert on films.

In his days as chairman of Granada Television, those in the know
would have named Denis Forman as one of the biggest men in British
broadcasting. I specify those in the know because he was never one to
seek the headlines. We have seen him earlier excelling as a leader of
troops in Italy; he was just as effective as a leader of the mixed mob of
talent that goes to make up a television company - and for the same
reasons, he could do their jobs, or at least understand them, as well as
they did. In his early days he produced programmes such as What The
Papers Say; The Verdict Is Yours; Family At War; The Christians; The
Odd Man; All Our Yesterdays, but even as chairman of the company
he led from the front and was personally responsible for the decision to
produce Jewel in the Crown. His deep knowledge of music led to the
production of a unique music programme. He became the dominant
figure in a company already dominated by Sidney Bernstein - no
ordinary feat.

* * *

After Alec Home's resignation Ted Heath was elected leader of the
Conservative Party and asked me to become Shadow Postmaster
General.

My opposite number, the Postmaster General, was responsible for
the Post Office, which in those days embraced the post and telephone

services and broadcasting. In addition to administering a large department he would be responsible for any legislation on these subjects that passed through the House and for answering questions, of which there were plenty, mainly about the postal service.

When I took over the Postmaster General was Anthony Wedgwood Benn, articulate, intelligent and courteous, but not there for long before he was replaced by Ted Short, a rugged and, in the House, deceptively humourless schoolmaster from Newcastle. In politics it is possible to rise to unexpected heights not on you own ability but because of the unacceptability for one reason or another of more able competitors. The Labour Party, with its constant divisions, was more susceptible to this phenomenon than the less fractious Conservative party and Ted Short's advance to be Deputy Prime Minster was a prime example.

The main Post Office legislation due to come before the House was the rather strangely entitled Marine Offences Bill which was designed to do away with the pirate radio stations, half a dozen of which broadcast pop music from ships anchored around our shores. Against all the evidence Carlton Greene, the Director General of the BBC, claimed that the pirates had a negligible audience but it was noticeable that once their stations had been expunged the BBC at once took over some of their disc jockeys and their style as well.

The pirate radio stations commanded a big audience, not because they were good but because they had hit upon a spot in the spectrum of entertainment unoccupied by the only other operator, the BBC. They were a rough and ready lot operating from leaking old tubs at sea, with Rohan O'Reilly on Radio Caroline the most notorious. In the course of my duty I got to know most of them and discovered one Phillip Birch, of Radio London, to be the only competent broadcaster. He was a professional who had been with J.Walter Thompson, the famous advertising firm in America, for 12 years and was the man I turned to whenever I needed reliable advice, My friendship with him bore fruit in 1973 when representing Granada in the team going for the Manchester Radio franchise. I managed to get him to join us and he was the critical factor in our success in winning the franchise and subsequently developing Piccadilly Radio, the best run of the first batch of commercial radio stations, and of which I became a director.

In retrospect the team I was given to deal with the modest Marine Offences Bill was of the 'sledgehammer to crack a nut' variety. My number two was Ian Gilmour, a brilliant writer, future cabinet minister and thorn in the side of Mrs Thatcher. My research assistants were Chris Patten, future cabinet minister, party chairman and governor of Hong Kong, and Patricia Hodgson, future top lady of the BBC. We had a lot of fun.

We could not, of course, oppose the bill for in using unauthorised frequencies the pirates were clearly breaking the law, so in order to give ourselves a more positive role than mere acquiescence I suggested to Ted Heath that we might use the bill as a vehicle to press the virtues of commercial radio. With his love and knowledge of classical music I rather wondered whether Ted would approve, yet he gave us the go-ahead and was indeed enthusiastic.

All the arguments against commercial broadcasting had been rehearsed with heat and vigour in the early fifties during the introduction of independent television. High standards produced by ITV, stimulating the BBC to greater efforts, had by now silenced all the prophets of doom so the government had to take a new line in their opposition to commercial radio. The contention now was that commercial radio was technically impossible due to the shortage of frequencies, all of which were fully taken by essential services and the existing and proposed local BBC radio stations. Time and again Ted Short rose at the dispatch box in the House of Commons quoting the evidence of his Post Office experts to pour scorn on our technical ignorance.

I was indeed technically ignorant, but after going to Australia and America and seeing their countless radio stations happily in action, I frankly did not believe him or his experts. I went to a firm of consultants in London, Urwick Orr, and asked them how much it would cost for them to produce a radio system which would produce 80 stations and they said that this could be done for £7000. This was quite a sum in those days and certainly not to be had from Conservative Central Office so I visited the main firms likely to be interested - Sir Joseph Lockwood at EMI, Pye Radio at Cambridge and others and had no difficulty in raising £7,000. Urwick Orr duly produced the plan which is the basis of the system which by now (1992), taking into account all the radio franchises on offer, will have reached our target of 80 stations.

* * *

On November 24 1966 the proposition 'That this house, taking note of the report of the Select Committee on broadcasting of proceedings in the House of Commons, approves for an experimental period broadcasting its proceedings on closed circuits, subject to any recommendations which the Select Committee on House of Commons services may make thereon.'

This debate was in effect to decide whether or not the House wished its proceedings to be televised, for nobody doubted once an experiment had taken place the real thing would follow. The proposition had been debated and rejected several times before, but with the passage of time and the arrival of many new and younger members there appeared a good chance that this time it would be approved.

Richard Crossman, as Leader of the House, opened the debate and I, as Shadow Postmaster General, led for the opposition, both of us speaking in favour of the motion. As this was not a party matter no advice had come from the Whips Office and members were free to vote as they chose. This being so Quintin Hogg, a former cabinet minister and very senior member of the party, asked Ted Heath's permission to speak against the motion - to which he was fervently opposed - from the front bench, and this was granted.

The antis argued in general that television would change the whole nature of our beloved and ancient House. The pros argued that since television was now acknowledged to be the chief source of information of the electorate it was wrong that they should be denied this source in respect of the activities of the representatives whom they had voted.

At the end of a debate members move off into the 'aye' or 'noe' lobbies and looking down on this process from the strangers gallery this milling about with members chatting to each other presents a somewhat disorganized scene.

Quintin and I having voted in opposite lobbies were sitting on the front bench and as members passed by us one Labour member came up to Quintin and said: 'I was going to vote in favour of the motion but having heard your speech I decided to vote against. Quintin let out a guffaw of laughter, saying that this was the first time in his whole life that he had consciously changed anybody's opinion.

This feat was more important than he then realised for when the votes were counted Hansard reported the results thus: 'Mr Speaker; order. This is not being televised. (Laughter). The ayes to the right were one hundred and thirty. The noes to the left were one hundred and thirty one.' So the motion was defeated. Had Quintin not converted the Labour member the result would have been: 'The ayes to the right were one hundred and thirty one. The noes to the left were one hundred and thirty.' - and the televising of the House would have been introduced in 1967 instead of 21 years later in 1988.

On retirement, Speaker Weatherill, after nine years in the chair, six without and three with television, was in a unique position to answer questions as to the effect of broadcasting on parliament. He remains in favour of television maintaining that the electorate has a right to see what is done in their name, as well as to hear about it on radio and read about it in the press. He also claims that it has had a beneficial effect upon standards of behaviour. This may sound incredible to those who watch 'Prime Minister's Question Time' but this is in fact a freak period, a tiny proportion of the days business and quite untypical.

The House of Commons is far quieter now than in various periods during my career there. As Minister of State at the Department of Employment I well remember the fierce all night debates on the 1970 Industrial Relations Bill. This subject, the taming of the trade unions, was all important to the Labour party. The very existence of the party seemed threatened and there was real hate in the air.

During the so-called 'winter of discontent' in the last months of the Callaghan government when, due to the strike of the public service unions, the streets of London were piled high with uncollected rubbish and hospital services were breaking down, once again the bitterness of the debates was genuine and the chamber of the House of Commons was where it erupted. There were also long, late and heated hours of debate on our entry into the EEC. Parliament has never been a polite institution.

Speaker Weatherill says that television has tended to make the chamber less well attended as members get more interested in select committees which, when televised, can make even better television than the proceedings in the chamber.

Television is only one cause of the emptying of the chamber. In my early days only senior members had offices and the House was much more of a club than it is today. One made a point of visiting the smoking room and the members' dining room was always full. All this meant that members were about the place more, and at the closing stages of a debate, would all crowd into the chamber to hear the winding up speeches from both sides.

The drink-drive regulations have also been a factor in emptying the smoking room so, in the Speaker's words, 'the old market place atmosphere of the House has tended to disappear - and that is also a sad loss.'

* * *

In the early days of television I asked Carlton Greene, the then Director General of the BBC, what was the effect of television on politics. He answered: 'It can only increase a tendency which is already there.' This has proved a valid judgement. After Harold Wilson won the 1964 election, the first election at which televison could be said to be dominant, one's constituents said: 'You will never win another election unless that man leaves the Labour party. He is so brilliant on television.' Within a couple of years Wilson's own colleagues were asking him to keep off television. He was neither better nor worse on the television than he had been during the election, but the news had got worse as the Labour government got into deeper and deeper trouble. When John Major first became Prime Minister he looked immeasurably better than Neil Kinnock in the broadcasts at Prime Minister's Question Time, but as the economic depression deepened and week after week Major was having to defend the ever deteriorating situation, the gap between them narrowed markedly. Neither of them had got 'better' or 'worse' at television. It was the news that had got worse for Major.

* * *

During my period as Shadow Postmaster General in the 1960s Richard Crossman, the then Leader of the House, instituted morning sittings on Wednesdays from 9.30 to 1 o'clock. On one of these Wednesdays I rose to speak from the opposition front bench at 11.40 to wind up the debate with a speech of about 20 minutes. When I had been under way for about five minutes a note was passed to me from the Whip on duty which read: 'Can you keep going until 1 o'clock?' In other words, could I extend my 20 minute speech to a speech of an hour and 20 minutes?

The debate was due to finish with a vote at 1 o'clock, but Post Office matters are not always enthralling and fewer members wanted to speak than expected. It looked like petering out at about midday - an hour before our members had been instructed to be there to vote and we would have had a very poor showing in the lobby.

My answer to the Whip's note, muttered in a stage whisper over my shoulder was: 'Yes, if you throw me some buns'. By that he knew I meant that he was to arrange for our own back benchers to keep interrupting me with questions which I could answer at length. Soon more and more people could see what I was up to, joined in the fun and by the time the House filled in readiness for the vote I was still going strong.

30
Happy Trinity

From an early age Libby had wanted to be a doctor and especially a children's doctor. She had a way with children, a certain kind of understanding firmness which seemed to win their confidence on sight. As a teenager at Park Farm she taught countless little boys and girls how to ride a bicycle. You would hear her asking: 'Can you ride a bicycle?' She would then disappear down the lane with the child protesting to begin with as Libby kept saying: 'Pedal, pedal, pedal,' and in an incredibly short time in would run a beaming little thing shouting: 'Mummy, I can ride!'

In 1960 she got into St Thomas's Hospital as a medical student, quite a feat in those days, for St Thomas's then only took three non-university girls per year. She stayed with me in our flat at Marsham Court, conveniently placed only 15 minutes walk from St Thomas's.

Libby's return home to Park Farm after her very first week at St Thomas's Hospital coincided with the Conservative Party conference at Scarborough. We had either staying or dining with us that night Willie and Celia Whitelaw, Michael Hughes-Young, Tony and Lesley Leavey, Martin and Anne Redmayne, Eddie and Lalage Wakefield, Richard and Pam Sharples, John Hill and, surprisingly, Denis Forman.

Libby burst in at the coffee stage of our dinner. I said: 'Well, how did you get on?' Out it all came and the company present were agog as she described her first anatomy lesson in which a naked man stood before the class whilst a lecturer illustrated his talk by chalking designs all over the poor man's body. I asked who was the naked man in real life? Answer: 'The fireman.'

In the general elections of the 1960s Libby, Felicity and their friends added glamour to the Bryan election team. The day after Libby passed her driving test she became my chauffeur for the next three weeks which was perfect for me but arduous for her. Elections are not light-hearted affairs for the candidate and to have a familiar figure, especially one of the family, constantly at one's side is a comfort. The months after Libby's driving test soon established her as an experienced driver for, having spent three weeks driving me around the East Riding, as a reward for her labours, she went motoring with Betty on the continent for a month in our Morris Minor, enjoying most of the time in sunny Italy.

At one election Joey Cayley, the youngest of that tribe, both attractive and intelligent, took the wheel. As company she was perfect: as a driver not reassuring to start with, for when I said to her: 'Are you a good driver, Joey?' she replied: 'Yes, but I do run out of road sometimes.' That she did not do, and her worst driving crime was a little damage to a branch chairman's front gatepost. She had an easily ignited sense of humour and every other day something would make her burst into laughter which could last for half an hour, and lighten the darkness of the apparently never ending campaign.

Felicity's forte at election time was the microphone. She would stand up on the front seat of our poster-bedecked estate car, her head and shoulders through the sunshine roof, a vote-winning little blonde figure, microphone in hand, her message ringing out over the wolds. Her standard patter went: 'This is Paul Bryan, your Conservative candidate. Paul Bryan has come to Driffield to meet you and answer your questions. Come and meet Paul Bryan.' She normally did this to perfection but things went wrong in the village of Thorpe Basset where the message that rang down the village street was: 'This is Paul Bryan, your Conservative candidate. Paul Bryan has come to - where are we, Daddy?'

Libby qualified as a doctor at St Thomas's Hospital in 1966 and then instead of carrying on there as a houseman like most of her colleagues she decided to do this in Scarborough Hospital. This was a great success for in addition to being near home and her Yorkshire friends she worked under Anthony Bacon, for whom she had the greatest respect. From the age of six she had wanted to be a paediatrician so she then moved to the hospital at York to work under Walter Henderson, a well-known paediatrician in the area. The next year she went out to Australia on a cargo ship as the ship's doctor. It was the maiden voyage and her ship's surgery shone bright with modern equipment. Traditional medicine was represented by a huge earthenware jar entitled 'pile paste.' I was rather alarmed at the idea of her as the only female in a crew of 50 but she pointed out that in an oversized syringe she had a ready defence against over-amorous sailors. In Sydney she worked in a children's hospital for nine months, staying with my sister, Helen, who was married to Dennis Rowe, one of the leading orthopaedic surgeons in the country. She worked in an African hospital then after another spell in York, this time as Registrar, she went to the Hammersmith Hospital to research on twins. This was a very formative period in her doctoring career, for twins and multiple births have developed into her speciality and today, now a Fellow of the Royal College of Physicians, she is probably the leading authority on multiple births in the country and is Director of the Multiple Births Foundation, which she started in 1988. She has written several books on the subject and this year her book *Twins, Triplets and More* has been published in America and the UK by Penguin and translated into Japanese.

Libby has also become a specialist on bereavement, particularly in the newborn period. When one of her child patients died she would often go to see the parents in their homes. When she had done this many times in homes all over the country she had acquired a deep knowledge of the suffering of the bereaved. This is not something you can learn out of a book. Consequently she finds herself frequently asked to address professional gatherings, such as doctors and nurses, to give them the benefit of her experience.

Sadly, though more than happily married to Ronald Higgins, she has had no children of her own.

Felicity slipped into Benenden with quite a struggle and much reluctance but her first letter made us hope that perhaps she might blossom there. It read:

Dear Mummy and Daddy,

You are bound to like something here.

This was factually true. The 'something' she loved was the arts department. But by and large she did not like Benenden, with its emphasis on games and competition. She left at 16; in her view not a minute too soon. She then spent a few months in Paris at an establishment for young ladies run by a Mademoiselle Anita.

The effect of Paris on Felicity was to convince her that the deb life was not for her, and for the first time gave her the idea of going to a university. This was quite a possibility for she had got three 'A' levels at the age of 16 and had apparently only to pick up a Latin 'O' level to qualify. This she did in the merriest way via a 'crammer' called Kirby Lodge near Cambridge where life was a brilliant social whirl and she shared rooms with another Yorkshire girl, Patricia Cockroft, who became a friend for life.

Things improved further when, having decided she wanted to get to the Courtauld Institute, she spent a summer in Italy. Assuming adequate 'A' levels, the main hurdle in the Courtauld entrance procedure was a gruelling interview with a panel chaired by the notorious spy, Sir Anthony Blunt. Felicity cleared this and so started the one part of her education which she really enjoyed.

At this point Felicity was thinking of a career in the art world and on leaving the Courtauld in 1967 had fixed herself up with a job on the *Burlington Magazine*. But her last long vacation, spent in America, changed all that. She worked for two months in the Scenic Design Department of CBS - a job kindly arranged by Denis Forman - and then took the Greyhound Bus across America to San Francisco and back. She was captivated by the excitement and openness of America and determined to return.

So by April 1968 she had found a job working as assistant to Joe Rogalay, the bureau chief of the *Financial Times* in Washington. Her journalistic experience so far was limited to a lively piece in the *Sunday Telegraph* describing her experiences as a volunteer clearing up after the disastrous floods in Florence. But she soon had pieces appearing regularly in the *Financial Times*, which I showed to my friends with fatherly pride.

She stayed in Washington for two of the most stimulating years of her life, arriving just after the death of Martin Luther King when Washington was smouldering, seeing through the election campaign of 1968 and the full drama of America at the height of the Vietnam War. Some of her most lasting friendships date from that time. She still runs a Fellowship - in memory of her friend Larry Stern - which sends a young British journalist to work on the *Washington Post* every year.

In 1970 she was asked to join the *Economist*, writing for The American Survey back in London. She took a break between jobs accompanying her friend Larry, who was to be the *Washington Post* correspondent in Saigon. She travelled in Laos and Cambodia, leaving Cambodia just before the coup in March 1970.

Back in London life on the *Economist* was not so stimulating and, while she had a perfectly interesting two years, she was quite happy when, out of the blue, she was approached by the Literary Agency, Curtis Brown, asking if she would like to train as an agent.

Life as a literary agent has suited her well. She has always loved the company of writers and reads widely. To her surprise the business side - negotiating contracts for clients - came naturally and she found it exciting. Much of her business is done in America, allowing her regular visits. Above all, she finds, like her sisters, that she enjoys being in a caring profession. In 1984 she set up her own agency in Oxford, with great success.

From her mother she inherited a love of gardening. For four years she wrote the *Evening Standard*'s gardening column and has since written two books on gardening.

In her childhood Bunny felt rather overshadowed by two bright elder sisters, but luckily my three daughters, if they excel, do so in entirely different areas. There is no competition and harmony reigns. Libby would be an unlikely deacon, Felicity most certainly could not be a doctor nor Bunny a literary agent.

This point was picked up by the *Sunday Times* colour magazine in an article about my daughters in the 'Relative values' series, entitled 'Happy Trinity.'

Bunny was not happy at Benenden. Duncombe Park had gone well for her. She loved the grounds, the riding and the music. She had good friends. She surprised herself by winning prizes for such things as diving and Greek dancing. Her final speech day was certainly the finest hour of her educational career for she was Head Girl and won seven prizes.

But Benenden was a depressing contrast. Bunny was very close to her mother and Betty's illness deeply affected her during all her time there. She lost confidence and uncharacteristically became quite a loner. With Betty ill holidays too were bound to be different, with less friends to stay and fewer parties at the farm.

However, she did well enough at Benenden to get into London University, where she wanted to study social administration with a view to becoming a medical social worker. In her final year she realized she was not yet ready for social work and what she really longed to do was to work abroad, so she went with the International Voluntary Service to Cameroon in West Africa for two years. She found this a wonderful experience. She taught English to bright Cameroonian girls in classes of 45 at a convent school and found that she was a good teacher. She writes:

During my stay in Cameroon I met some impressive Christians - black and white - and they challenged me in my own faith which was very flimsy at the time. I came home with a new commitment to God.

Now aiming to be a teacher she did her certificate of education at York University then taught for two years in a very go-ahead comprehensive school, during which she gradually realised that she was more interested in the home and community life of the children than teaching them English.

At this point she felt drawn to the Church and went to Cuddesdon, the Theological College at Oxford, to train as a Church social worker and in due course became a parish worker at a large lively church at Abingdon.

Though the opposite of assertive or a layer down of the law, Bunny turned out to be a good, at times almost brilliant, preacher. As she has a low voice and speaks slowly she by nature avoids the two main hazards of women speakers who tend to have high voices and speak too fast. She also speaks in parables and stories which hold your attention so much more easily than worthy exhortations.

The first time I heard her preach to a congregation of about 200 at Abingdon I thought she had done well. From a father who professes to speak I felt I ought to make some comment so I said: 'As far as your technique is concerned, Bunny, I shouldn't worry at all.'

'But, Daddy, I never do,' said she, and I then woke up to the fact that our speaking objectives were quite different. As a politician one speaks in hopes of claps or boos or questions or at any rate something to show that you have stimulated the interest of the audience. All she was interested in was conveying her message, which required a far simpler but just as elusive technique.

After another year at Cuddesdon, the first woman student there, she became a deaconess on a large council estate in Slough. Bunny's 'vicarage' in Slough was one of a row of little council houses. Most of this new industrial town seemed to be council houses, peopled by 'over-spill' from the East End of London. When Bunny arrived for the first time at her house she found that small boys had sprayed the entire small garden with weedkiller.

This in no way unnerved her, which was as well, for apart from her spell in the comfortable home county town of Abingdon most of her pastoral duties have been in Balsall Heath, the old 'red light' area of Birmingham, where prostitution is still a main problem, but in Bunny's words: 'It must be the holiest parish in England for we have four mosques.'

At Cuddesdon, where she returns from time to time to lecture (the first woman lecturer at that establishment), she met Rob, her husband, who became the vicar at Balsall Heath. They have two children, Elizabeth and Catherine.

Epilogue

On Cup Final Day 1971 I married Cynthia in the crypt chapel of the House of Commons. She was the widow of Patrick Duncan, son of Sir Patrick Duncan, governor general of South Africa. Patrick was in the Colonial Service in Basutoland and at the time of their marriage he was coming to the end of a three year secondment as private secretary to Sir Evelyn Baring, the British High Commissioner in South Africa. Patrick and Cynthia soon returned to Basutoland but in 1952 Patrick resigned from the Colonial Service to become one of the best-known leaders of the anti-apartheid movement. Cynthia's family came from Hexton in Hertfordshire. Her late father, Sir Patrick Ashley Cooper, had been a director of the Bank of England and was governor of the Hudson's Bay Company for 21 years.

Our wedding service was conducted by the House of Commons chaplain, Canon Edwards, a bachelor Fellow of All Souls' College, Oxford. He asked us to tea on the eve of our wedding day which we appreciated. Rather to our surprise, over the scones he gave us a little talk about the pitfalls of marriage - bold considering that we were a couple of old stagers at the game and he had not yet started.

By way of a dowry Cynthia brought four delightful and talented children whose Oxbridge promise has since been fulfilled in their several professions.

Patrick, a Ph.D. in ecology, is *Directeur de Recherche* of a programme in the French *Centre National de la Recherche Scientifique*. He is married to Alison, who is in charge of the information service of the *Ligue Française pour la Protection des Oiseaux (LPO)*. He has a son, also Patrick, by a previous marriage.

Alex, an agricultural economist, has made my daughter, Felicity happy by marrying her. They have three children, Alice, Max and Ben.

Ann, an economist in the World Bank, has married another economist in the World Bank, Akbar Noman. They have two children, Zafar and Natasha.

Emma, a well-known journalist on the *Economist* and author of a successful book on Pakistan, married Nick Harman, also a journalist, and has one son, Jack.

Jack Woodhead and Pat, our housekeeper, came to live in one of the cottages with their sons, John, David and Paul soon after our marriage. Over 21 years thay have become very much part of our family.

Frequently at Park Farm, Cynthia reigns over varying numbers of our happily joint family, sometimes rising to 20 or more at Christmas.

Appendix
Letters from my Father

Here are extracts from a letter written by father to my brother, Awdry, in the year that I was setting off on my North African adventure:

February 25 1942

My dear Awdry

We are so glad you did not get back to Manila before the Japanese attack. Now, do not be anxious to do anything that would sever you from the Sun Life. At your age you will get nothing after the war, so keep unbroken connection with the Sun Life. You know what a mistake Arthur made in being tempted to break with the Canadian Government; and had a hard time recovering his position, through me, though he does not know it, I think. We hear from Helen now and then; she seems all right so far, but what will happen if the Japanese get into Australia no one can tell. John is still in Kobe so far as we know, but have not heard from him since the break with Japan. But I feel that all foreigners in Japan will be well treated, as they were during the last war. I expect John will have to keep to his house a good deal and not go outside the city without police permission. There must be many English and Americans in Tokyo, Yokohama and Kobe still. Indeed it might have been better for Helen to have remained. The only danger is if Japanese cities are bombed by America, as they are sure to be eventually after America gets into war strike.

As mother has written you all the news of the family I shall not say more now. We are getting on fairly well. It is very hard on mother to have no house help, as she has been used to two or three maids all her life; and now at her age she is in no state to do hard work in a big house, especially in winter. But she is of an indomitable spirit and very difficult to control in the matter of work. I do what I can to help but it is very little. My own work is discouraging, as the war keeps many from Church and life is dull. We were very grateful for the nice parcels you sent us, in which you were really too kind, after all your own expense. The rations keep us well fed so far; it is only luxuries like sweets and sugar that we miss but the denial may be good for us, especially now in Lent. Mike is still practising operational flying, ready at any moment to shoot down an enemy plane. He now flies a 'Whirlwind,' the fastest made, and hopes no German can escape him. He has been promoted to navigation officer, leading his wing. He was here on leave a week ago and had a despatch from the Air Ministry ordering him to the south to fetch up a new Whirlwind to his own station north, just like a flashing thunderbolt. Paul is still awaiting embarkation; and Austin still at his aerodrome.

Give our love to Vi and Robin; how fast Robin is growing up. He will hardly remember us now.

Much love from your affectionate father.

J.Ingram Bryan

* * *

October 13th 1943

My dear Awdry:

In your last letter to Mother you said it was a long time since you had a letter from me. In this you are in the same case as the rest of the family; for as Mother writes all the letters and gives all the news, there is nothing left for me to say. But I am always interested in every letter from any of the family, and usually know what Mother writes. And it is quite a task for her to keep up correspondence with the eight sons and daughters. It often seems as if all her spare time, which is little, is given to these letters. Of course we are so anxious about those in the danger zone that we keep in touch with them more often than with those in safe places. Paul and Mike have been much on our minds, but so far they are safe.

But they have been through some bloody battles. Paul was in that great siege on Longstop Hill where victory opened the way for our march into Tunis; but he lost a lot of men and officers and for some time was exhausted. It was there he won the M.C. Then he was with his regiment, the Royal West Kents, in the break through in Centuripe in Sicily, which opened the way for the Canadians to split the German forces and turn their flanks, the beginning of the end in Sicily. For this he was made Lt-Col. Then, Mike has been in the thickest of it over France and Belgium. His brilliant record has won him the D.F.C. with bar, and advanced him to the rank of Squadron Leader. He tells us very little of what he has done; but his citation for honours mentioned a large number of locomotives, barges, mine-sweepers, E-boats and airfields destroyed, to say nothing of a very skilful dogfight in which he brought down a Focke-Wolf 190 the best of the German fighters. He had also brought down a Dornier 2319 before that. The F-W190 tried to evade Mike by diving to ground level as though out of action, but Mike's hurricane, the fastest in the R.A.F., dived on him, and followed him 50 miles hopping over tree tops, until he saw splinters flying off him and then his dive to earth in flames. Sometimes we do not hear from Mike for over a month which makes Mother very anxious.

Then the work of the big house is very hard on Mother, as she can get little outside help. I try to help her and to keep her out of heavy work; but she seems unable to let up. Perhaps it keeps her from worry.

Doris is still helping at the Admiralty office in Columbo, so far as we know. Philip has been suffering from eye trouble but is better. Austin is still chief padre over three or four air stations in Kenya sorry like you that he is not near the front; but I think it is lucky for both of you. Married men should not go to the front unless they have to. I expect you feel yourself a bit too old for the army, but you have a very important job to go back to when you are ready. It will be nice if you can see something of Sylvia and George in Ottawa. Sylvia seems to have had a nice visit with Vi and Robin. Robin is growing so fast we shall not know him next time we meet. Try to find his bent, guide him and make the best of his talents, with a strong moral and spiritual faith to support him. Show him that you take a deep interest in the Church; that the rector of the parish is one of the best friends. Teach him that the non-churchgoer is the cause of this war and the general enemy of mankind; that Hitler is the champion non-churchgoer of the world and nazism is the fruit of doing without Christ and the Church. All unbelievers are nazis; for if christianity be not true Hitler is right. His is the old pagan cult of the Roman empire; all pagan creeds are the same in reality; a worship of race and war. All who do not worship God worship themselves and then the devil gets his innings. This is the teaching of history and experience. If this war does not convince the world that unbelief is enemy NUMBER ONE man is hopeless and will never have peace. This judgement upon the rotten state of civilisation is our last chance for generations, to repent and seek true peace. The worst feature of war is that it kills off the best as well as some of the worst. Without the best we can have no proper government and so no protection from war-makers and infidels generally.

Well, you won't want many letters from me if this is a sample. But I believe the majority of people have not yet learned the cause of war and just want to return to the state of soul that brought the war on; which is about as crazy as to drink whisky to keep sober. Give our love to Vi and Robin when you see them. Take proper care of yourself. Cut out alcohol, tobacco and all poisons and keep your system healthy. I have done that and at 75 I am as well as I was at 20. Keep in touch with your padre and do all you can to help him. We've not seen any Canadians here yet but there are plenty of them elsewhere. With all our love, best wishes and many prayers, I am

Your affectionate father: J.Ingram Bryan

* * *

The following is a letter my father wrote to his children earlier that year, just before my mother died:

Milton Ernest Vicarage
February 6th, 1945.

My dear Children:

As I am too fully occupied with Mother now to write letters and keep you informed about her health, I am writing this general letter to all of you. Mother's condition is growing gradually worse and there is no hope that she will recover. By the time you get this she may have passed away, but the doctor says she might last some weeks. She is very weak and remains in semi-sleep most of the time, but fortunately has little or no pain, though rather uncomfortable.

Mother began to lose health after the servants left three years ago. She was always so cheerful and filling the lonely house with sunshine that I did not realize she was overworking; but she enjoyed going out in the car and carrying on as usual. But overwork and deep anxiety over some of the children wore her down, and when one is under normal any disease is likely to attack. It was hard to be so far from the children and to lose Michael. But she bore up wonderfully and never lost her old sweet smile. Two years ago when she began to ail I sent her to a nursing home in London for complete overhaul and even by X-ray they could find nothing worse than a floating kidney; but I suspect the fatal disease was then beginning; at least the surgeon who finally had to perform an operation thought so. But the disease had too far got hold of her for any operation to save her. So ever since last May when she left the nursing home after her operation she has been unwell but always praying and hoping for recovery. In the last three weeks she began to feel that recovery was unlikely. She asked me to write and tell you that though she would not see you again in this world you were all in her mind and she sent you her love.

She has been the most wonderfully perfect mother and wife I have ever known. Think of having had so many children, bringing them all up in the way they should go, sending them to the best schools, seeing them all in good jobs: 44 years of labour and thought for her family. She was life itself to me. In the 44 years together all my happiness came from her. Her inspiration enabled me to work for 22 years to get the money for the education of the family. She lived only for the welfare and happiness of others. She is loved by everybody. The people here have been very kind to her.

It was fortunate that Kathleen was near and that Betty, Margaret Macrae and Evelyn could take turns in the last days to come and stay for short periods to help out. A nurse comes daily to do the needful for Mother. We have not been able to find a nurse to live in. But Mother has not suffered in any way from this. We have done all we could to save her and to make her comfortable in spite of the disease: cancer of the intestines.

Evelyn is here at the moment. Margaret was here last week. I sit by Mother most of the time and attend to her at night. She seems brighter today: more wide awake and asked me if I had yet written this general letter to the children abroad. She desires to live until some of the children come home, but now feels it may not be so. The news that Doris might be home in the spring made her long for the spring. Austin is expected then too. Helen being so far away and alone was a great grief. The regular letter from Silvia and Awdry and Vi, as well as from the others gave her great pleasure. She always so looked forward to letters from any of the children.

At the end I cannot say yet what I shall do. I cannot stay here. But God will provide. Mother will sleep in the beautiful place here by the ancient Church. Do not be disappointed if I cannot answer your letters soon. Now Mother joins me in our deep love and blessings for you all and thanks for all you have been to us.

Your affectionate father,

J.Ingram Bryan

Among my father's papers I found this 'Biographical and Academic Record' which I would imagine was issued in about 1920:

BIOGRAPHICAL

AND

ACADEMIC RECORD

OF

1. **J. Ingram Bryan**, B.A., M.A., M. Litt., L. Th , B. D., Ph. D.

2. Educated at the Prince of Wales College and Normal Training College; the University of Toronto; Wycliffe College; the University of King's College; the University of California and the University of Pennsylvania, graduating in due course, after residence and examination, with the following degrees: Bachelor of Arts; Master of Arts; Master of Literature; Licentiate in Theology, Bachelor of Divinity and Doctor of Philosophy, the last degree being from the University of Pennsylvania, one of the oldest and foremost institutions of learning in the United States. The Major subject for the Ph. D. degree was English Literature, and the two Minor subjects Philology and Pedagogy. For the B. D. degree the Major subject was Apologetics and the Minor subjects Patristics and Greek New Testament. Dr. Bryan's courses comprised about ten years of university education; and he holds the university license for teaching in High Schools and Colleges.

3. **Experience :—** After teaching in the public schools for some time Dr. Bryan passed the Oxford and Cambridge Preliminary Examination for Holy Orders and took orders in the Church of England in Canada, being ordained by the Bishop of Toronto, on which occasion he was gospeller; and after holding various important rectorships in Canada and the United States he was finally elected rector of the Church of the Advent, Philadelphia, a former charge of the famous bishop of Massachusetts, Philips Brooks, where Dr. Bryan succeeded Bishop John Poyntz Tyler. As a preacher and lecturer Dr. Bryan has won wide recognition, receiving invitations to address special assemblies, to speak

the main facts directly and clearly, and has added a valuable contribution in true literary spirit and in a genuine literary form. . . . As an example of his breadth of view and his discriminating insight I may cite his treatment of Andrew Marvel and his reference of pastoral idealism to a general instinct in human nature. . . . I hope he will continue to give us more of such studies. . . ."

The **Ven. Archdeacon Coxe**, Diocese of Bethlehem; Pa : " On the two occasions when I heard Dr. Bryan speak on Japan his remarks were exceedingly interesting and instructive, and personally gave me the best information I had ever received on the social, moral and religious life of Japan."

SOME PRESS NOTICES

The Times, Reading, Ba : " The lecture was tremendously interesting, filled with personal incident and educative. The audience expressed their great pleasure and delight to Dr. Bryan at the close."

The Patriot, Charlottetown, Canada: " Dr. Bryan has taken a high stand as a student of English Literature, and his poems have appeared in leading papers and magazines."

The Times, Stroudsburg, Pa : " Dr. and Mrs. Bryan were in touch with many of the leading people of Japan, receiving invitations from His Majesty the Emperor to the Imperial Garden parties, to dine with ministers of State, and have much to tell of the Real Japan."

The Daily Record, Stockton, California : " Dr. Bryan plays on the English vocabulary with a deftness that draws therefrom passages of poetic beauty, which enables him to hold his audience spellbound to the end."

and so thoroughly competent to speak on Japanese affairs, as Dr. Bryan. His intimate knowledge of the people as the result of residence and work, his excellent equipment educationally and his literary skill, make him what I call an expert in dealing with Japanese and Far Eastern affairs. . . .

I have just been reading in the *London Athenaeum* his admirable article on one of the later Japanese writers; and it seems to me, from every point of view, a piece of work up to the very best traditions of The *Athenaeum*, which is saying a great deal. . . . I do not know of any one who has his command of the English language. . . ."

From Charles Vincent Esq. Mus. D. (Oxon) London. " I have been much interested in reading your article in " The Times " on " Songs of the Geisha " If you would give me permission I should like to set some of the verses you have written, they are so admirable for music."

From Dr. William Elliot Griffis: Author of " The Mikado's Empire," and many works on Japan : " I have a profound regard for Dr. Bryan's work as an interpreter of Japan. . . . To that work he has given himself with a penetration and zeal, a sympathy and patience with things little and things great, that are worthy of all praise."

F. E. Schelling, Esq , M.A., D. Litt., Professor of English Language and Literature in th University of Pennsylvania : " I have read your " Feeling for Nature in English Pastoral Poetry " with a great deal of interest and genuine pleasure in your charm of style and originality of expression. . . . You have shown a fine taste and appreciation of what you have read in poetry. . . ."

Professor Hancock, of Haverford College, Philadelphia : Referring to Dr. Bryan's book on English Pastoral Poetry, Professor Hancock says : " His treatment of Shelley's Queen Mab adds a most important factor to the chapter which I devoted to Shelley in my French Revolution and the English Poets."

Professor R. H. Fletcher, of Grinne. College : " Dr. Bryan has mastered his work thoroughly and has set forth

Curriculum Vitae

OF

The Rev. J. Ingram Bryan B.A., M.A., M. Litt., L. Th., B.D., Ph. D.

Index